#AMAZON BEST SELLER
20,00,000+ INVESTOR READERS

ALL ABOUT MONEY

BECOME MONEY SMART

SIMON DANIEL

INDIA • SINGAPORE • MALAYSIA

Notion Press

Old No. 38, New No. 6
McNichols Road, Chetpet
Chennai - 600 031

First Published by Notion Press 2019
Copyright © Simon Daniel 2019
All Rights Reserved.

ISBN 978-1-64546-847-9

This book has been published with all efforts taken to make the material error-free after the consent of the author. However, the author and the publisher do not assume and hereby disclaim any liability to any party for any loss, damage, or disruption caused by errors or omissions, whether such errors or omissions result from negligence, accident, or any other cause.

While every effort has been made to avoid any mistake or omission, this publication is being sold on the condition and understanding that neither the author nor the publishers or printers would be liable in any manner to any person by reason of any mistake or omission in this publication or for any action taken or omitted to be taken or advice rendered or accepted on the basis of this work. For any defect in printing or binding the publishers will be liable only to replace the defective copy by another copy of this work then available.

All about Money, Become Money Smart
Simon Daniel – Author

Simon Daniel had 35 years of experience in top companies in India and held senior titles such as CEO and Director amongst others and established eight highly successful new SBUs [business units] in these assignments. Some of these SBUs like in Gynaecology and Oncology reached No.1 status within India. He was also instrumental in creating a number of top brands in Pharmaceuticals.

As an investor, he has initiated two successful start-ups in healthcare which are being run by his two sons based out of Bangalore.

He had made many mistakes in investing personal finance early in his career and lost money. Later, he learnt the art and science of investing and got significant returns. He has good experience as an investor in real estate, shares, mutual funds and business start-ups.

He had been a source of guidance on personal finance and career development to thousands of juniors who worked with him. There are 12,000 of them, many in senior positions. He continues to be a mentor, trainer, public speaker and author after his long corporate career.

His answers elicited over 20,00,0000 investor readers and he is World's No. 1 writer on "Personal finance advice and investing advice" topics in QUORA#.

#June 2019 www.quora.com
A rare honour for an Indian.

This book is based on his life's investing journey and lessons. He lives in Bangalore with his family.

Contact:

Email – simondanindia@gmail.com

Website – www.simondaniel.in

Contents

CHAPTER 1	Outsmart Crooks and Scoundrels; Do Not Fall in Scams	5
CHAPTER 2	Become Money-Smart, Learn Financial Literacy	24
CHAPTER 3	Understanding Income and Wealth	33
CHAPTER 4	Psychology of Wealth-Creation	48
CHAPTER 5	Economy, Markets & Asset Classes	69
CHAPTER 6	Saving Habits and Investing	79
CHAPTER 7	Where to Invest Money & in Which Asset Class?	99
CHAPTER 8	Major Tax Saving Investments	167
CHAPTER 9	Great Investing Strategies	184
CHAPTER 10	Insurance – Protect Life and Assets	199
CHAPTER 11	Dealing with Banks & Loans	218
CHAPTER 12	Planning and Achieving Financial Life Goals	233
CHAPTER 13	Money, Friends, Relatives and Family	272

CHAPTER 1

Outsmart Crooks and Scoundrels; Do Not Fall in Scams

1.1 My Story

As my father was a Defence Officer, I had hardly any exposure to business or money management. Because of education, hard work and extraordinary values that I displayed at workplace, I climbed the corporate ladder quickly. Starting from being a Sales guy, I went on to reach GM, VP, Director and CEO positions faster than most guys. I earned an above-average income compared to my family and friends from the early days of my career itself. I did not have friends or relatives who were skilled enough to advise me about money. I did not come across any book which could teach me about money management. The only books were on stock market and tax investments. I took many immature or stupid decisions which failed; a brief list is given below.

SHARES – I invested in shares which I sold at the wrong time without making money. I gathered shares of rubbish companies which resulted in wiping out my entire investments. I had shares of many Companies of which I had very little knowledge. I had fallen for fancy advertisements and bought shares of worthless Companies, the share certificates of which cannot be sold even on paper value.

MUTUAL FUNDS – I bought sector mutual funds at peak and sold at bottom prices. I bought too many mutual funds without really understanding the differences.

REAL ESTATE – I booked a plot under fancy EMI scheme and lost a good amount of money. I booked an "Under construction" apartment and lost a huge amount of money by waiting for 7-plus years. I filed cases in consumer court for justice like a fool. Somewhere along the line I realised one can hardly get justice through courts in India. By the time you get justice, you may not be alive!

GOLD AND SILVER – I bought gold and silver like all middle-class homes and hardly gained anything. I bought silver bars at peak prices and sold at 35% lower prices!

After ten years of a series of stupid decisions and losses, I started learning the hard way. The first principle that I learnt is: DO NOT TRUST ANYONE WHEN IT COMES TO YOUR MONEY. I learnt to take charge of my life. I read dozens of books on personal finance and books written by famous investors. I subscribed to many physical and online journals. When it came to shares, I stopped believing every recommendation and 'tip'. I analysed each Company threadbare. I went against popular feelings about any sector and Company.

I learnt the importance of research and long periods of inaction and waiting. I do not get excited when my assets zoom and I do not get depressed if my assets fall by 10% as each decision is taken with a lot of thinking. I do not boast about my success and do not cry on anyone's shoulders too.

This book is written from my personal experience. I am happy to contribute towards your learning and self-discovery. Let us start with crooks, frauds and scoundrels from the world of Finance.

Why Are People so Gullible?

The world of finance, investments and wealth-management is filled with illiterates, crooks, frauds, and scoundrels. If you are not alert at all times, you will lose your money wherever you store it. Still worse, you may end up giving up your money and assets willingly, without any trace of violence! You may realise your loss only after a few months or even years. After losing your wealth you may not talk about it to anyone. And least of all, to the police!

Well, that's the way crooks extract money out of you. Very smoothly, cunningly and silently.

Why are people so gullible?

First, let us look at how to become rich.

Or how to earn income higher than inflation. How to create wealth greater than cumulative inflation

Becoming rich is a separate topic and I do not want to venture into that area by promising you the moon.

1.2 Ignorance vs. Greed

Ignorance and greed are the root causes of all scams

The root cause of all investment scams is ignorance or greed. A combination can make it worse.

Please read the chapter on income and inflation. Investment avenues like fixed income could give income around inflation rates only. Almost all fixed income investments offer returns around 7–8% p.a. If inflation is around 6%, Post-Tax, very often returns may be a little lesser than inflation!

> **Investing in fixed income generating instruments/assets can never make you rich!**

Essentially, there are six opportunities to get income or generate wealth faster than inflation. The higher you grow over rate of inflation, the faster you acquire wealth.

1.3 Six Inflation-Beating Instruments

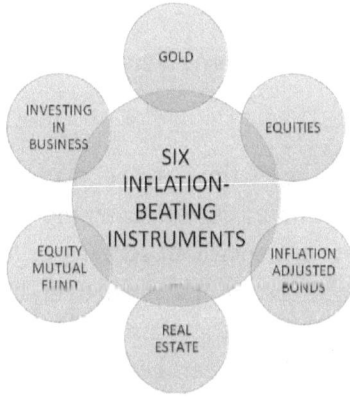

[INFLATION BEATING INSTRUMENTS – SIMON'S MODEL]

In all investment scams, frauds, crooks and scoundrels offer you return on investments far greater than these opportunities. Because you are ignorant you listen to them. Because you are greedy, you not only listen, you act on the baits offered.

1.4 Understanding Investment Scams

Investment scams usually involve getting you to put up money for a questionable investment or one that does not exist at all. In most cases you will lose some or all of your money.

Every scam is operated by a group of "smart crooks". It is often operated from make-shift office called "boiler room". To convince you that the company or its activities are real, it may have an elaborate FRONT which consists of websites, certificates, Approvals, Toll-free numbers, satisfied customers' photos and so on. Their address will be in a posh locality of a Metro city. Often, they will have a sweet-talking Lady Executive. English, for sure!

It will also have direct-contact people, usually innocent employees. Crooks prefer retired Government or Bank officers, teachers, religious leaders, etc., who are known for their integrity and good name in the community. They use communication baits – consisting of direct mail, newspaper ads, printed notices, billboard notices, brochures, SMS, phones and Email. Violence or threat is never used to extract money. They use smooth talk and great promises. They put up a show that you are one of the many clients that they have and they are not very eager to have you in. Their stories look so credible that you may visit their office and hand over your cheque.

1.5 Common Types of Investment Scams

1) Advance-Fee Scams

In an advance-fee scam, the victims are persuaded to pay money to take advantage of an offer promising significantly more in return. It could be a great gift or loan on easy terms without security or loan for those who have poor CIBIL scores or partnership in a great firm at "entry cost". Once the initial upfront payment is made, the scamster will ask for more amount as fees, commission and so on. If you pay, he will disappear. If you do not make further payment, he will disappear, for sure.

2) Pre-Public Offer Scam

In this scam, the victim is told about an impending public issue of a great company. "If you buy shares now, you will be getting it at face value. And once public issue is declared it will be available only at 5–10 times the face value!" They may or may not come out with a public issue. If they come out with a public issue, these shares will get traded much below their face value.

This is a "perfect scam". You have willingly participated to become a shareholder of this Company. Almost nothing can be proved in court.

3) Forex Scam

The foreign exchange (Forex) market is considered to be the largest and most liquid financial market in the world. The investors buy and sell currencies with the aim of making money on changes in the exchange rates. Forex Ad is placed to promote easy access to Forex market through online or offline courses. Many of these ads come in online news portals of well-known channels. I have seen such ads appearing in *www.moneycontrol.com*. You need to pay upfront to join the course. And, you need to fork out the commission while dealing through the brokers who operate in Forex Market. Since it is difficult to beat high standards of Forex professionals, you end up losing money most often. Many such firms are operated out of small one-room offices.

4) Offshore Investing Scams

In this scam, the victims are persuaded to invest in a foreign land; it could be in business, property or anything else. "Great property in the middle of London at ridiculous prices!" Or "Invest in Dubai Apartment through four easy instalments!" Offer would be too good to be true. The scamsters take money and disappear.

By the way, where will you file cases? Which jurisdiction? Sitting in India and filing a case in a foreign location? Think before you part with your money.

5) Ponzi or Pyramid Scheme [MLM] Scam

These schemes recruit people through Ads, Email or directly through "contacts". They promise everything from making big money, "work from home" to turning Rs. 1000/- into Rs. 10,00,000/- in just six months or you may be given the chance to join a special group of investors who are going to get rich on new "great investment idea". Investors, who get into the schemes early, may receive high returns fairly soon from what they think are "interest or profit" cheques. Each person is expected to add a few dozen people and these few dozen people are expected to add a few dozen more people as promoters. All these promoters are expected to add one dozen each of promoters. For each addition to the pyramid, the early entrant keeps getting a share. At some point of time, the money dries up or people in the chains disappear, leaving the rest. Since an entire chain of people is involved, it is difficult to pinpoint to an individual as the real culprit and hence, almost no one gets caught or punished. MLM (Multi-Level Marketing) scam is a variant of the scams.

6) Pump and Dump or "Hot Tip" Shares

This scam is generally operated during the bull period of stock market. You are advised to buy shares of a particular company through SMS and direct calls. Before the scam, the operators hold virtually all the shares bought from stock exchange at prices as low as Re.0.25 per share. SMS or direct "tip" will tell you that it will soon reach 30% higher within a week or so. When it touches higher level, you are tempted to buy on further "tips". The operators keep on rigging prices in the stock market. At some point of time, the shares would have touched astronomical values. Example: A shares of Re.1/- face value will be getting exchanged at Rs. 130/-, similar to ICICI Bank's or Tata's. The buyer and seller are the same group of people at early stages. At later stage, the buyers back out and you are left holding a huge amount of shares which has no buyers available even at $1/100^{th}$ of the price. So, you have acquired shares of Companies which do not have value equal to even toilet tissue paper! Since the whole transaction is hundred percent legal, nothing can be proved in court! If you go to Police, they may tell you two things. One, you have willingly bought these shares and no one showed you a knife to do it. Second, the call came from somewhere in Gujarat, outside the jurisdiction of even the Police Chief!

[Strange, but true, I have observed that many of these hot-tip shares come from Rajkot, Ahmedabad and Indore.]

7) Private Finance Company Scam

Generally, this scam is targeted at retired people soon after retirement. After retirement, people realize that bank deposits fetch only around 8% and there is hardly any avenue which is known to give returns higher than 8%. Here comes the friendly and very helpful Advisor who promises return of 15–20% PA. There is only one "catch". In the offer of 15–20% interest on deposits that they may give, only 10% is officially given as interest and the rest of the money is given as "incentives" or commission to circumvent the laws. At times "post-dated cheques" (PDC) are also given on the day of deposit to gain the confidence of the investors. The money collected is often invested into property development. An advance is paid for the land under housing plot development. As each housing plot gets sold, the scamster makes money and he keeps paying high interest rates. At some point of time, it becomes difficult to sell plots due to oversupply or economy's down-turn. At this point, PDCs start bouncing. One can file a criminal case for cheque-bouncing. But dealing with the police and judiciary is so difficult and time-consuming, that most people prefer to give up the money!

8) Gold Scheme Scams

In this scam, gold ornaments are offered on EMI basis. You are persuaded to deposit only 25% of the gold value and they issue a certificate for 100% value of gold at current prices. [Or some variant of this.] You are expected to keep giving monthly instalments till full price of gold is given. The money is utilised by the scamster for trading in commodities market and when the commodity market crashes he disappears. In some cases, he may return the money after adjusting making charges and admin. charges! Net amount would be less!

9) Investment Seminars

The scamsters invite hundreds of people to a seminar where he/she presents an unbeatable investment opportunity. Star hotel and free lunch are offered. You are told to bring cheque-book to book the great offer available on just that day. As the Chief person is leaving town after two days to a foreign location, you are advised to take the decision fast. Within 2 days, the money is gone; so is the person!

10) Housing Plot on EMI Scam

In this scam, the scamster offers housing plots in a great upcoming colony or township, named as "Defence Officers' colony" or "Doctors colony" or "Happy Valley" or such exotic name. Layout plan is shown which includes clubhouse, proposed temple [if the targets are Christians, proposed church!], proposed bus station, proposed English medium school, etc.

To book the housing plot, one has to pay only 10–15% of the site cost, rest is in easy instalments! Wonderful, is it not? Every 60–90 days, the instalment cheques keep getting cashed. Maybe 90% amount would be collected. 10% is kept for the time of registration.

After paying most of the amount and waiting for a few years, you would realise that they do not have permission from government Then there are series of stories:

- Office premises changed. [Now, it is located at a far-flung area]
- New Management or Committee will take over.
- Things will come through after elections, etc. Each time, a new story.

If you go to Consumer Court, it may take 10–15 years to get a verdict. Most likely, the verdict will ask them to return the amount with SBI SB account interest [3.6%]. If you work out legal fees and other charges, you would have made minimum 60% loss! That too, only if you are lucky to get back any amount!

11) Day-Trading in Stocks Scam

In this scam, you are promised Rs. 40,000/- plus income per day and a wonderful life by becoming a day-trader. They promise Mercedes car within a few months after becoming a day-trader. All that you have to do is to join a "Day-Trading training course". The fancy advertisement is linked to well-known sites like *moneycontrol* or similar ones. Believe me, you will not able to buy even a cycle, forget a Mercedes!

1.6 How to Spot a Financial Scam?

Here Are Some Clues to Help You Spot Financial Scams

1) Phantom Riches

A scamster may dangle the prospect of wealth, enticing you with something you want but cannot have it like this promise – "Your investment of Rs. 100,000 will produce Rs. 5,000 every month for 50 years". If it sounds too good to be true it probably is! You must view all promises sceptically, especially every promise which has annual return above 9% on invested amount.

2) Expert Credentials

A scamster might build credibility by claiming to be reputable expert. "Believe me, as Director of a reputed firm, I will never sell any investment that does not produce 20% returns." "As a Director, I do not get involved in amounts less than half a million rupees!"

3) Famous People Bought It

Any time a financial sale person tells you that cousins of Amitabh Bachchan and Rahul Dravid have brought these along with a few members of the local "temple committee" – run with your money! If the investment does not make sense on its merits, don't be fooled into thinking that a bunch of smart and well-connected people have already vetted it and forked out their cash!

4) Tit for Tat Offer

A scamster might offer you a small favour in return for a big favour. "I will give you a discount on my commission if you buy now – 50% off on my commission or price." Such heavy inducements are always a red flag.

5) Only a Few Positions Are Left, Only a Few Pieces Are Left

Be on the lookout for anyone creating a false sense of urgency by claiming:

- Limited supply of product/plots
- Limited days
- Limited positions

Reality is usually the other way around. If it is truly scarce, you do not have to "push" to sell.

6) Signs of a Ponzi Scam

- Investments' returns are abnormally high
- Company makes impossible claims and guarantees like "double your money" in six months
- Company makes it difficult to withdraw your money by having such clauses

7) Signs of Pyramid Schemes

- The emphasis is on recruiting new distributors, new agents, etc. and not product marketing
- The business has very high "start-up cost". Or it could be high "signing amount".
- The company will not buy back "unsold" inventory.

8) IT Scam

You get a phone call from someone claiming to be an I-T officer, claiming that you have an unpaid income tax. If you do not make immediate payment, the caller says "You will be arrested or face lawsuit in court. Or you pay _____ amount through me to settle the matter." Another version is asking you to pay _____ amount to get immediate IT refund.

9) Charity Scam

Following a tragedy [death of husband or child], you receive an appeal from someone claiming to represent a charitable organisation who asks you for a donation. You are in an emotionally weak stage and will offer to donate an amount in memory of the departed soul.

10) International Lottery Scam

You will receive SMS or Email or direct call saying that your Mobile has won an international lottery held at London held by a WALMART group or some big Company name. The amount is too big to be true. It may turn out to be half a million US$ or 20,000 UK pounds. Everything about them will be foreign-sounding – the address and the names. Also, they may tell you that if details are not given fast, the money gets surrendered as per UK laws. They want you to share your bank account details. Once you share your account details, you would know who won the lottery!

12) Inheritance Scam (Nigerian Email Scam)

You will receive Email from someone with a link, who claims to represent a rich old lady who recently died. Four million dollars can be shared by 50:50 if you help to take the money out of such and such African country. They want you to share bank details and you need to make initial payment for legal fees for dealing with RBI or something like that. There are many bulk email and Mobile sending companies in big metro cities. They peddle in these at very low rates. Such emails directories are available for various types of people's groups. Suppose, you want to target Credit Card users from class – 2 cities, it can be done.

13) Credit and Debit Card Scams

Scamsters do not need your credit/debit card to take out your money. In more than 90% cases, they steal the card details and then start spending using your card. They get the card details either from you directly or from unsecured websites, or from online shopping activities or installing spyware in your computers operated from remote location. This scam is pretty common these days.

Another variant of this scam is to call you on your Mobile, claiming to represent your bank and collect details like PIN or three digits behind each card.

1.7 Be Aware of Mutual Funds, Banks and Insurance Agents!

Mis-Selling by Banks

Many Banks are notorious for mis-selling of various products to customers. Some could be deliberate and many others are based on ignorance. Young officers simply follow instructions of seniors without realizing the financial impact that it will have on their customers.

If you make a financial advice or sell a finance product without taking into consideration the following factors, it can be termed a "mis-sale".

- Age of the investor
- Financial goal of the investor along with time frame
- Risk profile of the investor [Risk attitude and Risk capacity]
- Tax and other implications

If I have an old diabetic patient, will I offer fruit juice laden with sugar and ice? NO!

Similarly, I cannot offer finance products without taking into consideration the factors mentioned above.

Pushing Balanced Funds

Customer request	Fixed Deposit: Wants to invest in FD with monthly interest option
Bank official's suggestion	"Invest in balanced funds instead. You will earn higher dividend"
Why is it a mis-sale?	On long term basis: 5 year-plus, the return from Aggressive balance funds could be higher than 10%. But, on a short-term basis monthly dividend cannot be guaranteed.
What is the impact?	If the balanced fund has been booked at peak prices, the capital itself may show erosion after a few months. The dividend may not come about and the investor will be shocked.

Pushing Fixed Deposit & ULIP

Customer request	A retired person wants to open SCSS account with Rs. 1.50 million corpus.
Bank Official suggestion	Bank 1 – Invest in bank FD for 3 years as only people above 60 years are allowed into SCSS account.
	Bank 2 – Invest in ULIP and it offers insurance and capital growth.
What is the impact?	Bank 1: FD
	(a) – you will miss the difference in rate of interest between normal FD and SCSS.
	(b) – Normal FD is not eligible for IT benefits.
	Bank 2: ULIP
	Life cover offered by ULIP is too little. And for a retired person, life cover has very little meaning.
	ULIP investments go into equity market and with such investments, above-average returns happen only after 5–7 years.

Pushing ULIP Instead of Term Insurance

Customer request	Wants to buy TERM INSURANCE for himself as he is only 40 years and has a lot of loans.
Bank official suggestion	Invest in ULIP instead of a TERM INSURANCE
What is the impact?	Insurance content in the ULIP is very little and it does not cover the life of the insurer adequately.
	On a 10–15 years period, ULIP may give far less return compared to Multi-cap funds.
	There are exit penalties for ULIP.

Pushing Gold Coins Instead of Gold Bonds

Customer request	Wants to invest in Gold bonds for 7 years
Bank official suggestion	Invest in gold coins as it does not have a "lock-in period"
Impact of mis-selling	You will pay out a commission while buying gold coins. While selling the price may be upto 10% less
	You will miss the interest of 2.5% p.a. available on gold bonds
	Gold bonds can be sold at exchanges and it is not highly illiquid as claimed
	You will miss the IT benefit under LTCG which is available to Bonds.

Pushing ULIP & Insisting on FD While Giving Bank Lockers

Customer request	Wants a bank locker
Bank official suggestion	Take bank FD for Rs. 1,00,000/-
	Take ULIP for Rs. 3,00,000/-
What is the impact?	Pushing another product while giving bank locker is illegal.
	Both bank FD and ULIP will give far less returns compared to other options like Multicap or Balanced Funds.
	Insurance cover in ULIP is very little.

Pushing Life Cover or the Products While Selling Vehicle Loan

Customer request	Wants to take vehicle loan for Rs. 7,00,000/-

Bank official suggestion	Take personal cover for Rs. 10,00,000/-
What is the impact?	It is illegal to push another product as pre-condition for vehicle loan.
	If the person is already covered with a term insurance it is unwarranted.
	Premium charged is at "rack rates" which could be available at 30–40% less from online portals or from other insurance companies.

Mis-Selling by Insurance Agents

Insurance products are aggressively sold to customers.

The initial commission that the agent gets is pretty high and Insurance Company gets long term income from you. Because of these the following happen:

- They deliberately discourage taking Term insurance by investors on which agents get very little commission.
- Insurance agents often resort to gimmicks and outright lies to sell the products.
- Insurance Companies keep strong clauses in the policy document to prevent exit by customers. You may end up losing all or most parts of the premium paid if you exit early. If you take a wrong step, you will continue with the wrong track for decades.

The loss that you incur on 30-year period may run into Rs. 5 million to 10 million on account of stupid decision on Insurance product.

Hence, checking and evaluating Insurance product is essential before you write your first cheque.

- Do you really need an insurance policy?
- What are the different options?
- Which one gives the best offer in terms of coverage and least premium?
- What are the exit clauses and penalties?

Here are a few tips to spot mis-selling of insurance policies.

1) Selling short term policies

Basically, Life Insurance products are for long term. If anyone tries to sell it as for 4–5 years coverage with great investment vehicle, be on the alert! It could work out to be a risky proposition.

2) Beware of cooked-up illustration

Insurance Companies have standard illustrations to describe the product. If the data is cooked up by the agent, it may show fantastic returns in the short run which is grossly untrue.

3) Do not allow agents to fill up application

Very often, agents ask you to simply put in your signature and they fill up the rest. This could work out dangerous for you. And, you will realise it only after decades!

4) In Healthcare policy, make 'honest' declarations

To sell the healthcare policy, agents often fill up wrong data. It could be false medical claim or hiding some information. If you are not honest, your claim will get rejected and agent can do nothing.

5) Do not buy another policy unnecessarily

If you call up the agent with one product, he may try to push another product too. Be clear as to which policy you want and for covering what.

6) Do not fall for rewards and gifts

Do not fall prey to gifts and rewards offered by the Insurance agents. These could be baits to trap you with something bad and something big at a later stage.

7) Do not entertain imposters

There are many imposters who call claiming to represent IRDAI or similar agencies. Do not entertain these calls and offers. If you wish you can call the insurance company directly.

8) Single premium plans

Very often, ULIPs are sold as single premium insurance product to senior citizens. Your insurance coverage is very little and too much amount gets adjusted as premium for coverage. Net result is that, the end returns that you get from invested money would be far less than other investment options.

9) Guaranteed return promise

Except fixed income securities, 'guaranteed returns' cannot be promised for any insurance or related product. Do not fall for such sales talk. Except Fixed Income products, there are no "guaranteed returns" for any product.

10) Banks and Insurance products

Banks are for banking needs. Insurance is for personal and asset coverage. Please do not mix these two. Do not try buying any mutual fund or insurance through your Bankers. It may end up with mis-sale or you may end up paying huge commission to banks on long term basis.

Mis-Selling of Mutual Funds

Mutual fund mis-selling is done by MF Companies or agents. Let us look at some popular mis-selling of mutual funds.

1) New Mutual Fund NFO

This is nothing but a great marketing gimmick. Existing Mutual funds have many schemes targeted at various types of equities and debt instruments. Either it could be market-cap-based [large-cap, midcap, etc.], or it could be sector based [Banking, FMCG, etc.] or it could be any other sector or thematic. With this new NFO, the investors lose a huge amount of their money in terms of commission to Agents and Distributors. It could be as high as 5–6% of the money invested. Further, typical NFO being close-ended, your money gets locked for longer duration too.

2) Equity Funds Are Shown with Great Returns in Three Years

MF houses bring out huge advertisements in popular journals on great performance of the fund in 1 – 2 years. This is very misleading. After a bear market, equity markets may show good returns in the short period of 1–2 years. And, there is no guarantee that such returns can be sustained for longer period. All equity-related investments are for 5–7 or even 10 years. Short term success is no indication of its ability to sustain long term success.

3) Pushing Small Cap, Midcap or Sector Funds

All funds which operate in certain market caps like SMALL or MID or certain sectors like FMCG, INFRA, etc. go through cycles in the market. The performance may be attractive in the short run, but will it sustain for longer duration of 7–10 years? Can you hold for long periods? And, it is not for those who are in 50 years-plus bracket as the short term risks are high.

4) Dividend Announcement

Dividends have no meaning in mutual funds, as the mutual fund is for long term appreciation. The dividend declared is nothing but returning some of your own appreciated amount. Further, after paying IT on dividends, what you get is less than the appreciated amount. Such dividends are not sustainable in a depressed market. You can go in for SWP in case you want regular income from MF, which is more tax efficient too.

5) Investing in ELSS beyond Rs. 1,50,000/-

ELSS is one of the instruments to save IT, but, upto Rs. 1,50,000/- only. Beyond that it may appreciate, but, your money gets locked up for three years plus. You can as well go in for more suitable funds which do not have such lock-in period. Example: Multi cap funds.

If anyone is trying to push ELSS beyond Rs. 1,50,000/-, say NO.

6) Persuading to Shift from One Fund to Another

To achieve short term success, some agents or Managers may ask you to shift from one fund to another. While doing that the following need to be kept in mind.

- Have you looked at tax implication? You may end up with IT payments if not held for at least one year and some IT if held beyond one year too.
- What about the agent's commission for each new application?

7) Putting Multiple Applications for Same Fund

Please remember that for each new application there is a minimum commission that you need to shell out. Multiple applications mean multiple payments.

8) Suggesting MF Investments without Looking at Your Profile

Mutual funds are a great investment vehicle, but the following must be kept in mind. We do not give same food for all people with any age or health profile. Similarly, same MF cannot be offered to all.

- Risk profile of the investor. [Both risk-taking ability and risk-aversion.]
- Age of the investor, as some schemes are not suitable if you are older.
- Goal of the investor – like retirement, tax saving, children's education, etc.
- Minimum holding period may vary from 5–7 years to get decent returns.

9) Overselling MIP Mutual Funds

MIP [Monthly Income Plan] is nothing but a Hybrid fund with 25–60% equity content. If the equity content is less, the price fluctuation would be low and if it is high, the price fluctuation would be high.

There is nothing like "income" from MIP funds. The payment outflow is nothing but returning your own money either as dividend or SWP route.

Some agents push for STP with MIP SWP. This will result in multiple commissions for the same transaction if routed through an agent.

10) Offer to Deposit Your Mutual Fund Applications

Some agents and Banks offer "free deposit" of your MF application with the MF office. Please remember, there is nothing free and you end up paying commission on short term or even long basis.

This could work out to be millions at the end of 20–30 years!

CHAPTER 2

Become Money-Smart, Learn Financial Literacy

A financially literate person is less likely to get cheated by crooks and scoundrels. He is far less likely to fall for financial scams. Hence, the first step towards creating wealth is to become financially literate. Become money-smart; learn the art and science of managing money. Learn the basics of economy, inflation, income, wealth, different asset classes and the best investment avenues combining returns and at the same time evaluating risk.

2.1 What Is Financial Literacy?

First, financial literacy is far different from other education or expertise in other areas. Someone can be PhD in Physics or even Maths, but can be financially illiterate. It is similar to someone who can be PhD in Nutrition or Chemistry, but can be a bad cook. A lot of graduates and post-graduates assume that they "know" about money management, but I can say with almost certainty that a vast majority of these are financial illiterates.

Unfortunately, most Indians don't know how to manage money because they were never taught how to do it. And, most never tried learning too.

Most parents avoid discussing about money in front of kids as though it is a taboo subject. And, all through school and even in college, money is never discussed, unless you have joined for Commerce or Business Management course at undergraduate level. In school and college libraries there is hardly any book as to how to manage money. Most homes do not have any journals or books on money. The daily newspapers are mainly covering politics or news covering accidents and fire, and very little about money.

What is the result?

We are born into financial illiteracy within and around us; we are designed to lead the lives of financial illiterates. Still worse, we are made to believe that managing money requires great amount of intellect and shrewdness, and that only crooked and cunning people think and talk about money!

What is financial literacy?

Financial literacy is a range of personal skills which are required to manage one's money.

BUDGETING – This is about our awareness and management of income and expenses. We must know how and from where our income comes and where it goes.

SAVING – How to save money in each transaction and how the saved money can be deployed: in which instrument and how long to stay invested.

UNDERSTANDING OF INTEREST AND RETURNS – We must know the difference between simple interest and compound interest: must be aware of the principle of compounding.

DEBT MANAGEMENT – Understanding debt and its management. Managing loans, credit cards payments and maintaining good credit score.

ASSET MANAGEMENT – Understanding the differences in character, risk and returns of different asset classes. Example: Rupees ten million in real estate will be different from gold and it will be far different from shares or mutual funds.

PROTECTION – This is about personal and asset insurance or health insurance.

FINANCIAL AWARENESS – Understanding the sources of financial information. Developing skills to differentiate between clean and unclean financial transactions. The difference between Reasonable risks vs. Reward.

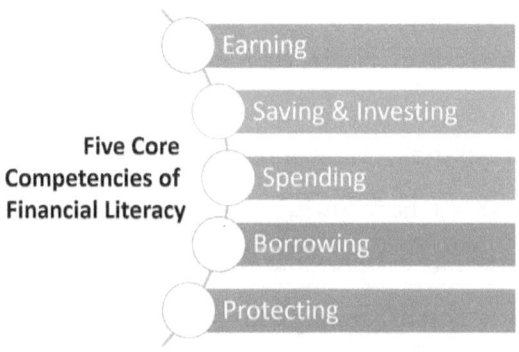

[FIVE COMPETENCIES OF FINANCIAL LITERACY]

These are the five competencies of financial literacy. A literate person will be able to:

- Earn better
- Save and invest better
- Spend wisely
- Borrow with best terms
- Protect his assets well.

2.2 What Are the Negative Impacts of Financial Illiteracy?

- People remain poor even though there is a clear opportunity to come out of poverty.
- People get into series of debts all through life leading a miserable life.
- People lose their earnings by investing into assets or investments which give low returns or negative returns.
- Families go through serious crisis while being sick and end up getting no treatment or mediocre medical treatment.
- Leading old age in poverty and misery.
- People spend a lot of their time in police stations and courts, fighting finance-related cases which may not have a happy ending.
- People lose their houses, properties and savings, grabbed by crooks or Banks.
- Leading an entire life of poor quality with hardly any good thing in life – houses, furnishings, vehicles, great white goods and holidays/picnics.
- Life of frustration, complaint, anxiety and tension.

Ask any 15–16-year-old the following questions:

- What is the rate of interest in Savings Bank A/C?
- What is the cost of running your home on a monthly basis? And what is the household income?

- If you meet with a motorcycle accident and there is one leg fractured, how much will it cost to get treated?
- If your Dad suddenly became unconscious, where will you take him for treatment? How you will pay for the treatment?
- Do you have a Bank account?
- How much money have you saved till now? And where?
- If you are planning to join for graduation how much will it cost? How will you fund it?
- What is the difference between income and wealth?

This is the real world. Are you satisfied with their answers?

Ask an adult working person the following questions:

- What is the difference between debit card and credit card in terms of rate of interest?
- Have you done sufficient investment to get the best I-T benefits? How much?
- Do you maintain a file/notebook to keep track of your investments?
- What is the difference between SB and CA of Banks?
- What is your CIBIL score?
- How much interest are you paying on your housing loan?
- What is the difference between PPF and FD of banks in terms of interest?
- What is the difference between debt-fund and equity-fund?
- Do you have any personal or family Mediclaim policy? How much?
- Do you have emergency fund equal to 6–9 months' salary?
- What is your net asset value?
- If you die suddenly, how will your spouse manage the next nine months?

- What happens to your house that your family stays in, if you die suddenly?
- Do you have any book at home which keeps track of your assets and finance?

Are you satisfied with the answers?

2.3 Development of Financial Literacy

Development of financial literacy is an ongoing, continuous journey. The first step towards development of financial literacy is realization of own inadequacies related to skills in making financial decisions. If an individual is able to accept that he/she needs development of skills and shows eagerness to learn, he/she will search for sources to develop these skills. It could be books, journals or even training from experts. Financial literacy cannot work without a certain degree of emotional balance in an individual.

2.4 Sources to Develop Financial Literacy

Let us look at various sources for developing our financial literacy to make us fitter, stronger and sharper. Sources that will make us money-smart are:

1) Financial Products' Brokers/Advisors

These could be insurance agents and distributors and agents selling Mutual Fund products. They may be operating in both online and offline space.

    a. Strengths

    They could be a good source of information and support for those who have less knowledge about various finance products. Usually they are situated in your neighbourhood and may be known to common friends.

    b. Weaknesses

- Most of the brokers, agents and advisors have an inherent interest to push financial products of the firm that they represent which may not be the most suitable for your needs. It could be due to their lack of knowledge about other financial products or non-availability of such products in their basket or profit motive.

- Very often, they push or promote products on which they get higher commission, often sacrificing suitability of the product.

- They deliberately or otherwise overlook other more suitable investment opportunities available to the investor.

Example – An insurance agent may try hard to sell a high commission-laden "endowment insurance scheme" and may not discuss with you about low commission-laden "Term insurance".

2) Chartered Accountants

They are qualified and trained in accounting, taxation and finances. They usually have good understanding of related laws too.

a. Strengths

- Generally, they have good understanding of various financial products and their implication from the point of view of appreciation and taxation.

- Because they are qualified, they can quickly learn about new finance products too.

b. Weaknesses

- Most often they are linked to annual income tax returns and their primary concern is proper filing of IT returns.

- They have only an indirect "understanding" about various finance products.

- Decisions on investments often have to be taken many times during the year and it cannot be linked or tied down to annual I-T returns. They cannot participate on continuous basis.

3) Real Estate Brokers

Real estate brokers play a major role while buying and selling properties in cities and small towns. They can provide useful information about properties consisting of current rates and probable development of the region in future, and also legality of the asset.

a. Strengths:

Knowledge of the geographical location and history of the seller or the location is the major strength that they offer. They can quickly gauge the customer's needs/background and make multiple offers or options.

b. Weaknesses:

It is rare to find 100% honest real-estate brokers. Often, they peddle in lies, half-truths and less than the information needed to force a sale. They wish to see sale taking place fast and then, there is a tearing hurry to collect their commission.

4) Certified Financial Planners [CFPs]

These are qualified professionals handling personal finance of individuals. They have passed qualifying examination from Finance Planning Standards Board of India and carry the title CFP. Normally they give an integrated financial planning for individuals:

Financial planning needs analysis, planning investment in terms of assets and products, planning retirement, planning real estate, planning Mutual Fund, planning Insurance, Taxation, Estate or will arrangements, etc.

a. Strengths

- They are well-qualified and have at least the minimum standards of subject knowledge.
- Usually they have ethical standards.

b. Weaknesses

- They charge on hourly basis or annual basis which could vary from Rs. 5000 – Rs. 50,000 for an individual, which will work out to be expensive for those in the low income bracket.
- They do not spend time in educating an individual and hence, unless you are well-versed in various finance products, you will be forced to follow their advice blindly. You need to have high

level of financial literacy to take part in the planning process and take most apt decisions.

5) Books on Investing and Personal Finance

Books are an excellent source of information and guidance for those seeking to become financially literate or those searching for higher knowledge in this area.

Some of the "must read" books are as follows:

- THE INTELLIGENT INVESTOR by Benjamin Graham
- SECURITY ANALYSIS by Benjamin Graham
- THE LITTLE BOOK OF COMMON SENSE INVESTING by John Bogle
- ONE UP ON Wall Street by Peter Lynch
- A RANDOM WALK DOWN WALL STREET by Burton Malkiel
- common stocks AND UNCOMMON PROFITS by Philip Fisher
- HOW TO MAKE MONEY IN STOCKS by William 'O' Neil
- THE WARREN BUFFET WAY by Robert Hagstrom
- BUFFETOLOGY by Mary Buffet
- IRRATIONAL Exuberance by Robert Shiller
- THE MOST Important THING by Howard Marks
- THE ALCHEMY OF FINANCE by Gorge Soros
- RICH DAD POOR DAD by Robert Kiyosaki
- EXTRAORDINARY POPULAR DELUSIONS AND MADNESS OF CROWDS by Charley Mackey
- THE RICHEST MAN IN BABYLON by George Clason

6) Print Magazines

- MONEY by OUTLOOK
- Money Today – INDIA TODAY group
- Moneylife

- Dalal Street Investment Journal
- Capital Market
- WEALTH by Economic Times

7) Online Journals

- www.moneycontrol.com
- www.valueresearchonline.com
- www.economictimes.com
- www.capitalmaster.com

8) Television Shows

- CNBC
- ET
- PROFIT TODAY

9) Newspapers

- ECONOMIC TIMES
- Financial Express
- BUSINESS STANDARD

Warning

* Never depend on a single or a few sources for developing your financial literacy.
* Check out with multiple journals, books and people.
* Keep a "healthy disrespect" for each opinion, meaning, check and recheck.
* When events and data change, you must change. Nothing is permanent.

CHAPTER 3
Understanding Income and Wealth

3.1 Understanding the Difference - Income vs. Wealth

We must know the difference between wealth and income.

What is the difference?

Income is a regular stream of money, which a person receives from different sources such as salary, rent, profit from business, interest, pension, dividend, etc. that helps in the creation of wealth.

Wealth is the current market value of all assets possessed, stored or saved by a person for future use.

Income Is Generated, Wealth Is Created

Basis For Comparison	Income	Wealth
Meaning	Income refers to the money received or earned on a continuous basis, as a return for work or investments. Salary, rent, dividend, interest, commission, fees and profit.	Wealth implies money or valuable possession accumulated by a person during the course of his life. Shares, land, building, gold, silver, debt funds, mutual funds and house.
What is it?	Flow of money.	Stock of assets.
Acquisition	Income is generated immediately.	Wealth is created over time.
Tax levied	Income tax.	Wealth tax.

Income – Expenses = Savings

SAVINGS ⟶ Appreciating asset [as below] OR Non-appreciating asset – Cars, household articles.

ASSET ⟶ Income producing wealth [Rental buildings] OR Non-Income producing [plot].

Types of Wealth

- Real estate – Houses, Flats, Plots, Lands, Ownership of Shops
- Gold/silver – Ornaments, gold bars, Gold ETF, Silver bars
- Deposits – Bank Fixed deposits, Company Fixed Deposits, SB A/C balance, Post Office Deposits
- Mutual funds – Equity and Debt mutual funds, Balanced Mutual Funds & Income Funds
- Company shares – listed company shares, Private Company shares, if saleable
- Govt Securities & related – PPF, NSC, NSS, Indira Vikas Patra, Kisan Vikas Patra
- Debt investments – Debentures and Bonds
- Art Collection – Paintings, Antique materials

What is real income?

Real income refers to the income of an individual or group after taking into consideration the effects of inflation on purchasing power. For example, if you receive salary increase of 10% and the inflation for the year is 7%, the real income only increases by 3%; conversely if you receive 7% salary increase and the inflation was 9% then the real income shrank by 2%.

Real income and consumer price index (CPI)

The "real income" measures the purchasing power of an individual's wages; financial analysts compare it with consumer price index (CPI).

Inflation and CPI [Consumer Price Index]

Inflation is the rate at which the general level of prices of goods and services are rising and consequently the purchasing power of currency is falling.

The CPI measures the average cost of basket of goods – food items, medicines and medical care, clothing, transportation, entertainment, education, etc., which is published on monthly basis.

3.2 Goals of Investment

The most important goal of any investment is to grow financially faster than inflation. If your investment does not keep up with inflation, your net asset value will be lesser. Meaning, you will be poorer.

MOST IMPORTANT QUESTION BEFORE MAKING ANY Investment-: Does it beat inflation? Will my investment grow faster than inflation, post taxes?

Most often, there may not be a 'guarantee' to grow faster than inflation. In that scenario, we must look at "what is best possible scenario" based on historical facts and current estimates.

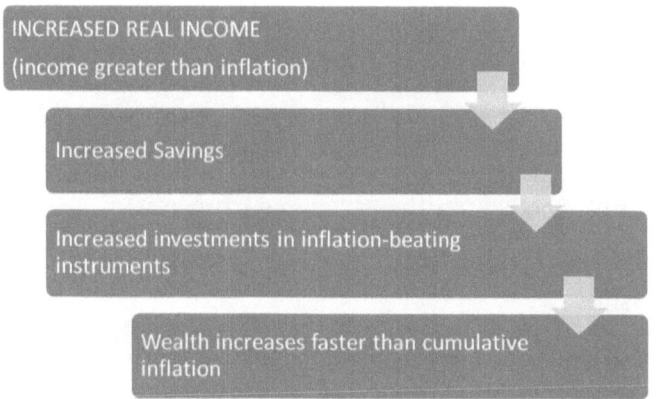

[GOALS OF INVESTMENT]

3.3 Strategies to Beat Inflation

The key to beat inflation is to plan investments in instruments which will grow faster than inflation.

However, each of these instruments has its advantages and disadvantages. Each has different risk vs. return profile. Unless you evaluate each one in the context of your strength and weakness, you must not opt for it.

a. REAL ESTATE INVESTMENTS

Real estate is considered a good hedge against inflation on long term basis of 10 years-plus. If it is an income-generating real estate like rented house or shop, it is even better.

b. DIVERSIFY – PORTFOLIO/GEOGRAPHY/ASSET CLASS

One of the best ways to protect against inflation is to diversify investments: geographically for real estate, classwise for assets (gold/equity/real estate) or market-cap wise for portfolio (Multicap/mid-Cap/small cap]. All asset classes do not grow similarly. Hence diversification is an important strategy to beat inflation.

c. IMPROVE CURRENT INCOME

Earn current income greater than current inflation. If current inflation is 6%, you need to get yearly salary/ income increase greater than 6%. This can be done by the following methods.

* Perform better at the current job and be eligible to earn wages higher than inflation
* Shift to a better performing company to earn wages higher than inflation
* Take up a higher position which can pay better
* Shift geographical location, i.e. a place where better wages are possible
* Learn new skill-levels or acquire higher education to improve chances to increase income

d. INVEST IN EQUITY/EQUITY MUTUAL FUNDS

Investing in equities (growth stocks) or equity MF is one of the best ways to stay ahead of inflation. Over the past 10 years NIFTY has returned close to 17% a year compared to average inflation rate of 6–7%. For all small investors and large investors who do not have time or expert advice, it is advisable to go for mutual fund route. To reduce risk, one can opt for SIP route and not lump sum investments to avoid entry at peak prices.

e. INVEST IN DIVIDEND-PAYING STOCKS

Another good way to stay ahead of inflation is buying stocks which pay good dividends. If you have a basketful of stocks paying good dividend, your net returns could be higher than bank deposits or inflation.

f. GOLD INVESTMENTS

Gold is considered an ideal hedge against inflation. Gold will not give recurring income like dividends from shares, but on long term basis [10–15 years] gold can beat inflation. This is subject to not wasting a lot of money at entry time like "making charges".

g. INFLATION ADJUSTED BONDS

RBI has issued IIBs (Inflation Indexed Bonds). These bonds protect the principal against inflation.

h. START A BUSINESS

If successful, most businesses will give returns much higher than inflation. All businesses have inherent risks associated with them. And, all people are not cut out for doing business.

3.4 Effects of Inflation on Life and Investments

Inflation is the sustained increase in the general price level of goods and services in an economy over a period of time. When the general price list rises, each unit of the currency buys fewer goods and services. Consequently, inflation reflects on the purchasing power of a unit of money – a loss of real value in the medium of exchange and unit of account within the economy. One can get consumer price index over a time from which one can understand the rate of inflation.

It is important to note the following:

* All products and services will not have the same rate of inflation. Example:- Medical treatment and higher education costs are going up more than 12%, whereas food inflation may be at 3–4%, transportation cost may go up by 10%, whereas Consumer Price Index may show just 5% inflation.

* The inflation change can happen month to month, quarter to quarter or year to year.

    a. Inflation erodes purchasing price: Same money in hand can buy far less items after a couple of years.

    Example:- Today, tea for two costs Rs. 20/-; however, after 10 years, tea for a single person would cost Rs. 20/-. For two people we may have to pay Rs. 40/- if inflation is 7% PA.

    b. Forces you to spend: Because the prices are going up people buy things and stock up thinking that at a future date, same thing would be costlier.

    c. It causes more inflation: High inflation forces people into spending mode which results in future inflation.

    d. Cost of borrowing goes up: Inflation makes borrowing costlier which reduces investments into business.

    e. Inflation destroys the future planning like retirement: With inflation, retired people find it hard to survive; with the stoppage of income and reduced purchasing power of the saved amount the retirees find it difficult to survive.

Inflation and Return on Investments

Let us look at three Scenarios of Inflation vs. Return on investments.

- If inflation is 7% and return on your investment is 7% the return after adjusting inflation is zero. You have retained the value of your capital.
- If inflation is 9% and return on your investment is 8% the inflation-adjusted return is -1%, though you got a higher return.
- If the inflation is 4% and return on your investment is 7% the inflation-adjusted return is +3%, meaning you have added wealth.

> **Every return on investment must be looked at through *the* prism of inflation "adjustment"**

> **THE ART OF WEALTH-CREATION IS CONSISTENTLY ADDING HIGHEST "INFLATION-ADJUSTED RETURN" TO INVESTMENTS MADE.**

3.5 Sources of Income

Each person gets income from different sources at varying proportions. The highest contributor of income to the kitty is called Primary income source. Then comes Secondary source, followed by Tertiary source.

Primary Sources

- ✓ Salaries for employed people irrespective of rank or position.
- ✓ Consultation fees for Doctors, Physiotherapists or Radiologists.
- ✓ Professional fees of Chartered Accountants, Company Secretaries and Lawyers.
- ✓ Service fees like for Architects, Engineers and Laboratory services.
- ✓ Service fees of personal services like Barbers, beauticians and tailors.
- ✓ Wages paid to Electricians, Plumbers and workers.
- ✓ Trading income like that of commodity traders, shopkeepers and owners of department stores.
- ✓ Commissions or brokerages earned by Insurance agents, Real estate broker and share brokers.

Primary income is generally 60–95% of the total income.

Secondary Income

- ✓ A Doctor can earn a salary by working in a Hospital and in the evening, he may do private practice and earn consultation fees.
- ✓ A person can earn salary by working in an office, but can add additional income by selling mutual fund or insurance products or working as a property broker.

The additional income earned is called secondary income.

The secondary income could be less than 50% of the total income.

Tertiary Income

A person can add further income by investing in other sources as follows:

- ✓ Income from interest on deposits with Banks and Companies.
- ✓ Income from rental properties – residential or commercial.
- ✓ Income from business as a sleeping partner or as an investor.
- ✓ Earns income from Company shares through dividends.
- ✓ Income by being a blog-writer or conducting classes in an institute during weekends.

The tertiary income could be less than 20% of the total income.

Fourth/Fifth Income Source

There are many smart people who get income from fourth or fifth source.

The sources of income and its contribution to overall kitty will vary from person to person.

Derisking Income Sources

A person can reduce his income risk by adding more sources of income over time. As one progresses in age, one should try to reduce risk by depending on only one source of income, say, primary source. At the time of retirement, the primary source will dry up and plans must be made to replace primary income through some other sources. A smart investor would have forecast his future and planned out his secondary and tertiary sources while hitting the age of 50 years. Retirement income planning is all about this. Since retirement is a certainty, why not plan it well in advance?

An example could be as follows.

Age	Primary %	Secondary %	Tertiary %	Fourth/fifth %
25	100	–		
40	90	10		

50	75	20	5	
60	0	55	25	20

How Much Income Do You Need?

This is to be answered by each person as it involves personal expectations, habits, place that you live, number of members of the family, whether you have own house or rented and financial commitment for members of the family.

What one person thinks as luxury may be looked at as "essential" for another person. Example: AC at home is a luxury for one person whereas another person looks at it as "essential". Getting bottled water by a person in a Metro is considered essential whereas a person located in a small town looks at it as luxury.

For most people sources of income are fixed, whereas the avenues for spending are many. One can even discover new avenues to spend. Let us look at types of expenses for a middle-class home.

House Rent	Medical expenses
Food-related household expenses	Social expenses (Marriages, Birthdays)
Utility expenses – Electricity, Water, Gas, TV, Phone bills, Internet, Mobile bills,	Entertainment (Movies, Shows, Picnics, Eating out, personal, Clothes)
Support staff- Servant, Gardener and Cook	Personal clothing
Children's education – Fees, Books, Tuition, transportation and uniform	Knowledge update – Newspapers, magazines and books
Furnishing of house	

Vehicle repair and petrol bills	
Building maintenance	
Apartment Maintenance charges	

Important Tips

- Saved income as Deposits and investments in appreciating assets are not expenses.
- Investments in non-appreciating expenses must be treated as expenses.

Example: Loan interest paid for housing loan cannot be entirely treated as an expense. But, loan interest paid for a car has to be treated as 100% expense as the value of asset falls over time.

However, both expenses must figure in monthly calculations for assessment of monthly budget.

3.6 Self Audit - Personal Income vs. Expenses

The first step towards becoming a financially literate person is introspection done by an individual about his sources of income, total income vs. planned expenses on monthly basis. You need to become aware of your current reality. Today is the reality and tomorrow is "wishful thinking" or a dream. We cannot plan day-to-day life based on dreams.

- How much do I earn?
- How much do I spend?
- How much do I save?
- Am I on debt or do I have surplus with me?

Income Vs. Expenses Monthly Audit

Sources of Income	Expenses
Primary [first]	Rent

Secondary second]	Utilities
Tertiary [third]	Children's education
Fourth	Medical
Fifth	Clothes
	Social expenses
TOTAL	**TOTAL**

SAVINGS _____ **OR EXPECTED GAP** _____

Income – Expenses = Savings [+] OR Possible Debt [–]

In savings, you can add the deducted PF money. But Income Tax deduction to be shown as expenses as this amount is unlikely to come back to your account.

3.7 Four Types of Wealth-Owners

Group – 1: Crisis State Income

If your income is less than expenses, you are in a state of financial crisis. To survive, you have the following options:

- Increase income suddenly – This is almost impossible unless you get into crime!
- Cut down expenses – This can be done almost immediately, particularly, the non-essential.
- Borrow if you have assets like Gold or Bank deposits from private parties or NBFC or Banks
- Sell assets – if you have assets!

[It is impossible to sell some assets on short-term basis].

Group – 1: Strategy

- Take up income-generating job
- Switch over to high-income job

- Encourage spouse to take up full/part-time job
- Do not use any credit card
- Try selling some assets

The objective of strategy is to end up with at least 10% of your income as savings.

Group – 2: Survival State Income

This is the financial state wherein an individual survives as good as on day-to day basis. At the end of the day or end of the month, if his/her savings are much less than 10% of the income, it can be considered a survival state.

The best option available for the individual is to cut non-essential expenses and increase savings to 10% or higher.

Group – 2: Strategy

- Evaluate expenses and look at what expenses can be curtailed or totally stopped
- Explore getting higher paying job
- Encourage spouse to take up full/ part time job
- The objective is to reach income state of at least 10% savings of the income

Group – 3: Wealth Creation State of Income

This is a healthy financial state wherein an individual saves 10–20% of the total income. The individual can now focus on creating long term wealth for self and family by deploying the saved amount in appropriate assets. This book is meant for those who are in this state of creation of wealth.

Group – 3: Strategy

This group needs to study investment avenues and carefully plan investments.

It is worthwhile spending Rs. 1000–3000 per year on the following

– Attend investment/personal finance training courses
– Read a few books and journals on investments

- Subscribe to a personal finance online journal
- Subscribe to Finance newspapers
- Consult CAs and CFPs
- You need to have software or tracking mechanism for all your investments and wealth.

[There are many online types of software and Apps available FREE.

Example: www.moneycontrol.com OR www.valueresearchonline.com]

Remember!

- Do not make investment decision simply based on advice given by friends, relatives and colleagues.
- Do not make investment decisions based on newspaper headlines.

Examples:

"SENSEX ZOOMS PAST 11000!

INVESTORS DANCE IN DALAL STREET!

AMBANI ADDS 50,000 CRORES WEALTH!

- Do not take an investment decision because someone else made great success.

Group – 4: Wealthy/Rich Income

If your savings are more than 20% of income, and if it runs into millions, you have the potential to be among top 5–10% of the Indian population in terms of wealth. In such a state of income, you need to plan and manage your wealth with professional help. Wealth management has to be done by allocating or reallocating wealth under different asset classes based on the growth potential at different phases of your life while looking at various economic opportunities that come up.

Group – 4: Strategy

- ✓ You need to have a software or tracking mechanism for all your investments and
- ✓ You must have the services of CA on annual retainer basis to file your Income Tax returns and take care of wealth tax and capital gains tax.

- ✓ You must have proper bookkeeping for audit purpose.
- ✓ You may need the services of a CFP to plan your investments and wealth.
- ✓ You may need the services of a good lawyer to protect your interests by drafting various finance documents.
- ✓ You need to study and plan your investment decisions carefully while taking into account return on investments and tax implications.
- ✓ Need to have a clearly laid up plan for allocation of asset in term of real estate/equity/debt/ tax saving investment, etc.
- ✓ You need to protect your assets with the help of various insurance plans.

3.8 Income/Wealth Paradox

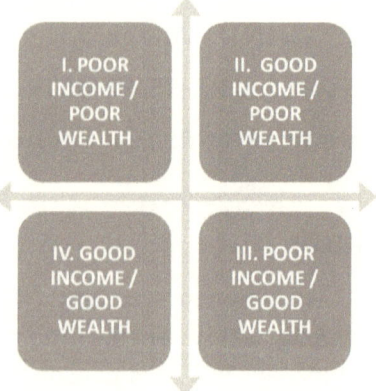

[INCOME/WEALTH PARADOX]

Income and wealth are paradoxical at times as shown in these examples. And, a person can figure in any of above matrix based on his income vs. wealth.

Example 1: HIGH WEALTH IS NOT A GUARANTEE FOR HIGH INCOME!

There is a lady who has inherited Rs. 200 million worth of plot in the middle of the city after her husband's death but she lives on monthly pension of

Rs. 10,000/- She finds it difficult to pay property tax or go for medical treatment.

Example 2: HIGH INCOME IS NO Guarantee FOR WEALTH OR ABILITY TO MEET EMERGENCIES.

This young man passed out of a leading institute and he is on salary bracket of 2 million p.a. He has no assets and even his fancy car is on EMI. He lives in a posh locality with monthly rent of Rs. 70,000/-. He is newly married and lives life to the fullest and has less than Rs. 100,000/- bank balance. He has life insurance worth Rs. 0.50 million and medical insurance of Rs. 0.20 million.

What if he meets with a fatal road accident? How will his wife handle it?

What if he dies suddenly? What will he leave behind? And what will his wife do?

3.9 Wealth Liquidity

Wealth can be broadly classified as liquid/semiliquid/poorly liquid. These classifications are not "cast in stone", but a few variations and exceptions are possible.

LIQUID	SEMI-LIQUID
• Cash in SB A/c • Cash in Hand	• PPF • Gold/ Silver • Insurance Policies • Bank FD/ Liquid fund
LOW LIQUIDITY	**FLUCTUATING**
• Houses/ Plots • Agri land/Comm bldg	• Mutual Fund • Shares

[ASSET LIQUIDITY]

CHAPTER 4
Psychology of Wealth-Creation

4.1 Three Hurdles Stop Us from Creating Wealth!

Who does not want to be wealthy? But only a few can reach levels of financial freedom and truly feel the power of financial wealth. Let us look at what is holding us back from financial success.

These are the three personal and emotional hurdles that are standing in our way, blocking our journey towards higher financial success.

1st Hurdle – Your Lack of Financial Literacy

The first hurdle towards financial success is your lack of financial education. You cannot delegate basic financial education. You have to take charge yourself.

To improve your body muscles, you cannot ask someone else to do exercise on your behalf. You need to learn different types of exercises and learn the science and art of building muscles. You need to undergo the exercises and learn by trial and error. At best, you can learn the steps from a trainer or pick up some tips from books. But, you need to sweat it out.

To learn financial literacy, you can learn steps from books like this. But you need to develop the skill through your commitment and experiential learning process. Even if you involve experts, you need to put the final signature.

First step to cross the hurdle: Learn the steps and take charge of your financial life!

2nd Hurdle – Your Psychological State of Blaming Family and Parents

I have seen some people blaming dead parents, family and friends for every failure in adult life.

Blaming one's parents for adult problems like poverty, inability to get a stable job, alcoholism, sexual infidelity, addiction to credit card, taking personal loans, emotional imbalance, etc. is irrational and takes away the responsibility from your shoulders!

I do not want to disregard the negative impact of a particular background or advantages of a privileged background on the lives of people. People with certain privileged backgrounds will have greater exposure to financial information than others.

Adults can make a whole lot of intelligent choices which can help one to overcome initial disadvantages and move forward. It is too late in life to blame parents, family and friends for all the current miseries in life.

3rd Hurdle – Blaming Current Income and Current Employer

Very often people blame their financial short-term inability to earn higher income for their current state.

Each person has to realize that there is no state of "satisfied income". If you earn Rs. 0.50 million p.a., you can be satisfied and with no debt; but even if you earn Rs. 2.00 million p.a., you can be dissatisfied and live in serious debt.

Most often, it is not the level of income, but what you do with your current income that matters. It has to do with how much you spend and how much you save and where you choose to invest.

Let us compare the life and financial status of two brothers –Ram and Shyam. Both have identical background, spouses and family size. But their income, savings and investments vary.

Types of Investments Can Make Us Rich or Poor

Rs. million	RAM	SHYAM
Annual income	0.80	1.00
Annual Expenses	0.60	0.80
Savings	0.18	0.20
Investments made	Equity/ELSS which gives 14% return PA	Bank deposits and PPF which gives return of 7.5%
Investment value after 20 years (Pre-Tax)	1,93,09,088	1,10, 80,366

Through Ram earned 20% lesser income compared to Shyam, at the end of 20 years he was 75% richer than Shyam, because he made wiser investment choices.

Key Lesson

> ❖ Each person's life and wealth is determined by the financial choices that we make today.
>
> ❖ **DO NOT BLAME OTHERS FOR THE POOR CHOICES THAT WE MAKE TODAY.**

4.2 Changing Personal Habits for Wealth-Creation

Development of financial literacy leading to creation of personal wealth involves major changes in your outlook and personal habits. Your financial behaviour changes slowly as you change each of your financial habits. Over a period of time, your financial personality itself will undergo change. If anyone told you that you can become wealthy without changing your financial habits and behaviour, he is fooling you.

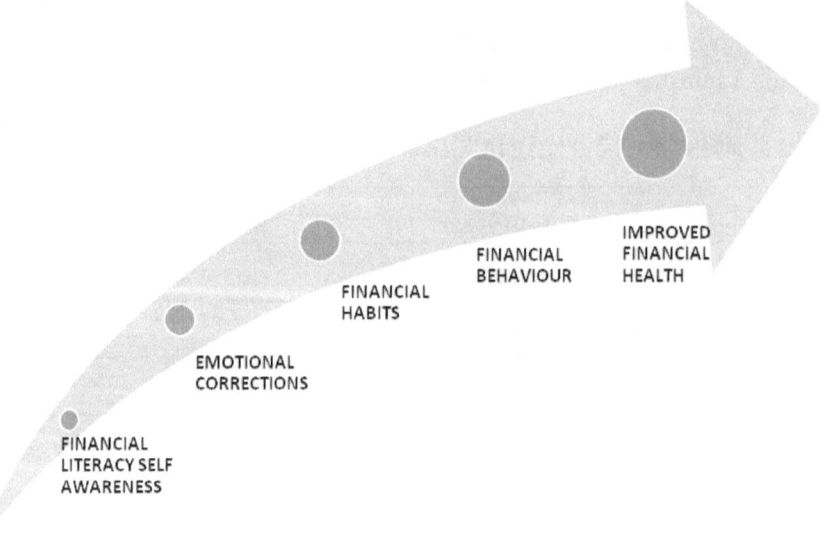

[DEVELOPMENT OF FINANCIAL BEHAVIOUR]

Changing Personal Habits for Wealth-Creation

Let us look at some of the current habits that require to be changed before trying to become wealthy. Each person has a set of personal financial habits and you need to discover these yourself.

The following example must be treated as a triggering point towards self-realization.

Personal Habit Change		
Savings on household	**Current habit**	**Proposed habit**
Food items	Current buying ½ kg – 1 kg	Can I buy in bulk for a month? Can I buy online?
Electricity	Normal bulbs/tubes	Can I install CFL bulbs/tube?
Mobile	Post-Paid	Can it be pre-paid?
Water	Packed containers	Can I install filters?
Purchase from mall	I buy what I see	I go to supermarket with a written-down list and stick to it
Savings on Cars – Fuel	Petrol	Can I switch to diesel? Can I install fuel-saving device?
Entertainment – Movies	First day First show	Can I see it later? Can I install online movies' channel at home?
Eating	I eat what I see or like	I order after seeing menu prices. I drink less at bars

Housing Loan	20 years with XYZ Bank	Can I renegotiate with another Bank for loan interest? Can I pre-close loan if there is no I-T benefit?
Vehicle Loans	5 years with XYZ Bank	Can I pre-close without penalty? Can I switch over to another Bank?
Credit card	Monthly payment of minimum balance	I read minutely to check for errors Can I close credit cards altogether? Can I use only debit card? Can I close credit card of spouse? I refuse free credit card offers
Debit card	I have debit cards of 4 – 5 banks	Can I restrict it to max. two banks' debit cards?
SB A/C with banks	I have six bank SB accounts	Can I close all except 1 – 2? Can I transfer above minimum balance to F/D account?
Utility bills	I pay at the counter	Can I pay online and get discounts?
Loans	I sign on dotted line	I visit minimum three HFC or banks. I make comparative statements on interest and major finance options.

Mediclaim	My company pays for my Mediclaim	I cover entire family including parents whether I work for company or not. I make comparative study of premium, coverage, etc.
Lottery	I am lucky with lottery and cards.	It is stupid of me to spend huge money on lottery and money-based gambles.
Bargaining	It is a shame to bargain.	Only smart people bargain to save.
Money discussion	I do not discuss money with spouse and kids.	I discuss money with entire family in varying degrees. I have fixed budget for everyone.
Income Tax	My company deducts.	I calculate, plan and "agree" for deduction by company.
Tax planning investments	Done in March every year after I get notice from Accounts department.	Done in April when financial year starts. I opt for SIP in ELSS.
Expense Tracking diary	I do not keep track of expenses.	I track expenses daily.
Saving Target	I save once a year.	I save daily and, on each transaction.
Credit card	I make minimum payment.	I do not use EMI mandate and I do not use credit cards for rewards.
Emergency Fund	I do not have one.	I keep six months' salary in emergency fund.

4.3 Fourteen Wealth-Killing Emotions: Beware!

"Money is not about finances, it's about emotions."

"We buy things we don't need with money; we don't have to impress people we don't like." [Anonymous]

A few months back I was at a store selling mobile phones. A man swiped his card while making a purchase and it returned with an error message. The man's response was in lightning speed to the pretty girl at the counter "But there is money. I have at least 1 million in that bank account."

Is it not the response of most of us when Bank card is denied by the swipe machine – embarrassment?

We are afraid the cashier will think we have no money! In this case, the man even let the lady know how rich he was!

Fear, shame and anger are common emotions surrounding money.

We all think that money is about our bank balance and cash in hand. Some people hate money and they think all their problems are due to money. Money has been the reason why some people have attempted suicide.

Money also influences how people treat you. A poor man walks into a high-end retail store or fast food joint and gets shooed out with contempt. A well-dressed man pulls up in a SUV and has a welcome mat rolled out for him. Pretty hostesses receive him. People have more respect for wealthy people: sad but true. That is the power of money!

- A bored housewife walks into a mall, carries trolley around, and keeps buying stuff her family does not need!
- An executive after a few drinks, orders a fancy mobile phone at midnight!
- A pretty girl offers "free credit card" at your Bank counter; you take it home though you do not require the credit card and any money or any other stuff on credit!

In short, we buy things that we do not need, at prices that are too high, from people who are not worthy to deal with and with terms and conditions which are rarely read!

We claim that we are rational in making financial decisions, but the truth is a large percentage of the financial decisions that we take are based on emotions and not with sufficient research or evaluation.

Let us look at various emotions that force us into bad financial decisions on day-to-day basis.

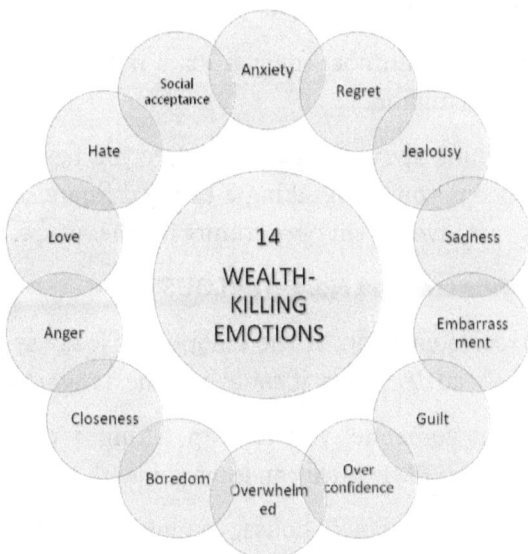

[14 WEALTH-KILLING EMOTIONS]

1. Money-destroying emotions No.1 – ANXIETY

Either you have lost money yourself or you saw someone close to you losing money while making investments in Company shares or housing plot.

Because of past incidents, now you are very anxious about the future. You are so terribly afraid that you end up taking no decision to invest even when market conditions favour you. Since you have limited knowledge about financial markets, you simply do not take decisions. With anxiety you sell financial assets after seeing mild fluctuation in prices. Either way, you lose out in the long run.

2. Money-destroying emotion No.2 – REGRET

A large percentage of Indians have regret about past financial decisions. Either they took a wrong decision of selling out an asset just before a climb in its value or did not decide to buy the asset when it was available at much lower price.

"I did not buy Infosys in 2000, when it was available at Rs. 50/- against current price of Rs. 1000/-."

"I did not buy housing plot in 2003 when it was available at Rs. 200 per square foot, against current price of Rs. 5000/-."

"I sold my 2BHK at Mumbai for just Rs. 2 million in 1998; look at the current price of Rs. 15 million!"

The more you think about the past the more you feel like a victim. This victim-mentality stops you from taking a rational financial decision today, which may be a great investment opportunity for the future.

3. Money-destroying emotion No.3 – JEALOUSY

Jealousy is a corrosive emotion. If the emotion of jealousy is the basis for taking various financial decisions, it could become dangerous.

After looking at someone, you end up taking a decision to buy an expensive car with high EMI which can leave you with very little savings.

After seeing your neighbour's house, you buy an expensive big LED TV, though you have been happy with a smaller version of TV.

You buy high-priced mobile phone with many advanced features even though you do not use even minimal features in your existing phone.

All these decisions are based on jealousy and not rational thinking.

4. Money-destroying emotion No.4 – SADNESS

There is this real, but, famous story of Kolkata industrialist's wife who gifted nearly Rs. 20,000 million worth of wealth including many big Companies to her Chartered Accountant friend! Current value is around Rs. 80,000 million. After the death of her husband, this lady became sad and a recluse as she had no kids. Her husband's CA was the single source of news and connection to the outside world. He was a nice and smart [and caring] guy. He kept her happy by visiting her often and managing small things like taking her to the doctor or taking her dog for a walk. At some point of time, she rewrote her will, gifting all her assets to the CA, who became owner of Rs. 20,000 million wealth including many publicly listed companies!

Divorce, accidents, sickness and death are sad incidents in a person's life. At this point, a person could take highly irrational decisions like gifting, selling or dividing assets unequally among kids.

5. Money-destroying emotion No.5 – embarrassment

Too often people put up a show of "Well-to-do" to avoid embarrassment. They go to expensive restaurants to impress people. They conduct functions like marriages and birthday parties at places which are too "up market" for their income. Have you not seen a junior Executive taking his girlfriend to a five-star hotel for lunch worth Rs. 5000/-, though his monthly salary may be only Rs. 25,000!

6. Money-destroying emotion No.6 – GUILT

Maybe you have been lucky. You got windfall profits from company closure or got a huge fortune after the death of a near one or you sold your software Company shares when the market was its peak and made a fortune. Now, you carry the guilt of this sudden wealth and you do not spend it. You start considering this as sin or ill-gotten wealth. Either way you are having wealth and if you do not want to get benefit out of it, why not gift it away to charity or religious trust?

7. Money-destroying emotion No.7 – OVERCONFIDENCE

Overconfidence comes from the gambler's instinct.

You get an SMS tip that investing in a particular share can give 30% return in 30 days. You make a quick decision of buying it. Gosh! The share has actually gone up by 30% soon after you buy. You are excited. From the same source you get the next tip that a scrip is likely to show jump of 40% within a month. Gosh! You have succeeded for a second time.

You start thinking that you are a brilliant investor. Now, for the third time, the same source tells you to invest a few millions of rupees, promising 50% appreciation and you are so confident that you put in Rs. 2 million, after cancelling your Bank FD and pumping into the share. After a few days, it drops by 20% from your purchase level. You are not shaken and you are confident that it will give 50% return. Within a few weeks, the share actually drops by 90% and you lose 90% of your original capital. You are devastated and depressed.

Overconfidence in yourself and market behaviour can have dangerous consequences.

8. Money-destroying emotion No.8 – OVERWHELMED/SENSE OF PARALYSIS

Whether you are a newly employed person trying to make a decision out of a dozen investment options or a person who has been submerged in a deluge of personal and credit card debts, you get confused and feel overwhelmed. You feel a sense of paralysis as to what decision to take and how to move forward.

Remember, you need to take a decision. Maybe you need to list down the list of issues confronting you and prioritize these.

A few decisions are better than no decision at all.

9. Money-destroying emotion No.9 – BOREDOM

People take a number of decisions because they are too tired to search for alternatives or are bored with details.

You try talking an OD/loan from a Bank. They will have a list of charges and clauses running into 1-2 pages. You are too tired or bored to go into details.

A bored housewife sitting at home orders various things online, many of which are not required by her family.

A fresh and active mind is needed to take rational and balanced financial decisions.

10. Money-destroying emotion No.10 – "CLOSENESS"

Imagine an Indian-looking guy speaking Hindi approaches you in a train in Paris.

You are happy to meet an Indian in a distant land. On the way he orders Indian food for you. He talks about old Bollywood movies. You are floored and you experience a sense of "closeness" and trust him. At the end of the journey, your bag is missing! You lost your cash and passport!

In a recent incident, a crooked couple's team led by a lady cheated hundreds of people in South India out of a few hundred million Rupees.

Virtually all those who got cheated were Muslims, and, the lady was a carrying a Muslim name! This happens very often when you trust people based on language, colour of skin, ethnicity, religion, and so on.

Whom to trust and whom you consider as "close" are very personal emotional decisions.

11. Money-destroying emotion No.11 – ANGER

Anger is an internal obstacle to wealth. If there is anger inside your soul, you are repelling money whether you are aware of it or not. When in anger, you end up taking irrational decisions on money which you would not have taken if you were in a cool frame of mind.

12. Money-destroying emotion No.12 – BLIND LOVE

Research has shown that financial difficulty was one of the biggest reasons for divorce among couples after infidelity.

Recently we read in the news that Jeff Bezos, the founder of AMAZON was paying Rs. 4.2 million worth alimony as part of divorce, because of his love affair with another lady! Love can destroy money!

Money cannot buy love. But money helps one to retain and nurture love. Those who are in blind love take highly irrational financial decisions.

13. Money-destroying emotion No.13 – HATRED

Hatred is another strong emotion which destroys rational decision-making. When you hate someone, you do not take a decision to deal with him or partner with him even though the relationship is likely to bring financial benefits to you. Hatred could be based on personal reasons or prejudices like caste or religion or language. Because of this hatred, you are unable to look at issues in the light of rationality.

14. Money-destroying emotion No.14 – SOCIAL ACCEPTANCE

We like to be respected and accepted by people. Because we have this need, we end up taking decisions which are not beneficial to us financially, but just for respect or acceptance. In a social group where bargaining by someone is considered "below dignity," one does not bargain even though you are likely to accrue benefits if you bargain or negotiate.

4.4 Understanding Risk Profile of an Investor

Broadly there are three factors which [must or should] influence an investor's decisions of investing. Together, these could be called the overall RISK PROFILE of the investor.

a. Risk attitude [Risk aversion] – How much risk do you wish to avoid?

b. Risk capacity – With your current financial status, how much risk can you afford to take?

c. Age of the investor – Are you young enough to cover up for probable losses?

Let us look at each of these factors to understand the overall risk profile of the investor.

The biggest drawback of many financial advisors is their inability to gauge the attitude of the investor to risks before suggesting finance products. If the financial advisors are not aware of investors' risk profile, chances are the investors will buy products by which the adviser will sleep well at night rather than the other way around.

Every investor has a different risk-attitude and risk-taking ability. You need to be aware of your risk-attitude before trying out any investment idea.

In the financial risk-taking ability, people can be conservative (Low-risk profile) at one extreme or very aggressive (high-risk profile) at the other extreme.

Risk-Attitude

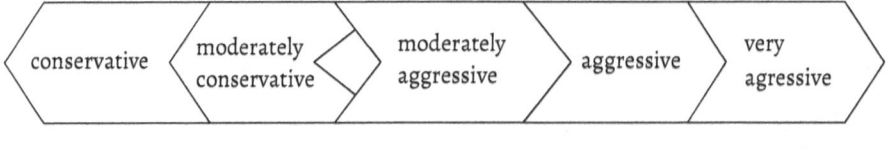

[RISK ATTITUDE]

This is an individual characteristic. Within the same family, an elder brother can have a "Conservative risk-profile" and younger brother could be having "Aggressive risk-profile". This individual nature comes due to varieties of reasons including influences in the childhood, friends, education, past experience, financial literacy and so on.

4.5 Five Types of Investors' Risk-Profiles

Conservative Investors

These are investors who are predominantly averse to risks. Investment losses in any given year will be unacceptable. Primary focus is on stability of invested amount. If annual returns are only 4–6%, it is ok, but loss of capital is strictly No! No! Such conservative investors prefer public sector bank FDs, post office products, gold and house located in a "known" geographical area.

Moderately Conservative Investors

Moderately conservative investors are those who do not mind a little bit of fluctuation in investment returns, but would be uncomfortable with significant ups and downs. They are willing to absorb some level of volatility and grudgingly can accept the same. They prefer predominantly cash-fixed-income investments like Banks FDS, Post office products, gold and moderate allocation to Mutual funds like balanced funds. Their understanding of stock market is very limited.

Moderately Agressive Investors

Moderately aggressive investors are those who wish to see consistent growth of their invested amount. They do not mind some amount of fluctuations in return, so long as it is growing on a long-term basis. They wish to strike a balance between portfolio-stability and portfolio-appreciation. They prefer to keep less of cash or cash equivalents. They prefer fixed income investments which give higher returns like company deposits, higher-FD interest-bank deposits, debt MF with some percentage of equity in it or balanced equity products, etc. They are long-term investors.

Aggressive [Growth Focus] Investors

These are the long-term investors who want to invest in products which offer good growth potential and do not need current income. They are willing to put up with higher levels of portfolio volatility and risk of principal's loss. They may be willing to have almost 45% of their investments in equities or

MFs with higher equity basis. They are also willing to invest upto 20% into small cup fund which has higher volatility. They may be willing to shift funds when time is ripe. Their understanding of all financial products and stock market is higher. They may have multiple sources of income too. They are also willing to lie low for long periods of 2–3 years.

Very Agressive Investors

They do not need current income and may have multiple sources of income and assets. These are the investors who are willing to take substantial risk. Their emphasis is on achieving above-average appreciation of portfolio over time which could be 4–6 years. They can take higher portfolio volatility and can invest into multiple financial assets enterprises, venture capitals, international shares and so on. They are typically leaders in a few fields – investments, business and so on and they have excellent access to financial information through research reports, analysis and so on. They bet high on sectoral funds, Small cap or Mid cap shares. They maintain "cash" in liquid funds with the intention of shifting to target companies or sectors when they feel that time is ripe.

4.6 Risk Capacity vs. Risk Aversion

Risk capacity of an investor refers to objective financial situation of the investor's sources of income and needs, regular income, wealth, type of wealth, investment horizons, tax rates, etc.

Example 1

Let us say there is the individual named Ramesh with total assets base of 50 million, and I believe this should be 10 million in fixed income funds. He has monthly income of Rs. 70,000 and does not have any dependant other than wife. He has risk taking capacity of Rs. 5 million which he can shift from fixed income funds as equity. Such shifting cannot challenge his current status significantly, but, he does not make this move.

Ramesh has risk capacity for Rs. 5 million and he is risk averse.

Example 2

Ashok is on the verge of retirement. He has 2BHK house (of Rs. 6 million) which still has two years of EMI left to be paid. He has PF worth Rs. 1.50 million and bank FD worth of Rs. 1 million. He earns Rs. 70,000/- p.m. and in his post-retirement period, will get a pension of Rs. 30,000/-. Someone advises him to shift Rs. 1 million FD to equity MF. Is it a right advice?

Ashok does not have risk capacity of Rs. 1 million considering his EMI and near-retirement situation. Ashok is not very risk averse, but has low risk capacity.

Risk aversion is the state of mind of the investor, who prefers lower returns with known risk, rather than higher returns with unknown risk. Risk aversion is a combination of psychological traits and emotional response that determines the investor's willingness to take a financial risk and the degree of psychological and emotional pain the investor experiences when faced with financial loss. Often, emotional and psychological factors are far more important than economic factors, which are difficult to understand. The combination of RISK CAPACITY and RISK AVERSION (risk ability) constitutes what is called INVESTOR'S RISK PROFILE

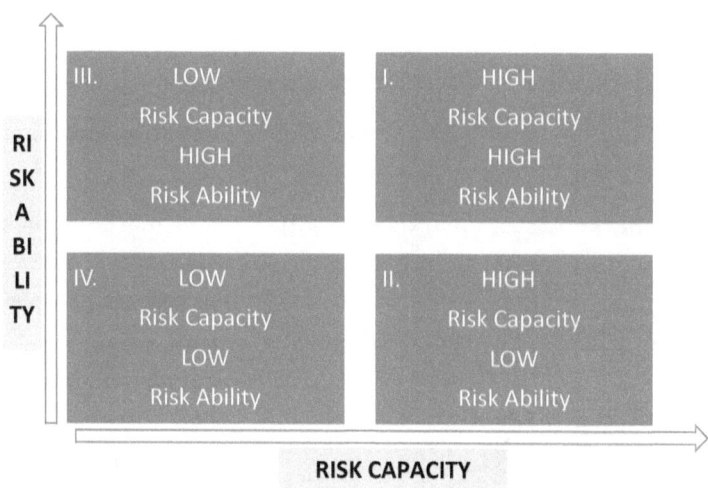

[RISK PROFILE MATRIX]

Quadrant 1 - Big Time Winners

Those who have both high risk-capacity and high risk-ability: They are aggressive, conquerors, big-time winners, and fighters. They are highly successful entrepreneurs and venture capitalists.

Quadrant 2 – Fearful

Those who have capacity to take financial risk. But, their high risk-aversion is stopping them from moving forward and adding significant wealth. They need support and guidance of a good financial advisor.

Quadrant 3 – Learners

Those in this quadrant have low risk-capacity, but are willing to learn and experiment. If they play their cards well, they will add wealth over time. They need to reduce their rate of failure by rational planning of their portfolio.

Quadrant 4 – Zero-Action People

Those who are in this quadrant are low risk-takers and are likely to remain where they are. They will listen to all and end up doing nothing.

Factors Influencing Risk Profile

1. Our genetic predisposition to take a financial risk.
2. The people we interact with and their influence on our views. Family, relatives, friends, colleagues, geographical area that we grew up in.
3. The circumstances that we experience in our lifetime, particularly, our formative years.
4. Business and stock market cycles: If the stock market is on bull-run, people are more willing to make investments. However, when the stock market is on down-turn or bear market, people are less inclined to take financial risk.

4.7 Risk vs. Reward Matrix

Please look at RISK PROFILE MAP as given below. Where do you figure?

In the Risk vs. Reward matrix, there could be "high risk/high reward"-oriented people like venture capitalists and entrepreneurs or those who do senior corporate jobs. The likely reward for them is likely to be much higher than for those who do "safe jobs" like being a clerk in a Government department or an assistant in a big private firm.

Then there are people who take big-time risk without proper analysis or maturity. These could be insane or idiots. Or just gamblers. A man in a junior job trying to make huge investments in small-cap fund is either an idiot or insane.

There are two groups who stand out in this matrix – those who hold senior corporate jobs and successful entrepreneurs. They strike a balance in terms of risk vs. reward.

RISK VS. REWARD MATRIX – WHERE DO YOU FIGURE?

Risks				
Insane Idiots Gamblers	Saints	Day Traders	VCs
Illiterates	Desperate	Senior Corporate Jobs	Entrepreneurs
Safe Jobs	Unsafe Jobs	Inheritance	
Unemployed	Part time Jobs		Politicians

Reward

[INVESTOR'S RISK PROFILE MAP]

Now, let us look at the "potential return" when you invest into certain investment classes.

4.8 Investment Strategy - Risk vs. Return

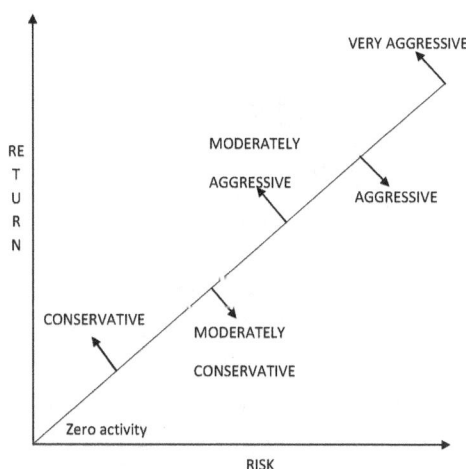

[INVESTMENT STRATEGY FOR RISK PROFILE]

Broad Asset-Allocation Strategy Based on Risk Profile

These are not "promised" or "anticipated" returns, but, returns likely under normal conditions.

The higher the risk of investment, the higher the return could be.

Example: When one invests into small-cap shares or small-cap MF, the probable return could be 20–25%. However, if stock market goes into a declining phase (bear phase) the return could drop to 30–35% lesser than invested capital itself. This is the kind of risk in return one must consider while making investments.

It would be foolish or highly risky if a person working as an Assistant in a private company or doing a junior Govt. job decides to opt for a small cap fund when he wants to invest. Further, if he invests major part of his savings into this fund, he is gambling beyond his economic state.

4.9 Risk Profile vs. Products Chosen

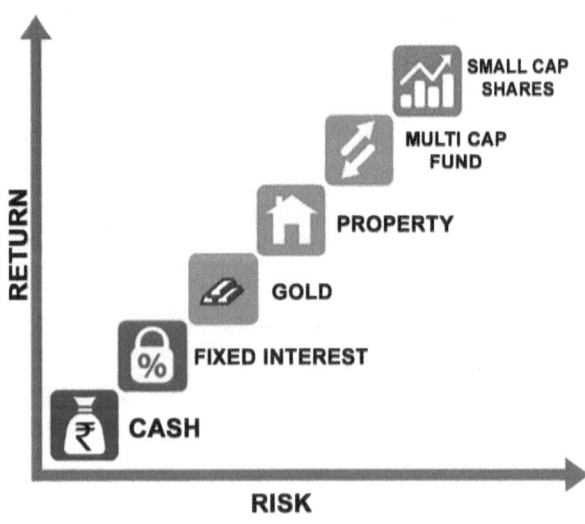

[ASSET CHOSEN VERSUS RISK/RETURN]

Conservative Investors

Returns – Average return 7.0%.   Best in year 8.0%.   Worst in year 6.5%.

Attitude – Investors who seek current income and stability; less concerned about growth of investments.

Products chosen – Cash in bank [3–5%], Bank deposits [6–8%], and PPF/Govt. savings [7–8%]

Moderately Conservative Investors:

Returns – Average return 8.0%.   Best in year 9.0%   Worst in year 6.0%

Attitude – Investors who seek current income and stability, with moderate potential in the growth in value of investments.

Products chosen – Debt MF-7–8%, High-debt hybrid funds – 8–10%, Company deposits – 8.5–10.0%

Residential rental – 2–3% PA

Moderately Aggressive Investors:

Returns – Average 10%   Best in year 20%   Worst in year [-10%]

Attitude-Long term investors who do not need current income and want some growth potential. Willing to accept some fluctuation in value but not significant erosion of value.

Products chosen – large-cap funds 9–12%, Multi-Cap funds-12–14%, Aggressive hybrid funds-10–12%

Commercial rental 5–7% p.a.

Aggressive Investors:

Returns – Average 13–14%   Best in year 30%   Worst in year [-30%]

Attitude – Long-term investors who want growth but do not need current income. Prepared for fair amount of volatility. Prepared to invest fair amount in equities.

Products chosen – Mid-Cap funds-15–20%, Businesses 20%+, Sector funds 20–30%

Very Aggressive Investors:

Returns – Average 16–18%   Best in year 30%,   Worst in year [-35%]

Attitude – Investors who seek high growth on long-term basis. Do not need current income. Willing to take big bets for high growth. Prepared for significant erosion of value in the cycle.

Products chosen – Small Cap funds 20–35%, Businesses 30% +, Venture capital – 40–50%

Before you choose a finance product for investment, please ponder as to where you figure. If you are a "moderately conservative" investor, you need to choose products which will go along with your profile. Your returns will be in the range of 9%. Because you have chosen certain class of products, you can never get returns higher than 10% and you can take safety of consolation that even in the worst scenario, you will never lose capital. If you are a "moderately conservative" investor, you can dabble in high debt-oriented hybrid funds. High equity-oriented funds are strictly NO-NO for you.

CHAPTER 5
Economy, Markets & Asset Classes

5.1 Types of Markets

In the economy, there are different classes of assets grouped together to be called **markets**.

Stock markets: Market where Company shares and debentures are traded.

Real estate market: Market where various types of real estate assets are traded. It could be apartments, housing plots and commercial buildings.

Currency market: Where various currencies are traded – Dollar, Rupee, Pound, etc.

Metal market: Where metals are traded – Steel, Copper, Tin, Brass, Aluminium, Zinc, etc.

Bullion market: Market where precious metals like gold, silver, platinum, etc. are traded.

Agricultural market: Agricultural commodities are traded – rubber, rice, pulses, wheat, corn, cotton, oats, etc.

Soft agricultural market: Market where coffee, sugar, cashew nuts, pepper, cardamom, etc. are traded.

Livestock market: Market where bulls, cows, buffaloes, goat, chicken, etc. are traded.

Energy market: Market where crude oil, Natural gas and Petroleum products are traded.

OTC Market vs. Exchange - Traded Market

In OTC market, the item is traded one-to-one or across the table. In this situation, most of the time actual delivery of the item takes place in physical terms.

In exchange-traded markets, the actual delivery of the item may not take place. Generally, it is less than 2% of the total deals. Based on the global and local demand, buyers and sellers take positions to buy and sell. It is more of a speculative position. There are currently four commodity exchanges approved in India of which MCX (Multi Commodity Exchange of India) at Mumbai is the biggest.

In these exchanges official contracts are exchanged between traders, giving legal sanctity.

All Markets Are Cyclical

Seasons are the best example of cycles. After spring, there is summer. After summer, there is autumn or winter. Similarly, commodities and financial markets undergo Seasons. In a bull-market, share prices zoom up. In a bear market, prices drop dramatically, the only difference being, each cycle length could vary from a few months to a few years. This is true in commodities' market too. Prices do not go up forever and prices do not go down forever. At some point, the trend is reversed.

Sensex [Share Market]

Between 2000 and 2014, your Sensex jumped from 3000 points to 22000 points.

Price fluctuations:

- There are hourly fluctuations
- There are weekly fluctuations
- There are monthly fluctuations
- They are yearly fluctuations in each of these markets

5.2 The Importance of Market Cycles and Price Fluctuations

Market Cycles

An understanding of market cycle is essential if you want to maximize investment and trading returns. Those who understand market cycles make most returns. And, those who ignore market cycles get the least returns. Let us look at the four components of market cycles and how we can recognize these.

1. Accumulation Phase

This phase occurs after the market prices have bottomed out and there is gloom all around. In this phase, valuation of assets is very attractive and the general market sentiment is bearish. Articles in the media talk about doom and gloom. Most investors have sold their assets at "available" prices and got out in disgust. There are trading experts, technical experts and veteran investors who are impressed by the low-priced, quality assets which can be picked up for a song! They start buying assets slowly over a few or many trading sessions. Since market is in depressed state, hardly anyone notices these and almost no one talks about this quiet buying and accumulation of assets.

2. Mark-up Phase

In this phase, market is beginning to move higher. Early majority is getting into the bandwagon. This includes technical and trading experts. Media talks about "worst phase is over" kind of stories. As the phase matures, the number of people getting into the bandwagon increases. Over a period of time, prices start peaking. As the prices peak, many who have been waiting on the sidelines enter. The market sentiment moves to a state of euphoria.

3. Distribution Phase

This is an emotional phase of the market. From previous bullish sentiment, this market is having mixed sentiment. Sellers dominate the market. Many expert traders sell and move out slowly. The market sentiment moves from complete fear interspersed with hope and even greed. Valuations reach sky-high and extreme prices start getting quoted. Smart investors dump stocks and move out of the market. A sudden geopolitical event or extremely bad economic news can break the market and push the slide downwards. Prices keep dropping.

4. Mark-down Phase

This is the fourth and the final phase in the cycle and is most painful for those who hold high bought-out position. When market drops more than 50%, they sell and surrender. All-round gloom sets in. Media gives kind of stories like "Bloodbath in Dalal Street". This phase can continue for weeks and months.

Meanwhile, smart value investors start picking up assets at very low prices. This accumulation of assets happens over a period of time. And, it heralds the next Accumulation phase.

An example of market cycle is given below. This is the way Sensex cycle behaved for the period June 2014 to July 2018. Those who bought at the peak and sold when the market came down, suffered badly. However, those who bought when the market was down, gained when market picked up and they sold their position. The problem is, almost no one knows when it is up or down. The only way to get the best out of the market is to stay on for long. Exactly the reason why experts suggest that the investor must stay on for 7–10 years to get best benefits.

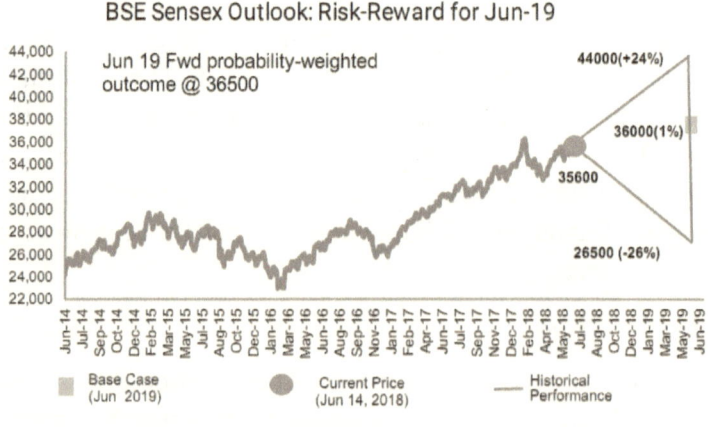

[BSE INDEX]

Timing

A cycle can last from a few weeks to a number of years depending on the type of market one is looking at. A day-trader may see such cycle 4–5 times a day. For a real-estate investor, the cycle could last 5–15 years period.

How Do Cycles Help?

Cycles exist in all markets and there are opportunities to accumulate and sell. For a smart investor, the accumulation time is the time to buy assets because he sees gloom all around and he sees assets are available at attractive valuations or very low prices. They take a contrarian view.

They sell when the market is peaking and take rest, while all others are madly buying. A smart investor does not follow the crowd and never takes positions based on "reports to buy" from newspapers and journals. By the time people talk about attractive valuations, he would have accumulated a good amount of assets at much lower prices.

Market cycles and price fluctuations offer the greatest opportunity to buy assets at low prices or sell at high prices. It is a blessing for a smart investor.

5.3 Speculation in Financial Markets

What is Speculation? Who are speculators?

Speculation is the buying of an asset or financial instrument with the hope that the price of the asset or financial instrument will increase in the future. Speculative investors tend to make decisions more often based on technical analysis of market price action rather than on fundamental analysis of an asset. Speculators are an important and valuable part of the world's financial markets.

A speculator is a person who buys assets, financial instruments, commodities or currencies with the hope of selling them at profit on a future date. So they're not really all that fundamentally different from other market participants who also enter the financial markets looking for financial rewards.

The speculator's active involvement is what keeps various markets on the move. They provide life to the market and influence prices on hour-to-hour basis.

Difference between investor and speculator

An investor is concerned with the fundamental value of his investment, whereas a speculator is only concerned with market price movement.

In other words, for example, a speculator doesn't really care if a company is performing well or poorly – only about whether or not he can profit from trading the company's stock.

Types of Speculators

[STOCK MARKET]

- **Bullish Speculator** – A bullish speculator expects prices of securities to rise. A bull is a speculator who buys the securities with the hope of selling them at a higher price in the future.

- **Bearish Speculator** – A bearish speculator is one who expects prices of securities will fall in the future. A bearish speculator sells short securities, aiming to profit from being able to repurchase them at a lower price at some point in the future.

Speculation in the Stock Market

Stocks that are considered highly risky in the stock market are known as speculative stocks. Speculative stocks offer potential high returns to compensate for the high risk associated with them. Penny stocks with very low share prices are an example of speculative stocks. Some stock market speculators are day traders who seek to profit from the intraday fluctuations in stock prices that occur within the trading day. As noted above, speculators are important to publicly-traded companies because they are willing to invest in unproven companies, providing those companies with equity funding that enables them to grow and expand their market reach.

Speculation in the Currency Market

The foreign currency exchange (Forex) market is popular with speculators because of the fact that there are constant fluctuations in the exchange rates between currencies, both on an intraday and long-term basis. The currency market also provides frequent trading opportunities due to the many different currency pairs that are available for trading. For example, the exchange rate of the US dollar can be traded relative to more than a dozen other currencies worldwide.

Speculation in the Commodity Market

In the commodity markets, speculation is important to control the price volatility of commodities because without speculators there would be only a very limited number of market participants. Commodities are much less widely traded than stocks. Speculators add significantly more liquidity to the commodity markets, thereby helping to facilitate trading among all the market participants. Speculation in commodity futures is popular because, like Forex trading, commodity trading offers traders high amounts of leverage.

5.4 Economic Asset Classes

Understanding asset class

There is no universally accepted standard or category of economic asset classes. However, there are the 5 types of Asset classes which have high acceptance in the context of middle classes to "well-to-do" category.

Asset Class Comparison

Asset Class No.1 – CASH OR CASH EQUIVALENT

When we say "cash" it does not means bundles of hard cash. It means money lying in SB A/C at Bank or liquid mutual fund – all of which can be quickly converted to "cash" and are liquid. The freedom with cash is very high. You can buy almost buy anything with "cash" – phones, TV, ornaments, plots, books, a flat, etc. Further, cash transactions cannot be tracked easily.

Caution!

Recently Government introduced a law which prohibits cash transactions above Rs. 200,000/- in any one single transaction. There are provisions for penalty equal to the cash transactions above Rs. 200,000/-.

Return

Among all asset classes' cash or cash equivalents give low returns. With hard cash at home or in lockers you get zero returns.

SB A/C – interest on SB accounts could be as low as 3.5%. Some new generation banks may offer 6% interest for SB accounts.

MF Liquid funds – These may give return of 5–7% p.a.

Asset class No.2 – FIXED INCOME

This is the most popular class in India, particularly among lower middle and upper middleclass. It could be Govt. products like PPF, NSC, SCSS, PO MIP, Bank FDs, Bonds or Company Deposits.

These are financial products where invested amount is more or less guaranteed to be returned. The returns are generally low, but prefixed or it is more or less predictable. Investing in FIXED INCOME ASSET CLASS is like lending money to someone with the assurance of return of capital along with pre-determined (more or less) "extra" (call it by any name – dividend or interest).

These financial products offer annualized return in the range of 5–8%, but many people do not realize that it is a pre-tax return. The income from these products, most of the time, gets added to an individual's income and is taxed accordingly. Hence, you end up paying 10–30% Income Tax on the returns received. The post-Tax returns are barely higher than inflation, which may amount to negative returns!

Asset Class No.3 – COMMODITIES

Commodities refer to various types of physical goods or products which we buy to hold or sell.

Long term investment commodities (Precious metals)

Gold and silver are long-term investment commodities. These appreciate in value over a period of time.

Commodities for trading

These are commodities which are bought with the intention to sell when you are able to reach levels that you anticipated.

Metals – Copper, Brass, Iron, Tin, Aluminium

Agro products-Pepper, Cardamom, Rubber, Clove, Cooking oil, Rice, Pulses, Cotton, etc.

Petroleum products – Petroleum-related products, Plastics, etc.

Asset Class No. 4 – REAL ESTATE

Real estate refers to all physical space in land and buildings.

Classification Based on Types/Usage

AGRICULTURAL LANDS – Paddy fields, coffee plantation (Rubber, coffee, tea, pepper & cardamom) cultivating dry land, etc.

COMMERCIAL BUILDINGS – Shops, godowns, factory sheds, office buildings.

HOUSING – Individual houses, flats, paying-guest accommodation.

CITY HOUSING PLOTS – Housing Plots approved by local governing authority.

REIT (Real Estate Investment Trust) – is a new development in India. These are shareholding in companies which own or finance income-generating real estate in a range of property sectors. It could be commercial buildings, residential complexes, hostels, etc. Internationally these shares are traded like any other company shares in the exchange.

Asset Class No.5 – EQUITY & EQUITY LINKED ASSETS

When you buy equity shares of a company you are buying a small percentage of the ownership of the company, though you have no controlling interest. It means, you let existing Directors or Management to run the company. Over a period of time company's revenue and profits grow. The profits generated and distributed among shareholders is in proportion to the shares that you hold. Further, with the increased profits, part of it gets accumulated as "Reserves". A good financially sound company will have significant reserves and low debt. This results in higher market value for its shares.

Four types of equity and equity-linked investments:

- Equity shares bought directly from stock exchange
- Buying mutual funds which have holding in equity shares
- Shares of privately held companies (Unlisted)
- Shares of self/family owned business

CHAPTER 6
Saving Habits and Investing

Saving Money

6.1 Marshmallow Experiment and Lesson for Saving Money

In 1960–70 period a Stanford University Professor conducted a series of studies on delayed gratification called "Marshmallow experiment".

In these experiments, kids were given marshmallow (a type of sweet) and offered choice to eat one marshmallow or wait for 15 minutes and then get one more marshmallow as a gift. Only $1/3^{rd}$ of the kids could wait 15 minutes. Meaning $2/3^{rd}$ kids could not delay their gratification.

In follow-up studies of the same children as adults, the researchers found that children who were able to wait 15 minutes tended to have better life outcomes, as measured by SAT [competitive exam] test scores, education attainment, BMI (Body Mass Index) to test whether they were overweight or not and other life measures. In short, they were able to control their body desires to have higher life achievements.

Similarly, saving requires will power to delay gratification. Those who have poor ability to delay gratification are unlikely to save enough. In practical terms, it means, not going for something which brings immediate satisfaction or pleasure, but settling for long term benefit with the money saved.

Choosing delayed gratification requires the ability to envision your desired future if you were to forego your current desire. If you cannot paint a vivid picture of your future, you will have little motivation to plan for it.

Saving Quotes for Thought

"Do not save what is left after spending, instead spend what is left after saving," says Warren Buffet, world's richest man.

"It's unfortunate how some people complain about being financially unstable, yet they use their last savings to acquire material things" –Edmond Mbiaka, economist.

6.2 Five Top Saving Habits of Millionaires

In various studies the following top saving habits were observed in millionaires from round the world:

1. Aggressive Saving Goals

Most Millionaires established aggressive saving goals early in life. They saved 20% or more of gross income. This may not be possible for everyone, but having an aggressive goal, yes.

2. Being Frugal Spenders

This does not require great intellect to understand. Being frugal means spending your money wisely. They are selective in their buying. They prioritize their buying, having less emotion-triggered buying. They are careful about the price at which they buy.

3. Avoid Lifestyle Creep

As one builds wealth, one adds up additional lifestyle products and activities to match the increased wealth: more expensive gadgets, vehicles, attire, house and so on. Millionaires are a little slow to increase lifestyle spending.

4. Keeping Expenses Low

Millionaires try to keep expenses low at every low. Not only their personal life, but also in the enterprises that they run. Many famous Indian entrepreneurs travel by economy class. [Example – Mr. Narayana Moorthy of Infosys]. World's richest man Mr. Warren Buffet drives his own car and he cuts his hair in a saloon near his house right from early life.

5. Surround Self with Right People

Millionaires surround themselves with the "right people". People who fit in their lifestyles and way of thinking. People who follow similar values in personal and professional life.

6.3 How to Save Money?

Visualizing Future

Every person must have a mental picture of self, family, wealth, assets for the future date.

A mental picture of what you wish to become, what you wish to acquire or where you wish to see family, etc.

A few examples are given below:

House
- I wish to stay in own apartment in another 15 years.
- I wish to stay in a 3 BHK Apartment.

Car
- I wish to drive my own car.

Children
- I wish to see my elder son joining MBBS/MBA.
- I wish to see my younger daughter getting married before 25 years.

Retire
- I wish to retire by 55 years with at least Rs. 20 million investments in MF, FD and others.

Future goal and current savings

Once you have a vivid future that you wish to see yourself in, you need to decide as to how you will reach these goals. There is no way you can reach these goals unless you have a strong-enough saving habit.

Saving is possible only if you delay your desire for gratification.

An example of your desire and how you control yourself which result in huge savings is given.

Desire	Actual Action	Net Saving
I wish to have dinner in a 4-star Hotel (Cost Rs. 4000/-)	I eat in a 2-star Hotel (Rs. 2000/-)	Rs. 2000/-
I will buy latest smart phone (Rs. 35000/-)	I will buy a one-year-old model Smart phone (Rs. 18000/-)	Rs. 17000/-

I will buy ABC brand shirt (Rs. 3000/-)	I will get the shirt stitched (Rs. 1500/-)	Rs. 1500/-
I will buy a luxury car for Rs. 1.20 million	I will buy another model for Rs. 0.70 million	Rs. 0.50 million
I will take an AC Taxi to go home (Rs. 500/-)	I will take an auto to go home (Rs. 200)	Rs. 300/-

There is an ongoing battle between your desire for gratification and what you actually do. It depends on your willpower and discipline.

What do you think about yourself?

Most often your mental perception is far different from what others think about yourself. For example, when you wear a Rs. 0.1 million-worth watch, you may feel that all others have noticed it.

The following may be the likely Scenario:

- 5% people have noticed it and thought that you could be a "rich man".
- 20% of the people noticed the watch and thought that the value is not more than Rs. 10,000/-
- 20% of the people noticed the watch and thought the value of the watch is not more than Rs. 3,000/-
- 35% of the people did not notice the watch at all.
- 20% of the people may have thought you are wearing a duplicate watch bought from the roadside.

So, if your circle of contacts has 50 people, hardly 2 people noticed the value of the watch to be Rs. 100,000. If you will not see both these people for the rest of the life, you would have lost the perception battle by 100%!

Three Important Points about Saving

SAVE REGULARLY - Make monthly "saving and investment" a habit.	SAVE AS OFTEN AS POSSIBLE - Save money daily. Try saving money on each transaction. Make monthly investment of ad-hoc saved amount.	SAVE TILL IT ALMOST HURTS - Do not try to save a fixed % like PF only. The PF may be 8-15% of the basic pay. If you can save more, save till it almost hurts.

[THREE POINTS ON SAVING]

Celebrate saved amount every month

Look at the saved amount on monthly and cumulative basis. Talk to your family and announce as to how much you saved. This will give you a lot of social support and make you feel good about it.

Keep Shifting from low-yielding to high-yielding investments

This is a very important decision. You need to shift the saved amount from low-yielding investments to high-yielding investments.

Example – 1:

Bank A gives 6.9% interest on RD for one year.

Bank B gives 8.0% interest on FD for one year.

If this is happening to you, after one year, shift the accumulated RD amount in bank A to FD of bank B for one year. You will earn 2% higher interest. On Rs. 1 million, you will gain Rs. 20,200/- more as interest.

Example – 2:

If you have an SB account with a bank which gives only 3.5% interest, shift major part of your savings to a Bank which gives higher interest of 6%. If you hold Rs. 100,000 in your SB, the saved amount in 15 years will swell to Rs. 37,500 [2.5% yearly × 100,000 × 15 years].

Remember!

> "Little drops of water make the mighty ocean"

6.4 The Magic of Compounding

> "Compound interest is the eighth wonder of the world. He who understands it, earns it; he who does not, pays it!"
>
> – **Albert Einstein**

Compounding is the ability of an asset to generate earnings, which are then reinvested in order to generate their own earnings. In other words, compounding refers to generating earnings from previous earnings. Money multiplies money.

Suppose you invest Rs. 10,000/- into a company 'X'. The first year, the share rises 20%. Your investment is now worth 12,000. Based on good performance, you hold the stock. In Year 2, the shares appreciate another 20%. Therefore, your 12,000 grows to 14,400. Rather than your shares appreciating an additional 2,000 (20%) like they did in the first year, they appreciate an additional 2,400, because the 2,000 you gained in the first year grew by 20% too.

If you extrapolate the process, the numbers can start to get very big as your previous earnings start to provide returns. In fact, 10,000 invested at 20% annually for 15 years would grow to nearly 8,65,000.

Interest is often compounded monthly, quarterly, semi-annually or annually. With continuous compounding, any interest earned immediately begins earning interest on itself.

Albert Einstein called compound interest "the greatest mathematical discovery of all time."

Unlike complex mathematical formula that we studied in school, principle of compounding can be applied to everyday life.

The wonder of compounding (sometimes called "compound interest") transforms your working money into a highly powerful income-generating tool. Compounding is the process of generating earnings on an asset's reinvested earnings.

How Reinvestment of Interest Adds to Multiplication

If you invest 10,000 today at 6%, you will have 10,600 in one year. Now let's say that rather than withdraw the 600/- gained from interest, you keep it there for another year. If you continue to earn the same rate of 6%, your investment will grow to 11,236/- by the end of the second year.

Because you reinvested that 600/-, it works together with the original investment, earning you 636, which is 36 more than the previous year. This little bit extra may seem like peanuts now, but let's not forget that you didn't have to lift a finger to earn that 36. More importantly, this 36 also has the capacity to earn interest. After the next year, your investment will be worth 11,910.16. This time you earned 674.16, which is 74.16 more interest than the first year. This increase in the amount made each year is compounding in action: interest earning interest on interest and so on. This will continue as long as you keep reinvesting and earning interest.

Great Principles of Compounding

Starting Early Can Make a Major Difference

Consider two individuals; we'll name them RAM and SHYAM. Ram and Shyam are of the same age. When Ram was 25, he invested 15,000 at an interest rate of 5.5%. For simplicity, let's assume the interest was compounded annually. By the time Ram reaches 50, he will have 57,200.89 in his bank account.

Ram's friend, SHYAM, did not start investing until he reached age of 35. At that time, he invested 15,000 at the same interest rate of 5.5% compounded annually. By the time SHYAM reaches age 50, he will have 33,487.15 in his bank account.

What happened? Both Ram and Shyam are 50 years old, but Ram has 23,713.74 (57,200.89 33,487.15) more in his savings account than Shyam, even though he invested the same amount of money. By giving his investment more time to grow, Ram earned a total of 42,200.89 in interest and Shyam earned only 18,487.15.

Great Principles of Compounding

Frequency of Investments Makes Difference

The effect of compound interest depends on frequency. Assume an annual interest rate of 12%. If we start the year with 100 and compound only once, at the end of the year, the principal grows to 112. If, on the other hand, we compound *each month* at 1%, we end up with more than 112 at the end of the year. Specifically, we end up with 112.68. The final amount is higher because the interest is compounded more frequently.

Great Principles of Compounding

Selecting the Right Asset Can Make A Major Difference

A marginal interest rate of 0.5% p.a. can leave behind a huge difference in a period of twenty years as you can see below

Amount	Interest Rate (%)	Years	Interest	Total
1,00,000	7	20	3,00,638	4,00,639
1,00,000	6.5	20	2,63,116	3,63,116

Let us look at another example:

Let us say, your grandpa gave you a gift of Rs. 1,00,000/-; you take it to the bank to make a fixed deposit. The banker will give a form asking you to tick the following:-

- Duration
- Interest pay-out/cumulative

Many people tick these in 'semi sleep' and let us see how these impact returns:

- 91 days duration may earn 4.5% interest
- 365 days duration may earn 6.5% interest

[A] Rs. 1,00,000 * 91 days * 4.5%

  Rs. 1,00,000/- reinvested at every 45 days

  Interest paid out = Rs. 4,500/- per year * 5 years = Rs. 22,500/-

Net capital after 5 years is Rs. 1,00,000/-

[Plus interest received – Rs. 22,500/- TOTAL – 122,500]

[B] Rs. 1,00,000 * 365 days * 6.5% * 5 years = Rs. 1,38,000 [cumulative]

Years	Rate % 7	Rate % 8	Rate % 10	Rate % 14	Rate % 18
5	14,197	14,859	16,386	19,897	24,117
10	20,015	22,080	26,850	39,592	58,163
15	28,318	32,810	43,998	78,780	1,40,274
20	40,063	48,759	72,095	1,56,757	3,38,301

Interest paid out = Nil

Net capital after 5 years = 1,38,042/

In situation [A], the person spent the received interest of Rs. 22,500/- and net balance after 5 years is Rs. 1,00,000/-

In situation [B] the person got Rs. 1,38,042/- which is significantly higher than situation [A].

This is the power of compounding, which is interest on interest on interest.

Money multiplies at rapid pace.

Two most influential factors to maximize multiplication:

- Rate of return on return – Even 0.5% higher return can make a major difference
- Duration – The longer the duration the higher the possibility of returns

From the following chart, we can see how rate of interest and number of years impact net return at the end of the term.

Let us look at how 4%, 7% and 10% can make a huge difference in 30 years period through the following chart. On longer term period, the effect of compounding is phenomenal. With investments on assets with higher return rate the impact of compounding is almost magical.

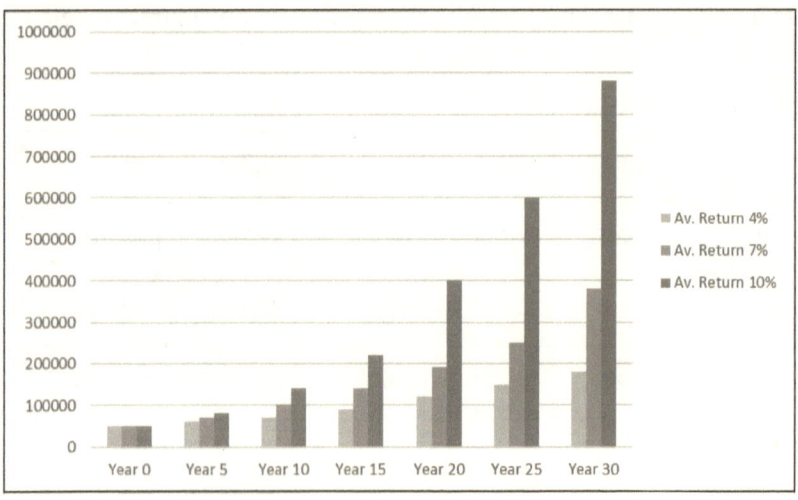

[EFFECTS OF COMPOUNDING]

TO MULTIPLY WEALTH

Start early and get early benefit of multiplication

Choose a high [but reasonably safe] return of instrument

Choose as long number of years as possible. The longer, the better.

6.5 Trading vs. Investing in Assets

Investing and trading are two very different methods of attempting to profit in financial markets. This book is for those who want to invest. But, let us talk about the concept of Investing vs. Trading.

Investing

The goal of investing is to gradually build wealth, over an extended period of time through the buying and holding of a portfolio of funds, shares, basket of shares, mutual funds, gold, bonds, debentures, real estate and other financial investments.

Investing is like a rollercoaster ride. You hold on to the chair as the assets go through ups and downs on a daily basis. Do not panic and jump out in between. Be courageous. Be patient.

When the time is ripe after a few years or even decades, you can switch to another asset or encash the assets. Investors are generally happy to get 10–15% annualized return.

Trading

Trading involves frequent buying and selling of shares, commodities and even real estates and generates profit within a short period. Traders hold a short term view of the asset. They may hold on to the assets for a few hours or even days or weeks. Most often trading is done with shares in the stock market. However, there are traders in real estate who hold on for a few months or a year and get out later. Similar trading takes place in commodities like Gold, Silver, Oil, Agri-products, etc.

Let us look at two famous people who did INVESTING (Warren Buffet) and TRADING (George Soros); both made huge fortunes from stock market.

Warren Buffet

It is estimated that Buffet is worth close to US $ 100 billion through long-term investment in companies which he held for decades.

His investing philosophy can be summed up in the following quote:

"I will tell you how to become rich. Close the doors. Be careful when others are greedy. Be greedy when others are fearful".

"Calling someone who trades actively in the market an investor is like calling someone who repeatedly engages in "one-night stand" as romantic!"

George Soros

He is worth US$ 30 billion acquired mainly through countless number of trades in various financial assets. He deals in currencies, commodities, shares, bonds, etc. based on macro-economic analysis. He bets across geographies and is credited as the man who almost broke the Bank of England.

George Soros' philosophy can be summed up in the following quote:

"Markets are constantly in a state of uncertainty and flux money is made discounting the obvious and betting as the unexpected."

Let us look at the difference between INVESTING & TRADING in broad terms.

	TRADING	**INVESTING**
Goal	To generate returns by frequent buying and selling of shares.	To steadily build wealth over a period of time through buying and holding financial instruments.
Belief	Share price will move only in one direction.	The company will perform in future and come up with return in the form of dividends.
Profit	Buying shares at a lower price and selling at a higher price. Or selling at higher price, and afterwards, rebuying at lower price.	Re-investing dividends and profits on shares into additional shares of the company.
Period	Very short period – minutes or lower max lays	Long period of time years or decades
Return	10%+ return every month	10–15% annually
Tools	Moving average oscillator and technical graphs	Market fundamentals, Earnings ratios, PE multiple, Book Value, Management forecast
Strategy	Buy to sell	Buy to hold
Protection	Stop loss orders, sell at pre – determined prices if there is anticipated loss	Survive the ups and down and hold to long periods of time

Orientation	One-night stand	Marriage
Cost of operation	High	Low
Investment	Low	High

Trading or Investing, What Should You Do?

This writer is comfortable with "investing" only and I never do any trading –either in shares or commodities. However, each person has to decide as to what he is comfortable with, and for that, try to answer the following questions:

1. How much time can you devote daily?

Trading in shares or commodities requires a few hours daily. It involves reading some charts on daily basis. You need to keep daily track of economic news, RBI monetary policy and political developments whereas as an investor, you can track the quarterly results and management performance review for a given period and day-to-day price swings in the shares need not be bothered about. After zeroing in on the right company and buying in the shares, you can be on a holiday for long periods.

A. The amount of equity and market research required for trading is much higher than for investments in shares.

B. Size of the capital also matters. For most small investors, long-term wealth creation is far more important than short-term gain in the stock market.

C. Trading is far riskier than long-term investing. Even with the best of company shares and even Gold you could lose large sum of money in short period. It is similar to gambling.

D. With profits if any, earnings from trading are added to your income and are taxed. You may end up losing 30–35% of the profits through taxes and broker margins. On the other hand, with investing you are eligible for LTCG benefits, if held for more than one year.

2. Can you do both – Trading and Investing?

Both require different sets of attitudes and emotional responses. However, if someone desires, he can do both – Trading and Investing. But the following aspects must be taken care of for smooth operation.

- Need to maintain separate accounts both for banking and Income tax purpose for smooth working. Mixing both transactions can complicate transactions and I-T calculations. Usually, trading may have multiple transactions even during a day, whereas investing may have only a few transactions per month.
- Fix very low capital deployment for trading as it is highly risky.

Conclusion - Trading vs. Investing

If you want to create long-term wealth, focus your energies with sound long-term investments.

Leave trading to people with right temperament and experts.

6.6 Two Popular Ways to Save Money on Monthly Basis: Bank RD vs. MF-SIP

If we ask our grandparents or even parents about the best way to save long term, most likely they will recommend RDs (Recurring Deposits). It has a pre-set investment plan that you contribute to monthly. Typically, these RDs are operated in Banks where one's salary is credited. Interest rates vary from time to time and bank to bank. For example, a leading PSU bank offers 6.9% and another Private Bank offers 7.30% for one year RDs.

Fixed Deposits (FDs) are traditional investment option for lump sum investment and RDs for monthly investment options. There is nothing fundamentally wrong with these, but there are far better investment options available now.

RDs offer assured returns over long or medium period of time. It is unaffected by the day-to-day fluctuation in the stock market or any other factor.

However, the returns will be invariably lesser than equity linked SIP-MF investments. Let us look at how returns are different for RD and SIP in MF.

Note: The following calculation is based on a set of Standard assumptions and must not be taken purely mathematically.

Rs. 10,000 invested per month for 15 years:

Rs. 10000 PM	Interest%	Actual invested	Gross gain (Rs.)	Taxation	Net Amount	Amount (Rs.)
Bank RD	7%	18,00,000	13,77,000	20% on the interest	2,75,000	29,02,000
MF Multi-cap SIP	14%	18,00,000	42,32,000	10% of the Appreciated amount after indexing	1,90,000	58,42,000

The interest earned from RDs is treated as "short-term gain" and is added to the slab of the I-T payee to work out I-T of the individual. However, appreciation from Equity-based MF is treated in the "long term capital gains" category and only 10% of the appreciated amount above indexed value is liable to be taxed. Hence tax outflow will be much lower than RDs.

Net result is that, in 15-years' period, there is a strongly possibility that SIP investments into Equity-based mutual funds like Multi-Cap will result in doubling the amount.

6.7 Planning Mutual Fund SIPs

We have discussed as to how investing into equity mutual funds is the best way to build long-term wealth for most investors. For equity investment, SIP (Systematic Investment Plan) is the best way to save.

SIP builds saving discipline.

SIP "forces" you to a save a fixed amount every month, taking away laziness or effects of bad habits.

SIP helps you to "cost average" your purchase. This means, if you bought Mutual fund at peak, since you are buying regularly it will catch the market when it is down; thereby you get the benefit of average pricing.

With SIP, you can reasonably forecast your net corpus; thereby you can plan major events of your life

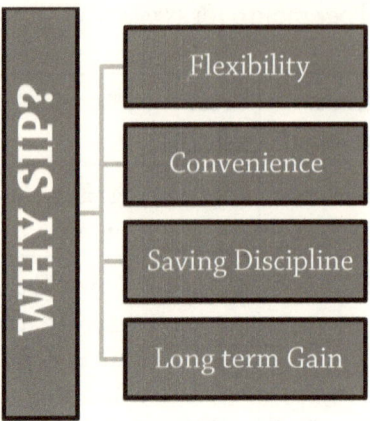

SIPs and long-term Performance-Scientific study

In a study conducted by Value Research Online (Nov 2018) on the long-term returns with SIP, the following were noted and we quote:

"In 2017, Value Research decided to dig into 25-year-old data on mutual funds to take stock of SIP returns actually experienced by fund investors in diversified equity and aggressive hybrid funds with more than 10 years' history. For every single month starting from their launch date, we simulated SIPs on all possible rolling time periods from one to ten years. We then calculated the interval rate of return on these 3.67 lakhs possible SIP accounts, running from 1992 to 2017 across the 217 schemes.

We found that investors who invested in SIPs for just one year suffered losses in 22.5% of the time. As they lengthened the period of SIPs, the incidence of losses fell dramatically. SIPs that lasted 2 years subjected investors to losses 16.2% of the time. Three-year SIPs suffered losses 9.8% of the time. But 4-year SIPs were able to lower the probability of losses to just 6%. These findings essentially tell us that if you run a SIP for 4 years or more you had a 94% chance of ending up with a positive return."

Other findings from the scientific study by Value research online

Most bear markets in India are between 12–24 months, hence three-year SIPs help you to neutralize the impact of fall and 4-year SIPs help you to come to positive territory.

In 25 years' history 5-year SIPs managed an average return of 15% and never gave investors less than Savings Bank return of 4%.

Buying a theme or category after it has just delivered great performance is a great danger while investing.

Shifting investments into different themes or category (because it is the flavour of the season) is a very bad idea for long-term creation of wealth.

Wealth creation through SIP

If Rs. 10000 monthly SIP is done for 5–20 years, what will be the total wealth created?

Years	SIP (Rs. PM)	Return %	Total Wealth [Rs. million]
5	10000	10%	0.78
10	10000	15%	2.79
15	10000	18%	9.19
20	10000	20%	23.00

Assumptions:

As the number of years increases, overall returns increase from 10% for the first 5 years to 20% for the 20 years

SIP has remained constant @ Rs. 10000/- PM.

Most Important:

- Choose the right funds/right mix
- Stay for long periods to create wealth

Points to remember while planning SIP

1. Timing

One can start SIP at any given time. In fact, studies have shown that even those who started SIP at the peak of stock market also have "broken even" after 3 years. Start SIP and stay on with it for a long time.

2. Do not stop SIP

If the stock market has crashed, do not stop the SIP. In fact you will be benefited by continuing with the SIP.

Example

Let us say, the unit price of the MF was Rs. 500/- and with Rs. 10000/- SIP you managed to get 20 units while the market was at its peak.

After six months, let us say the market has crashed and now unit price is Rs. 400/-; hence you will get 25 units.

Now, the buying average price will be Rs. 444/- per unit

3. Do not shift to another fund

Unless there is a strong reason do not shift from one type of SIP to another type based on the flavour of the season.

At different periods different themes became 'HOT'-Infrastructure, IT, Pharma, Energy, Automobile, Export and so on.

If you are part of a Multi-cap fund, your fund Manager would take care of opportunities at marketplace. Since you do not have technical or financial understanding of each sector, you will end up making major blunders: That is, entering when the sector is at peak and shifting when the sector is very attractive: Exactly the opposite of what you should be doing.

Assess performance of the fund for long period of time, i.e. 1–3 years before shifting to another fund SIP. If your fund has performed badly compared to the index or category consistently, you can consider shifting.

Example: Your Multi-cap fund has returned 10% and 12% only when the market was returning 13% and 16% respectively.

4. Diversify rightly

There are two principles that must be followed while planning SIP.

* "Do not put too many eggs into only one basket" (**over-concentration**)
* "Do not put too few eggs into too many baskets" (**over-diversification**]

Over-Concentration

Over-concentration means any or all of the following.

- All MF investments under one fund-house [Over-trusting one fund-house]
- All MF investments under one Fund Manager [Over-trusting one individual]
- All MF investments in different fund houses, but under one category (Example: Someone who has invested into three small-cap funds of three fund houses. On closer look one can notice that 80% of the portfolios of all three fundholders have similar companies) [Over-trusting one category]

Over-diversification

- Half-a-dozen MF investments under different fund houses, under same category (Example: Multi-cap investments into six different houses
- Half-a-dozen MF investments spread among three different categories (Large-cap/Midcap/small-cap) in different fund houses
- Going for a mix of balanced funds and debt funds ending up with disproportionate debt component in the portfolio (This may be OK if you are 55 years-plus, but not for a young man)

1. Do not exercise option for dividend mindlessly

If you want regular income from MFs opt for SWP (Systematic Withdrawal Plan) instead of Dividend plan. By opting for dividend plan, you end up losing part of your investments as taxes.

In any case, while going in for SIP, your objective is creation of wealth. Hence opt for "Growth option" instead of "Dividend" or "Reinvestment" options.

2. Doing SIP by "Regular" route

All SIP investments come with two options – Regular or Direct. When you opt for "Regular", you end up paying a small commission to the intermediary for a long time. Yes, if you have opted for 15–20 years, you will keep paying "commissions" for 15–20 years!

3. SIP based on labels

All MF house are good marketers. They keep on coming with different labels at different points of time. For example, Govt. of India announced some sops for Agricultural Sector; soon a few fund houses came with "Rural focus Sector Fund". Investing into such sector funds could become a highly damaging decision in the long run.

Do not get attracted or distracted with aggressive Ads and hard selling by any MF sellers.

4. SIP from multiple SB accounts

It is better to have one "first choice" SB account. This account must be used for principal income like salary and all SIP payments or it will become very confusing for you.

CHAPTER 7
Where to Invest Money & in Which Asset Class?

Asset classes

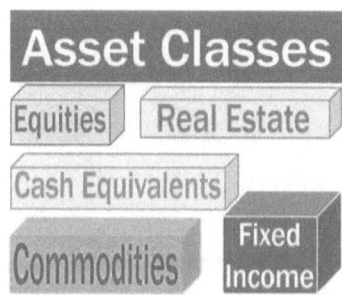

An asset class is a group of financial instruments with similar characteristics and similar behaviour in the marketplace. The income that we receive is in "cash" or cash equivalent into Bank accounts. Our future wealth and well-being will be determined by what we do with this income.

- What type of asset classes do we deploy?
- How much do we deploy into each asset class?
- How long do we deploy into these asset classes?
- With whom do we maintain these asset classes?
- When do we deploy into these classes? Season, time or cycle?
- When do we shift from one asset class to another?
- Which asset class do we give higher weightage in various life stages – Youth, Middle age or Old?
- How do we protect our assets? etc.

With almost similar types of income levels, people will end up with different levels of wealth in another 20–30 years! One may be worth Rs. 50 million and another may be at Rs. 10 million.

This is no exaggeration, but the hard truth.

WHERE DO INDIANS PARK THEIR MONEY?

In a study published by SEBI [see below], it was shown that:

- 95% Indians park their money in Bank deposits.
- 30% Indians invest in Gold jewellery or similar products ["Dead investments"]
- Hardly 10% Indians invest in stock market and/or Mutual funds.
- Except investments in stock market or related investments and real estate, most investments go into assets which yield returns less than 8–9% p.a. Exactly the reason why majority of Indians remain poor or average as they are not able to get returns significantly better than inflation rates.

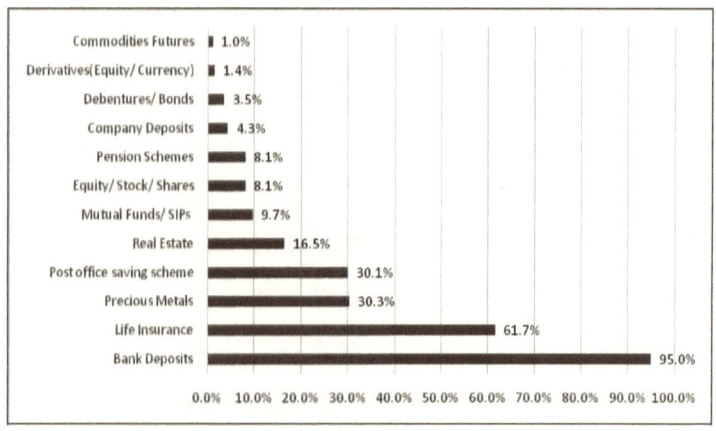

[WHERE DO INDIANS INVEST?]

Let us look at different asset classes and their strengths and weaknesses.

There is no standard or category of asset classes. However, here are the 5 types that are widely accepted in the context of middle classes-"well-to-do" category.

This is the most important decision that you will have to take to become wealthy on a long-term basis. This decision can make you rich or poor.

Let us look at the pros and cons of investing in each of the asset classes.

7.1 Cash & Fixed Income Assets

Hard Cash

When we say "cash" it does not mean bundles of hard cash. It can mean, money lying in SB A/c at bank or liquid mutual fund – all of which can be quickly converted to "cash" or are liquid. The freedom with cash is very high. You can buy almost anything with "cash" – phones, TV, ornaments, plots, books, flat etc. Cash transactions are difficult to track, which is the preferred mode of transaction in various deals which are outside the legal system, particularly large transactions.

Caution!

Recently Government introduced a law restricting cash in any one single transaction to Rs. 200,000. There are provisions for penalty equal to the cash transactions that you did above Rs. 200,000.

Returns

Among all classes of assets, cash or cash equivalents give lowest returns. With hard cash at home or lockers, you get zero returns.

SB A/C – interest on SB accounts could be as low as 3.5%. Some new-gen private banks may offer 6% interest on SB accounts.

Liquid funds with Mutual funds – these may give return of 5–7% p.a.

Fixed income asset class

This is the most popular class in India, particularly for lower middle and upper middle class.

These are financial products where invested amount is guaranteed to be returned. The returns are generally low, but prefixed or it is more or less predictable. Investing in FIXED INCOME ASSET CLASS is like lending money to someone with the assurance of return of capital along with pre – determined (more or less) "extra" (call it by any name – dividend/ interest).

These financial products offer annualized return in the range of 6–8%. But most people do not realize that it is a pre-tax return; the income from these products can get added to an individual's income and get taxed accordingly.

Hence, you end up paying 10–30% I-T on the interest earned. The post-tax returns are barely higher than inflation and often less than inflation.

Fixed income assets:

Government saving products [For details see under TAX SAVING PRODUCTS]

Bank FDs [see under Banking]

Mutual Funds – Debt products [See under Mutual Funds]

Company Deposits, etc.

Company Deposits

Company deposits are unsecured investments and carry relatively higher risk than Bank FDs. Such deposits are offered by manufacturing and non-Banking finance companies (NBFCs) with varying tenures and different frequency of interest payments. Typically, company deposits offer interest rates a little higher than Bank deposits if they have good credit rating, and significantly more interest if credit ratings are lower than the top bracket.

Features of company deposits:

1. Minimum deposit will vary between company to company from Rs. 5000/-

2. Online deposits may yield higher interest than offline deposits.

3. For renewals, additional incentives may be offered.

4. The ratings may be A, AA or AAA or similar. The higher the rating, the lesser may be the interest.

5. The minimum tenure is 6 months to one year and it could go up to 5 years.

6. Interest could get credited to your Bank A/c.

Tips for investing into company deposits

1. If you invest, go for highly reputed names with high rating [AAA or similar]

2. Spread among 2–3 companies
3. Stagger deposits in different tenures like 6 months/ 1 year/2 years. Avoid long-duration deposits. This improves liquidity and reduces interest opportunity loss while reinvesting
4. As interest from company deposits are taxable, I-T limits must be rechecked especially in the light of limits fixed for senior citizens.

Mahindra Finance, LIC Housing Finance, Bajaj Finance, HDFC, and Shriram Transport are some reputed Companies accepting Company deposits. For a minimum deposit of Rs. 5000–10,000, interest varies between 7.75% – 8.10% p.a. For senior citizens additional 0.25–0.40% is offered.

Recommendation:

* Fixed income assets are ideal for those in low Income Tax or no Income Tax paying group.
* Good for retired people who wish to get monthly income, but do not mind paying I-T.
* Fixed income assets can never give returns higher than inflation.
* Fixed income assets can never make you wealthy.

7.2 Gold Investments

Traditionally, Indians have been investing in gold jewellery as an investment. However, with the availability of other investment avenues many other options are available now. Let us look at the pros and cons of investing into gold, and also, how it has performed over the years.

The impact of gold prices on your investments is determined by the nature of the gold investments that you hold.

As prices vary for **physical gold** there are two options:

- Gold jewellery and
- Gold bullion (bars/coins)

For non-physical gold, there are three options.

- Gold bonds

- Gold ETF
- E-Gold.

a) Physical Gold Products for Investments

i) Gold Jewellery

This is the most common form of owning Gold. There are two major factors which are pushing its sale. One, Indian women have a special affinity for gold. This is generally in the possession of women and gives a sense of security to women. Second, Gold merchants promote sales through advertisements and promotions. Hence, most of the decisions relating to investment of Gold jewellery are not taken based on sound financial calculations.

When one purchases gold jewellery, he/she has to pay 3% GST and "making charges". For normal jewellery "making charges" could be 10% and for more intricate designs, it may go up to 20%. If there are precious stones attached to it, one gets that much less gold.

Soon after buying gold jewellery, within days [or even hours] if you sell, what are you likely to get?

Let us say, you spent Rs. 100,000 for purchase and see the financial impact below:

Amount spent: 100,000+ tax 3000	=	103,000
Less GST paid Rs. 3000 [which is non-refundable]	−	97,000
Less 10% making charges of selling price. [10,000]	−	87,000
OR Less 15% making charges of selling price. [15000]	−	82,000

If, there were precious stones worth Rs 10,000/ the price could be further reduced by Rs. 5000 [50%].—Rs. 82,000/ or Rs. 77,000/

The gold you purchased for Rs. 103000/ is worth Rs. 77,000 within 24 hours!

Even if gold appreciated by 7%, it may take 4–5 years to recover your invested amount! If you have hired Bank locker to store Gold, locker charges have to be added.

Recommendation: Do not invest into gold jewellery as an "investment" but if you buy as a beauty-enhancing product, it is fine.

ii) Investing In Gold Bars/Coins

This is another method of holding Gold in physical form. The advantage is that it eliminates making charges unlike gold jewellery. However, there are two distinct disadvantages.

1. Jewellers charge 2–3% commission while buying or selling.
2. Many banks do not give loan against Gold bars/Coins.

Then, there are charges for holding in Bank lockers.

How much gold can you hold?

Jewellery and ornaments to the extent of 500 grams for a married lady and 250 grams for an unmarried lady and 100 grams for a male member are allowed. If you hold beyond that, it could be seized by I-T authorities if you have no proof as to how you acquired these.

Taxation on Physical Gold

If you are lucky and gained appreciation in gold jewellery, if you sell within 3 years of buying, you will have to pay I-T @ your taxable income limits/slabs. If you hold it for 3 years plus, you need to pay I-T @20% of the appreciated value, after working out indexation.

Conclusion:

Gold ornaments have certain emotional value, but, from pure investment point of view, it may not give return even as much as Bank deposit. The appreciation may take place only after 4–5 years.

Gold bars/coins are OK for people with unaccounted wealth.

b) Non-Physical Gold Investments

Traditionally, one had to depend on investing into physical gold only. In the last couple of decades, three non-physical gold investment options have come up. These offer many advantages over physical gold. Let us look at each of these.

i) Gold-ETF [Exchange Traded Fund]

These are open-ended MF schemes that invest money collected from investors in standard Gold bullion of 99.5% purity. These funds are traded in stock exchanges like shares of individual companies; hence investors can buy or sell Gold-ETF anytime, but need a Demat account to operate. When investors invest in Gold-ETF, gold of the same value is bought in the fund and stored with the custodian. Investors do not get physical gold into their hands, but investors need to pay fund-management expenses including security cost which could be between 0.65% – 1.25%.

The Gold-ETF prices will vary depending on the physical gold prices in the same proportion. Further, if there is capital gain, it is taxed along with your income, if held for less than 3 years. And, if held for more than 3 years it will be taxed @ 20% after working out indexation.

ii) E-Gold

E-gold is an electronic way to buy gold. Experts say E-gold will always beat gold-ETF in return as the latter's NAV (Net Assets Value) is computed after deducting fees of the Asset Management Company plus storage and custodial service charges, which will vary from fund to fund. The cost of trading in E-gold is also nominal. In E-gold, there are no recurring expenses such as management fees and custodial charges. This reduces cost and income returns year to year. E-gold is traded at prevailing market prices. It can be traded at market prices at given time.

iii) Sovereign Gold Bond [RBI]

These are bonds issued by RBI on behalf of Govt of India. These are substitutes for physical gold for those who are interested in investing in gold.

Highlights:

- Bonds are issued 1–2 times a year when the window is open for applying through leading banks
- Min 1 gm and maximum 54 kg per year can be applied per individual per year.
- Can be held in paper or online form.
- Bonds are sold and redeemed at prevailing market prices of Gold.
- There is a lock-in period of 8 years; however, it can be prematurely encashed from 5th year onwards with certain conditions. These are traded in the exchanges.
- An interest of 2.5% is offered p.a., payable biannually.
- SGB's can be offered as collateral for taking loans.
- Taxation: Interest earned on bonds is taxable on the tax bracket of the individual. However, on maturity, redemption is exempted from capital gains tax.
- These can be gifted or transferred.

Recommendation

- Hold bare minimum gold as ornaments to serve social and emotional purposes.
- Don't hold more than 10% of your total assets in gold of any form.
- Hold maximum as E-Gold or as SGB if it is a must to hold gold.

(Gold may give an annual return 5–7% in the next one decade and it can be considered a hedge against inflation or market fluctuations in currencies or stocks.)

7.3. Real Estate Investments

Famous quotes on real estate:

> **Mark Twain, writer and humourist:** "Buy land, they're not making it anymore."
>
> **Franklin D. Roosevelt:** "Real estate cannot be lost or stolen, nor can it be carried away. Purchased with common sense, paid for in full, and managed with reasonable care, it is about the safest investment in the world."
>
> **John Paulson, investor and multi-billionaire:** "If you don't own a home, buy one. If you own a home, buy another one. If you own two homes, buy a third. And, lend your relatives the money to buy a home."
>
> **John Stuart Mill, political economist:** "Landlords grow rich in their sleep without working, risking or economizing."

Notwithstanding any type of financial argument that is put forward against owning real estate assets, I will strongly recommend holding real estate for everyone. I am willing to debate about the percentage of real estate that one should have in his or her asset portfolio. Either of the extremes – too little or too much – is bad.

Owning a Home [Independent/Apartment] to Stay

I have seen a number of financial calculations to put forward the argument that renting a home is far better than owning one. Let us look at the advantages or disadvantages of owning a home.

OWN OR RENT	ADVANTAGES	DISADVANTAGES
Ownership of home	greater privacy and freedom usually good investment on long term fairly stable housing-cost over time tax benefits assets build up (wealth) emotional satisfaction pride of ownership stronger community ties	long term commitments maintenance and repairs cost lack of flexibility cost invariably more than renting high upfront cost bother of shifting to another house
Renting	lower housing cost commitment for shorter term minimal maintenance and repair cost wider choice	no tax benefits no fixed housing cost not building assets (wealth)

i) Owning vs. renting:

I strongly recommended ownership of a house for everyone. This gives tremendous emotional satisfaction to all members of the family, particularly sense of security for women. In the Indian situation, neighbours and society in general are more likely to make more social connections if you are an owner of a property. Over a period of time you would have created a valuable asset in your name. This is in addition to various tax benefits that you get.

Prerequisites to consider before planning your own home

For most people, owning a home is the fulfilment of the great Indian dream. For a few it could be a source of income. Purchasing a home is one of the biggest financial decisions that you make in life. For a large number of middle class and lower middle-class people, such decisions are made once in a lifetime only. So, before you choose to buy a home, the following issues need to be thought about.

➢ **EVALUATE YOUR INCOME/ SAVINGS**

Do you have sufficient savings to buy a home? Do you have sufficient savings to buy a plot to build a home?

Do you have a stable job or source of income to afford to take a housing loan?

Do you have an income which has been reflected in I-T returns for 3–5 years which can be shown to HFC?

From the current source of income, what are your other financial commitments?

➢ **WHAT ARE YOUR FINANCIAL COMMITMENTS?**

- Living expenses for self/family.
- Children's education expenses.
- Emergency fund.
- Retirement fund in which at least 8% of your income must go.
- EMIs of loans for luxuries, post retirement –vehicles, white goods, holidays, etc.
- No credit card dues.
- Minimum 35% of the net income is freely available to give as EMI from income of self plus spouse.

➢ **WHAT IS THE NATURE OF YOUR JOB?**

If you are holding a job which is transferrable within three years, it may not be worthwhile to buy a home at the place of your current posting. It takes a lot of time to search and finalise a home and considerable time has to be spent for possession and furnishing of the property. With all these, you may end up staying at your home for just a few months. If it is an "under construction" property, you may get transferred to another location even before you get possession of the property. God forbid, if there is any dispute on the property it might become a nightmare for you in the coming decade.

> **FINANCIAL GAIN/LOSS [COST OF ENTRY FOR NEW HOME]**

When you acquire a house or apartment you end up spending money on various things which are virtual 'write-offs'. Cost of registration of the land along with GST/service taxes may be high as 10% of the cost of the property. Cost of internal furnishing, club-house charges, certain security deposits, etc. will further add to your cost of entry. These could add another 5–10% to the property cost. For many of these costs you may not have bills or receipts too. Hence, 15–20% of the initial cost spent on acquiring property will have to be written off and will not fetch any value at market place.

In the best scenario, you may "break-even" [No profit/No loss] only 3–5 years after acquiring a house. In case there is some appreciation during this period, you may be left with very little after working your I-T, in case you choose to sell. If you choose to hold it for more than 2 years, the clause of long term capital gains tax will step in and the I-T will take away 20% of the gain after working out indexation.

Important Recommendation – Never acquire any property even by remote chance if you have to sell it in less than 5–7 years. You may end up with negative return.

Housing loan

The first step before taking a decision to buy/build a home is to check your home loan eligibility.

Please read details under Banking/Loans.

> **FACTORS TO CONSIDER BEFORE CHOOSING A HOME**
>   o GEOGRAPHY

The part of the country/City you choose to live in will have a major impact on your lifestyle, quality of life, your career and your children's education/ future. If you want to stay in your home for a long time, make that decision carefully, considering the factors which are most important to you, such as average home prices in the area, job opportunities, climate and social situation that you are comfortable with.

- CITY VS. SUBURBS AND NUMBER OF BEDROOMS

The place that you choose will decide the size of your home in terms of square feet, number of bedrooms and its size, apartment or independent house. A 2BR house at Worli in South Mumbai may cost Rs. 40 million, whereas a 3BR house in the Western Mumbai suburbs like Borivili may cost you Rs. 20 million. If you travel another 30 Kms, you may get an independent house and 1200 Sq. plot-cum house at the same price.

- EDUCATION AND HEALTH

Access to the educational institutions like schools and colleges is a very important consideration if you have children. If the school is far away, there are issues like transportation time and cost. And, children may not be able to participate in life-skills programmes. If you have people in your family who require frequent or quick hospitalisation, proximity to a good hospital is essential.

- ACCESS TO WORKPLACE

The place of your work and its distance from home will determine your free time and quality of life. If you spend too much time for commuting to work, very little time will be left for various essentials and pleasures of life. If you have to start for work much earlier in the day, you may spend less time for morning walk and sports. You may not be able to eat the breakfast of your choice. If you return home very late in the night, you may spend less time with spouse and kids and there will be emotional gaps at home.

- SAFETY AND SENSE OF SECURITY

This is a very important consideration while selecting a home. You will certainly wish to have a locality which has less crime and less social tensions. It would be preferable to settle for a home where there is good policing, is reasonably crowded and with good lighting of streets. Your home must give you a sense of security.

- NEIGHBOURHOOD

Within a particular area itself different neighbourhoods will have different characteristics. You will have to pick up which is closest to your lifestyle and personality – a place you will feel comfortable and where you are likely to get along with neighbours.

What kind of people live in the neighbourhood you are considering? Will you feel comfortable in the community? If they are 100% pure vegetarians, will they feel comfortable having you, if you are non-vegetarian? If they have strong political and religious feelings, will you be comfortable in that group?

The chosen locality must be visited during night and different times of the day to find what is happening, the movement of vehicles and people. Does the neighbourhood offer essential things of life like grocery, rickshaws, taxis, doctor, saloon etc.? If you need a particular type of religious institution, does it have it?

Does it have sufficient parking for your visitors? A crèche or similar arrangement to leave behind your kid when going to work?

How do you find the people? Are they comfortable talking to your family? Are they the welcoming type or snobbish?

- LEISURE ACTIVITIES

Does it offer leisure activities that you enjoy like Movies, Sports, Parks, walking areas, swimming pool, club etc.?

- PROXIMITY TO FRIENDS AND FAMILY

The best home may not make you happy if you live far away from friends and family. Your friends and members of your family may move out at some point of time, hence, make sure that, it is not the only reason you choose the locality.

- RESEARCH NEIGHBOURHOOD

You need to choose the neighbourhood with lot of caution and research. You must visit a number of times without estate agent or similar people.

ii) Option-1 Building Independent House

This will consist of buying a residential plot and building an independent house. You need to get a housing plot and plan construction. Let us look at the option of building an independent house. Starting stage is getting a housing plot.

- **GOVERNMENT HOUSING PLOTS**

These plots are sold by a Government Agency directly to the people. Government agency acquires large tracts of land from landholders, develops into housing plots and sells based on criteria different from one agency or state or city to another. Some of the known such agencies are as follows:

- Bangalore Development Authority
- Tamil Nadu Housing Board
- Jaipur Development Authority
- WB Housing Board
- Army Welfare Housing Organisation

There are many such government agencies or government approved agencies who sell housing plots.

Each agency has criteria laid down which may be as follows:

– Number of years' residency in a particular city/ state
– Employment
– Not having any house/housing plot elsewhere

Generally, there is a waiting period to get such plots. Allotment of plots is based on how many times you may have applied. Many applicants wait for decades to get plot.

Advantages:

– Clear document of land without litigation
– Pre-planned layout with specific areas for parks, schools, roads, clubhouse etc.

- Choice of plot sizes – 1200/1800/2400/4000 sq. ft. etc.
- "100% white deal" which is possible without I-T problems.

Disadvantages:
- Long waiting period
- Development may take long periods

- **APPROVED PRIVATE LAYOUT PLOTS**

There are Government agencies which give formal permission to private parties to plan and develop housing layouts in the outskirts of metros and other cities.

For example: The following are the Government authorities in different part of India:

- BMRDA – Bangalore Metropolitan Regional Development Authority
- DTCPTN – Directorate of Town at Country Plan of TN
- MUDA – Mysore Urban Development Authority
- LDA – Lucknow Development Authority
- SUDA – Surat Development Authority

In most cities, there are master development plans for comprehensive development of the city and suburbs. Since Govt. Departments cannot develop all land and housing colonies, they sanction layouts based on pre-determined plans. In most cases, once a plan is approved, changes in plan in terms of road, recreation, park, school, etc. cannot be carried out.

One has to check out availability of such layout plots.

Caution: There are private parties who try selling plots claiming that "Plan is pending for approval." Invariably, the buyer gets into trouble. Be careful!

- **PRIVATE LANDS OUTSIDE CITY: APPROVAL PLANS**

There are plots which have been in the possession of people for generations or for decades. These must have been agricultural land in the past. At some other time, they must have been notified and later denotified for industrial or road or some other project.

Caution: Be very careful before buying these types of plots for housing without getting NOC from a Govt. Agency. Do not buy such plots under normal conditions.

- **DOCUMENTS TO BE VERIFIED**
    1. Original registration document of the seller
    2. Certified true copy of the original from registration office (as original may be fake!)
    3. Receipt for tax paid for three years
    4. Possession certificate, if any
    5. Land ownership certificate (Name may vary from state to state. It must clearly show that the land is in the name of the seller.)
    6. Encumbrance certificate 30 years up-to-date (this will show history of transaction of the land for 30 years)
    7. Sketch of the plot from Tahsildhar office if it is a private land
    8. NOC from Govt. Dept. for layout plan (or plan approved for housing)

       Note: If it is agricultural or industrial land they will not issue such an NOC.
    9. If it is inherited property, names of all possible claimants. This is a very tricky area in the buying. After you register the property, other claimants may step in to harass you.

       Caution: It is mandatory for you to get this vetted by a lawyer. Remember! If you spend a few thousand rupees, it is worth it. Further, the reputation of the seller and his history must be verified from independent sources. The clerks operating out of registration office could give a mine of information if you "please" them!
    10. Release letter from bank if it was hypothecated
    11. Copy of the complete layout plans, preferably "true copy" certified

Caution – 2

Some sellers may blackmail you emotionally with statements like "If you do not trust me, it is difficult." You must see every single document and all your documents must be vetted by a lawyer.

Caution – 3

The same seller may drop names of political leaders and police officers or film stars/cricketers in the conversation. Listen to all these, but 100% documents and 100% vetting by a lawyer is a must.

Caution – 4

You must keep in mind two important rules/ laws

   a. Minimum rate – there is something called minimum rate/ circle rate below which if you buy property, it will land you in trouble. Please check out.

   b. As per I-T laws, cash transaction above Rs. 2 lakhs is not permitted; in case you do, there is heavy penalty on the transacted amount. Be careful!

Caution – 5

HFCs or banks may finance only 85% of the land value excluding registration charges for funding as per documents. If the plot is a few years old, you can get it revalued using an official valuer of the banks.

- **INDEPENDENT HOUSE BUILDING PLAN**

Building housing is a complex, emotionally and physically draining experience which could take 1–2 years of your life. It will consist of the following:

   1. Broadly define what you want to the Architect or Builder.

Cost per square foot of construction may vary between Rs. 1500/- per sq.ft. – Rs. 2500/- per sq.ft. Depending on the size of the plot that you have, maximum "allowable" construction may vary from city to city.

   Example: If your plot size is 1200 sq. ft. you may get permission to build 960 sq.ft. if it is only ground floor and 1900 sq. ft. if it is ground plus 1st floor.

If you are trying to build third floor, the allowable area will vary from city to city. Get a broad idea as to how much you are allowed to build.

2. Define exactly what you want

Looking at your family situation as on current date as well as 10–15 years from today, how much space will you require? How many bedrooms will be required? Will you occupy entire complex as house or be renting out part of it? Do you want single entrance or two entrances? If all your bedrooms are on the first floor, how will you climb the steps when you get old? Do you want a mini-lift? Do you want a separate entry/exit for your maid servant? Think of each of these elements and define exactly what you want.

3. Finalise an Architect

As most people are not experienced it will be desirable to get an Architect to help you with house building plan.

If you are also working with low budget, it may be advisable to get an Architect who is willing to work on fixed fees or they may charge 7–10% of the total project cost.

Ideally, the same Architect can deal with government authorities or this may result in time wastage – running from table to table at the government offices.

Caution: Verify credentials of the Architect and visit a few projects which he has designed/completed.

4. Budgeting and financing

The architect will give you stage-wise project expenses. You need to plan financing with internal savings and bank loan. Ideally, maintain a separate bank account for all transactions related to house construction. As much as possible issue A/c payee cheques.

HFC or banks may ask for the following:

a. All documents related to land

b. Plan approval

c. Proof that you have the ownership contribution part of the building cost. Example: If the building costs Rs. 10 million, the bankers may give Rs. 8 million loan. You need to show possession of nearly Rs. 2 million or banks will not release any amount.

5. Finalize building contractor

After finalizing Architect, this is an important decision. Ideally you need to explore relationship with 2–3 building contractors. You need to find the following details:

- Construction cost
- Stage-wise payment schedule

(Ideally spread payment scheduled in 15–20 parts, payable every 15 days.)

Caution:

You need to visit a few constructed projects done by the proposed constructor. Probably talk to the customers/clients to get confident about the contractor. Specifically check whether the contractor has negative reputation like incomplete or disputed projects.

iii) Option-2 – Buying an Apartment

There are three options while buying an Apartment:

a. Under-construction Apartment
b. Almost ready-to-move-in apartment
c. Ready-to-move-in Apartment (old/new)

A. Under-Construction Apartment

Such apartment can be booked under two types of stages:

- **PRE-LAUNCH PERIOD**

In this period, the builder has not received a formal permission from Govt. authorities to build the apartment complex. There are frequent instances wherein the builder has not even purchased the land or entered into "agreement to sale" with the owners of the land. All that they may have will be colourful brochures with drawings. Invariably, such brochures will have notes with "Asterisk mark" and comments like "for example purpose only", "pending approval", "the final drawing or plan may undergo changes and builder will have right to make changes," etc.

The builders may ask for 10–15% of the apartment cost as "booking amount"; another 10 – 15% will be collected within 90 days of booking. Remember, you may have already parted 30% of the flat cost in the first day for an apartment for which the builder is yet to take procession of land!

A few builders may issue an "allotment letter" which also may have the usual "Asterisks" and notes.

Advantages

- The offered flat will be priced much lower than then prevailing prices in the locality, hence look very attractive for the middleclass buyers.
- Buyer may have choice of apartment in terms of direction (north or east) and floor (lower or upper).

Danger of booking apartment in the prelaunch phase:

1. It may take a very long time for the construction of the flat to start and final delivery to take place. It has not been uncommon to start construction after 3 years and delivery to take place after 10 years.
2. Once the construction starts, do not be surprised with massive changes in the drawing. They may add one more floor. They may cancel the club-house and make one more tower next to your block!
3. If you approach courts, you may not get justice for decades.
4. After making you run around courts for a decade, they may return the booking amount without interest. If courts give verdict in your favour, they may be asked to add 4 – 5% simple interest to the principal. Out of desperation, you may even settle for principal amount.

My recommendation:

Irrespective of the builders, never book apartment in the pre – launch phase. Do not trust anyone.

○ **BOOKING APARTMENT AFTER FORMAL LAUNCH**

Ignore the "sales talk" by the builders while selling an under-construction apartment to you. Remember the following hard facts based on history of majority of projects:

1. Almost no project has been completed on time. The delay can be from six months to a few years even after the construction has reached $2^{nd}/3^{rd}$ floor out of seven floors of the building.
2. The agreement that you sign with the builder is highly one-sided, favouring the builder. In the worst case, if you approach court, you may not get the flat for a decade. Do not be surprised if the builder cancels your flat after nine years, by returning the money that you paid!
3. The payment schedule is framed in such a way that almost 90% of the agreed amount will get collected when only 50–60% of Construction is completed. This means, for latter part of the construction you may be providing their entire working capital! Meanwhile, for all practical purpose, the builder is using your ability to take loan to run his business and you are funding his business!

Precautions to take while booking apartment in under construction period

1. Check reputation of the builder by visiting completed projects and talking to 3–4 customers who dealt with them in the past.
2. Consider projects which are already approved by leading banks like HDFC/ICICI/SBI. See if any leading banks are missing from the list of banks that have approved it. It is preferable to go for a project which is financed by HFC/Bank.
3. Very low booking amount, as low as 5% and avoid those who have high % at the initial stage, unless it is in the final stage of construction.
4. Make it a "construction-linked plan" spread around 10–15 stages and not just 5–6 stages.
5. Must go for projects which are RERA registered.
6. Book only if at least 25% of the projects are sold. Verify it.

7. Let all documents be vetted by a lawyer before paying the booking amount particularly for projects which are not yet approved by any HFC.

8. Keep all communication via email for records.

B. Almost-"Ready to Move"-Apartments

This is the kind of apartment that I will go for my personal investment. When we say "ready to move" it means, the possession can happen in maximum six months' period. The basic structure and walls are ready. It is at a finishing stage with plumbing, painting, flooring, etc. At this stage, the risk of non-completion or delay is very low. Since builders get 90% of the total apartment cost within weeks, you can negotiate prices to attractive levels. You can do a "take it or leave it" approach while negotiating. Quietly find out, how much of inventory they have. The more the inventory the more discounts that you may get. With fewer inventories, the builders may not give much discount if you are not good at assessing and negotiating. Take an experienced person along for negotiation.

Caution:

1. If only columns and beams are completed it does not mean "almost ready to move", though the builder wants you to believe that. From this level, it may take 1–1.5 years or even a few years for completion of the project.

2. Visit the project at odd days and times to find if active construction work is going on.

[There are builders who deploy a few workers only at weekend!]

1. Build relationship with other 2–3 buyers to understand what is going on with the project.

    (I will recommend forming of a "WhatsApp" group on the day you give token advance.)

2. Start with a "token advance" before giving actual "booking amount", which gives you time to study and evaluate before going forward with further financial commitment.

C. Ready Apartments/Resale Apartments

Advantages

1. Very low financial risk
2. You can take the decision after visiting flat, complex, locality, etc.
3. HFC/banks will extend loans fast if you are eligible
4. Ideal for "self-use"

Disadvantages

1. You may not get a discount compared to "going prices" in the locality
2. Some sellers may demand high "cash" component.
3. You may have to redo interiors if it is old or not to your liking
4. Appreciation in 3-years-period is very limited; hence not an ideal investment for appreciation

Recommendation

Keep track of apartment prices over 1–2 years period. Enter when the price trend is favourable to you: that is, prices have dropped by 5–10%.

b) Real Estate Investment for Rental Income

i) Option-1 – Residential rental properties (flats/independent houses)

While buying any residential property, we need to keep in mind whether it is for "self-use" or for renting out. If it is for "self-use", there are tax benefits available for self-occupied property.

Further, while selecting properties for self-use one needs to look at various factors as mentioned in the earlier part. Also, you need to be clear as to who will be your prospective tenant: couples with kids, IT professionals, office employees, etc. For rental properties for the target groups, goals and strategies would be different.

Low cost of entry

Whether it is 900 sq.ft. 2 BR flat or 775 sq.ft. 2BR flat, the rent difference will be marginal, whereas the cost of purchase will be at least 15% higher.

Whether there is club-house or swimming pool or not, the rental value is unlikely to be more than a few hundred rupees, whereas you would have shelled out Rs. 2–3 lakhs more per flat and monthly maintenance also would be higher.

Whether you paid for luxury class interiors or not, the rental value would be only marginally different.

Locality and parking may be two major influencing factors.

If you want to get rent as a source of income, go for a flat with "low cost of entry". Also try to go for "almost ready-to-move-in" property to get value for money.

Sensible furnishing

You need to furnish the flat, keeping in mind the targeted prospective tenant. For certain type of tenants, better furnishing and fixtures may be required. But for others, bare minimum furnishing is OK.

In some cases, providing beds, dining table and A/C will fetch you much higher rentals. If the going trend is not favourable, if you provide a "furnished flat", it may remain vacant for long periods of time. Hence, before taking a decision to furnish, you need to evaluate investment vs. potential benefits.

Type of tenant

There are societies which have restrictions for renting to non-vegetarians, bachelors, owners of pets like dogs/cats and so on. If you want to have less trouble, keep these irrational demands and sensitivities in mind.

Getting a tenant

Depending on the city that you live in, you can use services of brokers, social media like FaceBook, online advertisements or traditional press advertisements you need to evaluate the cost of tenant acquisition before jumping into any arrangements.

Verification of the Tenant

This is very important before agreeing to rent out the place:

a. Various physical proofs like PAN, address, etc.

b. Place of employment, position and number of years.

c. Office references from HR or colleagues.

d. Previous place of stay or even details of previous landlords' name and contact details.

e. In western countries, landlords obtain CIBIL score details, which is a good idea for India too.

Residential rental agreement

There are a number of residential rent agreement formats available online as well as with lawyers/ estate agents. However, the following is to be kept in mind.

1. In some states if the agreement is made on a plain paper it is valid if it is for 11 months. In most states, the rental agreement needs to be registered after paying stamp duty and registration charges if it is for a period beyond 11 months. Please take advice from a lawyer in your city.

2. Essential elements in the agreement:

    a. Duration

    b. Monthly rent

    c. Electricity/ water and parking charges

    d. Security deposit

    e. Monthly maintenance

    f. Painting charges if tenant shifts before 11 months

Additional points

1. In case of dispute, jurisdiction of courts

2. Whether you wish to add "arbitration clauses"

Recommendation:

1. Considering long delay with courts and high cost involved, it is advisable to add "arbitration clause" clearly mentioning who will be the arbitrator.

2. If it is a private party, it is advisable to collect PDCs (post-dated cheques). If you are a busy person, it is difficult to keep track of electronic payments. Legal position of "cheque bouncing" is stronger than "non-payment" of rent.

ii) Option – 2-Paying guest accommodation

Paying guest accommodation is a lucrative business proposition if you live in a city which has large number of freshly qualified employees or students. The most important thing to remember is that, it is a full-time business activity and not a 'hobby'.

1. You need to take formal license from municipal or Govt. authorities.
2. You need to pay electricity, water and gas charges at commercial rates.
3. You need to provide cleanliness and security as per Govt. Rules.
4. You need to file I-T returns in consultation with C.A.

Where to start PG Business?

1. Near professional colleges where a lot of outstation students come to study.
2. On a land or building which you have built with economical rates.

Occupancy rates?

You will make significant profits only if you have high occupancy rates. For achieving high occupancy rates, you will have to advertise – online portals, Facebook and traditional press.

Employees and structure

You need to employ full time people – warden, office staff and cooks. Please remember! It is 24*7*365 days' activity.

If you are retired and wanting a peaceful life, this may work against your interest.

Caution

If you are weak in money collection, you will lose a lot of your income. The kinds of people who stay in P.G. are people who can walk out anytime without paying you. You need to be very skilled to manage such people.

iii) Option-3 – SHOPS AND OFFICES ON RENTALS

Commercial properties like office and shops yield much higher rental income than residential properties. It could be 5–8% p.a. of the current property value. If the current value of the property is Rs. 10 million, you may get Rs. 40,000–70,000 rent/per month.

Pros:

1. High yield of rental income.
2. Long-term lease, you need not search for a new tenant frequently (example:- Banks may take premises for 10–15 years).

Cons:

1. High cost of entry
2. Tenants often resist vacation of premises which may end up in courts. This means having strong rental agreement drafted by a lawyer and including "arbitration clause".
3. Fluctuation in rentals due to business cycles; hence if you enter at a wrong time, you are stuck with low rentals for a long period.
4. If you rent out the premises to a loss-making business, you could land up in serious trouble for a long time. No rent but legal expenses.

Caution

1. Check out the history and financial status of the tenant.
2. Draft agreement in consultation with a lawyer. Add "arbitration clause".
3. Take high deposits as a precaution against default [12 months plus rent as security.]

iv) Option-4 – REIT [REAL ESTATE INVESTMENT TRUST]

This has been in vogue in western countries for a long time. Embassy group has come out with India's first REIT. REITs collect investors' money and invest into rental space – commercial or residential. The rent earned is distributed among shareholders.

From the current estimates, REITs may give around 6–7% rental yield. It is too premature to judge the performance of REIT in India. Let us wait for a decade before jumping into this new idea.

7.4 Direct Share Market Investments

i) Basics of Share Market

If you want to earn much higher income compared to inflation, you need to establish a successful business enterprise. If that is not possible, the next best possible option is to take part in the business world through owning shares of business companies. For all practical purpose,s you will become the owner of the Company. As a small shareholder, you will not have these benefits:

- You will not have "controlling ownership" in the Company.
- You will not have fancy titles like 'Director'.
- You will not get a salary by working in that Company.

If you hold more than 1% shares in the Company, you may stand a chance of deciding the DIRECTOR. Otherwise, you will get two benefits:

- You will get dividends like all shareholders in proportion to the shares that you hold.
- Your share value will get appreciated if the company performs well.

As an investor who is interested in creating long-term wealth, investing into share market is almost unavoidable. There are two ways such investments can be made:

- Mutual Fund route
- Direct share investments by having a Demat account.

Either way, some basic understanding of share market is mandatory for everyone who seeks to benefit from the market.

Face Value of share

Company shares come in different face values. It could be Rs. 1/-, Rs. 2/-, Rs. 5/-, Rs. 10/-, or Rs. 100/-. A Rs. 5/- face value share is getting quoted at Rs. 100/-, which is different from a Rs. 10/- face value share getting quoted at Rs. 100/- In terms of market value per share, the former is valued double.

Market Prices

Shares are generally traded at trading hours and prices fluctuate from deal to deal. If there are few sellers and buyers are more, the prices rise. Conversely if the sellers are more and buyers are less, price could fall. Prices keep going up and down every minute. However, then it could be a rising trend or falling trend or more or less static price. No one knows what is going to happen one hour later. It is possible that after you sell your shares at 10 AM, the prices may go down by 2% within 2 hours and after another 2 hours the prices can jump up by 5%.

Stock Exchange and SEBI

There are two stock exchanges in India where shares are officially traded: NSE (National Stock Exchange) and BSE (Bombay Stock Exchange). Because there are inherent risks involved, Govt. has a separate wing as a regulator for these stock exchanges called SEBI (Securities and Exchange Board of India). To protect the interests of investors and ensure proper system and discipline, SEBI monitors and administers through various rules, regulations and systems. This helps in maintaining transparency of trading but also ensures increased participation of investors with more money flowing into the market and which will finally result in overall development of economy, employment and develop GDP (Gross Domestic Product). Improved GDP means better quality of life for all citizens.

Difference between Primary market and Secondary Market

When a company comes out with IPO (Initial Public Opening) it is called the primary market issue. The normal purpose is to list the company in the stock market and collect money from the general public and to establish "market price". Secondary market is the shares which are already listed and being traded in the market.

Stock Indices – Sensex/Nifty

Thousands of companies list their shares in the Indian share market; from these, a few similar stocks are grouped together to form an index. The classification may be on the basis of company size, industry sector, market capitalization or other categories. BSE India includes 30 stocks and NSE comprises of 50 stocks and others include Sector Indices like Bankex (Banking) BSE Midcap, BSE small-cap, etc.

Trading in Shares

One can do online trading of shares or offline (through broker). Brokers get a fixed commission for working as intermediaries. Trading can be done by anyone having a Demat A/C. Settlements are done within three working days (Trade day + 2 working days).

Derivatives Market

The derivatives market operates within the stock market but with a futuristic point of view. That is operating through F & O (Future and Options)

Futures and options are for highly experienced traders who thrive on speculation. This is certainly not investing with a view of creating long-term wealth.

Benefits of Investing in shares

After you invest in shares you can choose to sell any time to manage your profits. You can also sell at lower price to cut your losses. However, there are many additional benefits one can get, depending on the quality of shares that you hold.

Dividends

One could get dividends on annual, half-yearly or quarterly basis. This could be as little as 5% of the face value or 100 – 500% of the face value.

Bonus Shares

The company may declare bonus shares (free shares) from time to time; it could be 10 + 1 or 1 + 1 or similar depending on the company.

Splitting of shares

The company may choose to split the value of each share to increase trading by small investors. Shares of face value Rs. 10/- can be split as two shares of Rs. 5/- face value or ten shares of Re. 1/- face value.

Such splitting can increase trading and on long term basis, the market price can improve.

Right Shares

The existing shareholder of the company could get an opportunity to buy shares of one of its subsidiaries or associates at an attractive price.

ii) Prerequisites for Successfully Investing in Shares Directly

Legally almost all adults with money and Demat A/C can buy and sell shares. But, to be successful in stock market the following are the prerequisites. For all others, it could work out to be a gamble or buying a lottery ticket. We wish to warn you that your good intellect or technical skills elsewhere cannot be applied here easily. You may be able to pick up skills to invest into stock market if you have an open mind and humility to accept your mistakes and lack of perception.

PLEASE DO NOT SIT ON YOUR PRIDE. IT IS YOUR HARD-EARNED MONEY!

[1] Good understanding of economy

Each little event [economic, social or political] can leave the share market and individual shares with an impact. The impact could be positive or negative. It could be small or big. It could be short-term or long-term.

YOU ARE A SPECTATOR OF EVENTS AND NOT AN INFLUENCER OF EVENTS!

A few examples are given below:

	Positive Impact	Negative Impact
Agriculture	Government has increased budget allocation to agriculture	Government allowing free import of Agri products
Dollar	Rupee is becoming weaker and is likely to quote much higher prices against dollar. Helps export driven industries/sectors	Rupee becoming strong. Lesser rupees are available against dollar. Damages industries dependent on import
Interest Rate	Falling interest rates can help increase borrowings to SSI [Small Scale Industry] and MSME [Micro, Small & Medium Enterprises]	Rising interest rate can negatively impact SSI and MSME

[2] Good understanding of financial statements of companies

Various financial statements of listed companies are available online and offline on quarterly and annual basis. Companies also bring out revenue and profit forecasts in addition to other events like expansion, diversification, debt-structuring, product-introduction, etc.

Various changes in the financial and marketing situation of the company can bring out positive or negative impact. Such events keep happening on a continuous basis. You need to be updated on these.

A few examples are given below:

	Positive	Negative
Revenue	Introduction of new products are received well and the company's growth is expected to be higher than previous years	Products which contribute high % to the current revenue are being discontinued due to regulatory issues. Revenue is likely to fall
Profits	Company is increasing business in the highly profitable sectors or geographies may result in improved profits	Company's business will be negatively impacted in the sector or geography where high % profits are generated due to some factors. Profits are likely to fall
Employees	Some high-quality senior people are likely to join in the company	Some key seniors including CEO are likely to leave soon
Debt	Decreasing debt in the coming year because of internal profits generated	Increasing debt in the business disproportionate to revenue growth

[3] Understanding Company leadership and culture

Company leadership and culture can have a major impact on the long-term performance of the company. Hence leadership and ownership changes can have great impact on the future performance.

A few examples of such changes are given below:

	Positive	Negative
Directors	Ex-HDFC Bank MD joins the board of a leading Pharma company	Ex-Ranbaxy directors are likely to join the board of a successful Pharma company
Takeover	TATA group is likely to take over XYZ Airlines	Scam accused Director is increasing stake in ABC company

[4] Understanding of sector of the company

Every sector and every company work differently from one another. To understand the positive or negative impact of any event on the sector, one needs deeper understanding of the sector in terms of technological changes, competition, raw materials used, the dependence on import or export, etc. Even the best of investors in the world have rarely ventured out of certain sectors.

The legendary investor Peter Lynch used to say "Invest in what you know." Another legendary investor Warren Buffet kept out of technology shares and focussed on FMCG, Insurance, Tobacco, etc. When one does not know the basics of biology or chemistry how will you take a decision whether to invest into SUN Pharma or BIOCON? If you rarely purchased products from online stores, how will you take an investment decision in an E-Commerce company? Understanding means in-depth understanding of the sector and its dynamics in terms of competition, financials, etc.

[5] Reading, Researching and Consulting

To understand the companies, competition and sector, one needs to spend considerable time on the following:-

- Read reports of Analysts
- Read business newspapers and journals
- Visit customers who use such products
- Speak to competition, consultants

Unless you have deep understanding of economy, money policy, Company, Sector, etc., you cannot take rational decisions which must be based on facts and beyond normal emotions.

Let us look at the reading habit of 80 years+ old legendary investor Warren Buffet.

Warren Buffet's Reading habits
- He is over 80 years old and spends 80% of the day reading
- Reading consists of several newspapers, books, journals and finance reports
- He reads 500 pages of books everyday

What makes Millionaires?
1. The self-made millionaire Steve Siebold interviewed 1200 of world's wealthiest people to find out what traits they shared. There was one trait common to all. They read everything from self-improvement books to autobiographies.
2. Author Tom Corley spent 5 years studying daily activities of 233 rich people and 128 poor people. He found that 67% of rich people spend far less time on TV compared to poor people.

[6] Emotional Balance

Warren Buffet
As an investor, it is wise to be "fearful when others are greedy and greedy when others are fearful."

This quote by Warren Buffet sums up the emotional balance and maturity required to succeed in the share market. The "herd mentality" is ingrained in us from early childhood. We follow what others do. We need "social approval" for what we do. We are unwilling to take a position different from what is acceptable as a "popular position". This is the single big danger an investor can face in the stock market.

We buy shares when the prices are the highest in the market and sell when prices have dropped or hit the bottom.

[7] Be careful about media frenzy, "Experts", Self-appointed Advisers and other distractions.

We are bombarded with news and opinions about companies and stock market through newspapers, journals, television and online news portals. Then, there are grapevine news, SMS alerts, "expert" views and so on. Let us look at the types of news or messages that reach your eyes and ears every day:

Media/Newspaper Headlines

"Market plunges 600 points"

"Bloodbath in Dalal Street"

"Bears kill Bulls"

"Ambani's wealth grew by Rs. 100,000 million"

"Top five richest Indians are from Bombay"

"FII's getting out of India"

"Oil companies bleed"

"Time to invest in Mutual funds"

"Mutual fund investors make a killing"

The list goes on...

Now Listen to "Experts" in TV Studios

"Buy HDFC Bank, sell ICICI" – Mr. _____

"Sell HDFC Bank, buy DHFL" – Mr. _____

"ITC to touch Rs. 400/- by Diwali" – Mr. _____

"Sell DHFL, buy LIC Housing Finance." – Mr. _____

"Sell HDFC Bank, buy Federal Bank" – Mr. _____

If you keep track of all that all experts have said in the past 30 – 60 days, it would be hilarious!

- Opinions of many "experts" are contradictory.
- Some experts change opinion within two weeks.
- Same set of experts come to same set of TV studios.
- CNBC says buy Ambuja Cement and
- Times Now says sell Ambuja Cement (!!)

Let us look at what online news channels say

"Look at top 10 stocks bought by MF, do you own any?"

"Stocks sold by Reliance MF – ICICI Bank, L&T Fin and Sun Pharma"

"Stocks purchased by HDFC MF – ICICI Bank, L&T Fin and Sun Pharma"

"What Rakesh Jhunjhunwala purchased in the past 3 months"

"Dolly Khanna increases stake in Rain Industries in the past 6 months"

Let us look at SMS tips

SMS tips come from Rajkot and Indore far more than from the rest of India.

[I do not know why so many social service crooks settle down in these two cities. Due to the weather?]

"Buy FEKU Company at Rs. 8/-: guaranteed to touch Rs. 20/- in 15 days."

"Buy ULLU Company at Rs. 2/- today and sell at Rs. 10/- in another 10 days."

"ULLU FINANCE is tipped for takeover by Surat Bank; buy at Rs. 8/- for 300% return in 7 days!"

Let us look at telephonic advisors

Invariably the advisor will be a lady and she says that she is from Rajkot or Indore.

They start conversation as follows:-

"Aap trading karte ho? (Do you do trading?")

If you continue with the conversation she will "help" you with hot tips for investing into the stock market.

Most likely she may not be a matriculate and she will give tips on Biotech companies. For fun I asked those ladies question like:

"Is it midcap or small cap?" "Is it operating in bioinformatics?"

"Do they make such and such product for pneumonia?" (Ha Ha!)

How can they know, when they barely know the difference between botany and zoology!!!

Let us listen to "expert" friends in parties

When you attend cocktail and other parties, we meet many "experts" on stock market.

There are two types of conversations.

Those who boast:

"I made a killing in XYZ Shares."

"I purchased ABC shares at Rs. 20/- and sold at Rs. 25/-; made Rs. 50,000/-"

Then there are those who give free advice:

"Buy Sun Pharma, it will Rs. 1000/-"

{If you innocently ask why, they may tell that shortly they are entering into Philippines market." By the way is Philippines market bigger than Kerala? (Ha! Ha!)}

"Sell Airlines shares. Govt. is planning taxes on airfare" [All people switching to trains?]

iii) Basic Company Analysis

When we buy vegetables, we show a high degree of care. We look at competing sellers. We analyse each piece. We ask questions and give reasonable thought. For a decision for as little as Rs. 50/-, we show great care. Why not such serious thoughts when you invest your money to buy a Company share?

The following are basic Company analyses that must be done before trying to invest into any Company share directly. This is neither exhaustive nor a complete list. If you have not done serious homework, do not buy shares of any company. Do not trust anyone, except your own intellect and rationality. If you cannot do it, invest through mutual fund route only.

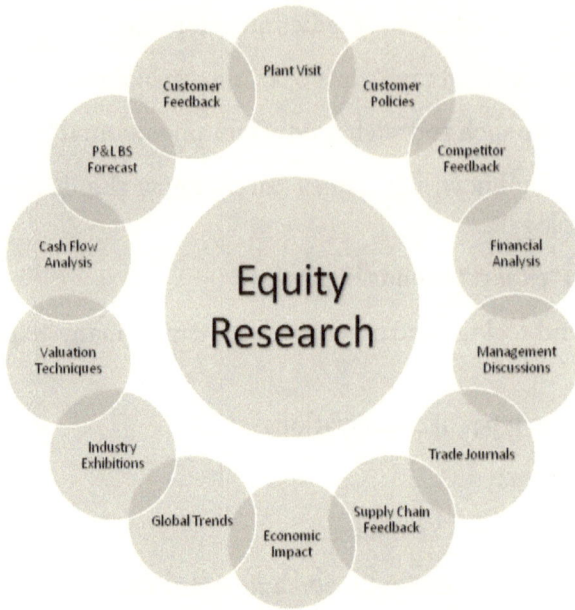

[BASIC EQUITY RESEARCH]

Equity Research

My Guarantee:

If You Do Not Do Serious Study of Shares, You Will Lose Money!

Revenue

- What is yearly revenue?
- What is the current year's growth? How has it grown in the past five years?

Net Profits
- What is the % Net profit to revenue?
- How has the NP grown in the current year?
- How has the NP grown in the past 5 years?

Reserves
- What are the reserves?
- How have reserves grown in the past five years?
- How much is the reserve in relation to revenues/profits?

Debt
- Does it have debt? – Short term or long term?
- What % of share capital is constituted by debt?
- Is debt growing?
- How does debt compare with peers in the industry?

Competitive Analysis
- Look at short term and long term competitive position of the company.
- What is the competitive strength and is it sustainable?

Book Value/PE Multiple
- What is the book value and PE multiple?
- How does book value and PE multiple compare with competition?

Dividend/Bonus History
What is the history of dividend and bonus in the past 10 years?

Directors/Major Shareholders
- Who holds the majority stake?
- How is the reputation of the Directors?
- How is the shareholding by leading MFs or FIIs?

Share Prices
- What is current share price in comparison with last 1–3 years?
- Is the share price post-bonus or post-dividend?

Experts' Views of Company and Industry
- Have you looked at experts' views and their research reports?
- What is the forecast of researchers and experts?

Your Long-Term View?
- How long will you hold these shares? 3/5 years?
- [If your view is less than 3 years, do not buy at all!]

iv) **Why Most Investors Lose Money in Stock Market?**
1. Most investments are in equity and very little in debt instruments.
2. "Over-focus and concentration" in a few Companies and a few sectors, sometimes as little as 2–3 Companies or 1–2 sectors only.

   [A typical Multicap fund run by a MF will have shares in 12–15 sectors and in 30–40 Companies with differing market cap]
3. Shares are bought without strong financial analysis, based on news and "tips".
4. Shares are purchased when market is at its peak and sold when market is at bottom, exactly opposite of what should have been done.
5. Buying and selling based on "emotions" rather than "cold facts" as given in equity analysis above.

7.5 Investing in Mutual Funds

i) Understanding Mutual Funds

As we discussed earlier under share market, if anyone wants to get investment returns much higher than fixed income instruments, the only option is taking part in the equity market. But, direct investments into equity market are highly risky and most people are neither equipped nor skilled to do it. But, they can get equally good returns through mutual fund route. And, in most cases, the returns will be better than direct shares investments with far less risks associated with it.

What are Mutual funds?

A mutual fund is a collection of investment pooled from a lot of people to be invested for a specific objective. When you invest in a mutual fund, you buy shares and become a shareholder of the fund. The fund manager and his team of assistants determine which specification securities (for example: shares, bonds, debentures, etc.) they should invest the shareholder's money in, in order to accomplish the objectives of the fund and keep shareholders happy. Because good mutual funds take most of the hassles and cost of figuring out which securities to invest in, they are among the best vehicles for investment ever created.

   a. Mutual funds allow you to diversify your investment, i.e. in many different industries and companies instead of just one or two or a few. By spreading the risk over a number of different industries and companies mutual funds lessen instability of our portfolio and chance of large loss.

   b. Mutual funds enable you to give your money to the best money managers in the country, some of the folks who manage money for the rich and famous.

   c. Mutual funds are the best "couch potato "investment with very little effort and low study and at times, you can get rich reward.

Top 10 mutual funds houses in India

1. ICICI Prudential Mutual Fund
2. HDFC Mutual Fund
3. Reliance Mutual Fund
4. Birla Sun Life Mutual Funds
5. SBI Mutual Fund
6. UTI Mutual Fund

7. Kotak Mahindra MF

8. Franklin Templeton MF

9. DSP BlackRock MF

10. Axis MF

ii) Structure of Mutual Fund House in India

Mutual funds in India are regulated by SEBI (Securities and Exchange Board of India). SEBI prescribes comprehensive set of guidelines on the functioning of mutual funds.

Fund sponsor

The sponsor is the main body that establishes the mutual fund; it can be compared to a promoter of a company. The responsibility of the sponsor includes appointing the trustees with the approval of SEBI and setting up AMC (Asset Management Company).

For example: ICICI Bank and PRUDENTIAL are the sponsors of ICICI MF.

Trustee

The main role of Trustee is to ensure that the interests of unit holders are met by making sure that mutual fund complies with SEBI regulations. The trustees ensure proper funding, function of AMC and supports key personnel and right processes, procedures and systems.

Asset Management Company (AMC)

The AMC is the Investment Manager of the trust. It manages day-to-day operations and takes care of investors' money. AMC may consist of CIO [Chief Investment Officer], Fund Managers and analysts. Example: HDFC AMC is the AMC of HDFC MF.

Compliance Officer

The Compliance Officer ensures that all the activities of the AMC are in line with SEBI rules and regulations.

Custodian – The Custodian is responsible for safekeeping of all the securities. Custodian is also responsible for the investment account of the MF.

Registration and transfer (RTA) – They maintain update of all investor records. They manage investor's application, purchases and redemption of various schemes and plans.

Basically, mutual funds use investors' money for buying shares or other securities. There are day-to-day expenses for running a mutual fund. It has to pay various people employed, [most of them highly qualified and experienced] and manage the office. Each AMC must make profits to sustain and progress.

iii) Charges for Investing into Mutual Funds

There are broadly two types of charges:

One-time charges

Entry load – these are charges received when the units are purchased. The mutual fund would sell the units at price higher than NAV. At present mutual funds cannot charge any entry load.

Exit load

The mutual funds would buy back units at rate lower than the NAV. The exit load varies between fund houses and between different schemes within fund houses. The current practice is the funds charge anywhere between 0.5% and 3.0% depending on the holding period. If the investor holds the fund for the minimum holding period, no exit load is charged.

Entry/Exit load on mutual fund

Entry load has been discontinued for all Mutual funds. However, the following exit loads exist:

Equity MF	–	Below one year: 1%
Balanced MF	–	Below 1–1.5 years: 1%
Ultra short term debt funds	–	Below one month: 0.5%
Some other Debt funds	–	Below 6 months: 0.50%

	ONE UNIT	1000 UNITS
Current NAV	90.00	90,000
Exit load 1% of NAV	0.90	900
Redemption	89.10	89100

If the investor has redeemed 1000 units he will be paid Rs. 89,100/-. If it is redeemed, Rs. 900/- will be retained by MF towards exit-load charges.

Transaction charges

These charges are one-time charges applicable when the money is invested as it will be paid to distributor or intermediary. It could vary from Rs. 100–150 per application.

Expenses ratio

The main income of a mutual fund comes from charging an expenses ratio on the funds it manages. The higher the fund it manages the more it earns in terms of value. However, for individual fund the ratio depends on the value of fund it manages. It could be as high as 2.5%. Expense-ratio-structure is stipulated by the regulator, and it varies based on the size of the net asset of the fund. The higher the net assets the lower the expense-ratio. This in turn impacts returns generated by the MF vs. another fund.

iv) Direct vs. Regular Mutual Fund Investment

All MF investments come in two flavours – regular plan and direct plan.

They are exactly the same scheme, managed by the same fund manager and investing in the same set of shares and bonds, but, there is only one difference.

Regular plan – In a "regular plan" a part of your profits is paid to the broker and it will cost you more. In short, you will earn less from the money you have invested.

Direct plan – In this plan, all the profit that you earned will come to you without parting with brokerage to any agent. It will cost you less and you will earn more from the money that you invested.

NAV difference between regular vs. direct:

The brokerage commission which otherwise would have been paid to broker are added to the NAV of direct plan over a period of time; this adds a huge difference in NAV.

Let us take two scenarios.

Ashok with regular plan:

Ashok is a 35-year-old who put Rs. 1.0 million into regular plan of MF for his retirement at the age of 65 years. Let us assume that the fund grows by 8% every year and net of commission of 1% it grows by 7% every year. In 65th year Ashok gets Rs. 7.60 million.

Ramesh with direct plan:

Ramesh is a friend of Ashok and is also 35 years old. He also put Rs. 1.0 million into MF, but direct plan for his retirement at the age of 65 years. At 8% growth every year, without paying any commission, he gets Rs. 10 million at 65 years!

Rs. 2.40 million was handed over to the broker by Ashok for broker's retirement!

Who should buy a regular plan? Can we switch to direct plan?

Regular plan may be required for those who are first-time investors to MF or those seeking investment advice from brokers. For most first time investors, going through a well-established broker or distributor would be better than making poor decisions. Your loss could run far greater than the commission that you paid. It is almost like self-treatment for a dangerous illness. Newcomers can take the help of "fees only" CFP professionals if the planned invested amount exceeds Rs. 500,000/-.

One can switch from regular plan to direct plan after taking into consideration exit load and "lock-in" period. If you exit before due date you may lose further 1% instead of gaining and if there is lock period. In ELSS Scheme you cannot exit before 3 years.

Recommendation:

Review all your MF investments and switch/redeem regular plan wherever possible.

How to invest in direct plan?

In direct plan the investor does not have the help of an advisor and he has to complete the paperwork himself. Also, he has to make the papers reach MF office.

KYC FORMS

These are simple forms which require you to affix your photo and attach proof of Aadhaar card, PAN card, and address proof. Also keep your bank details like A/c no., branch name and place.

Mutual fund applications:

- ❖ Fill up all columns properly.
- ❖ Clearly mention if you want it in single name or joint name.
- ❖ On top of the form where distribution details are to be filled, write "Direct plan".
- ❖ Attach cheque.

Recommendation for making direct investments into Mutual fund.

If you are doing things for the first time, you can personally visit the MF office to complete the formalities.

You can also opt for online application as all mutual funds are available online. Please ensure that all your MF investments in one fund house figure under a single Folio number. Multiple folios are difficult to keep track of when the investor is alive. And, it will be a greater problem if the investor leaves behind the folios to his spouse or other claimants.

v) Direct Investment in Shares or through Mutual Funds?

This is the question that most investors ask. Answer is very simple:

- * If you meet the "prerequisites" [as given above] of investing directly into share market, **YES**.
- * If you do not meet the "prerequisites" of investing directly into share market, **NO**.

Where to Invest Money & in Which Asset Class?

> **TWO RULES OF WARREN BUFFET**
>
> **Rule No 1:** Don't lose money.
>
> **Rule No 2:** Don't forget rule No. 1.

Performance Comparison – Direct Shares vs. Mutual Fund route

We only hear stories of great money made by people from share market by buying and selling shares; we hear big names from the list of share market investors.

- Rajesh Jhunjhunwala
- Vijay Kedia
- Dolly Khanna
- Chandrakant Sampat
- Ashok Kacholia _____ are a few names

Such star investors may be one dozen and may be a few thousand more have made decent wealth. Or 100,000 more! But, the vast majority (+95%) of direct investors have lost money in share market or made less money compared to MF investors. We do not hear the names of losers.

> **"History is written by the winners"**
>
> – Napoleon

If you lost a huge amount of money in the share market by direct investment, will you go up to your in-laws and say that you lost a huge amount of money? Will you talk about it in a cocktail party?

The 95% of the investors who did not make money from share market have a chance to create wealth through MF route.

vi) Mutual Funds Are Preferred over Direct Shares by Most People. Why?

The MF houses have an inherent advantage compared to ordinary investors. Let us look at the advantages:

1] Fund Managers are well-educated and well-trained

All fund houses deploy fund managers with excellent education and decades of experience. Typically they carry qualification like CFA (Chartered Financial Analysts), CA (Chartered Accountant), MBA (Finance) and so on. A large number of them are from premier institutes like IIT and IIM.

Leading Fund Managers

Name	House	Education	Experience (years)	AUM [Rs. Mln.]	Returns %
Chirag Setalvad	HDFC	BSc./MBA	20	1000	25
Neelesh Surana	MIRAE	BE/MBA	20	550	25
Mrinal Singh	ICICI	BE/MBA	14	900	22
Jani Karan	FRANKLIN	BE/MBA	20	740	28
Sohini Andani	SBI	B.Com./CA	21	480	23
Vinit Sambre	DSP	B.Com./CA	18	370	28
Krishna Kumar	SUNDARAM	BE/MBA	24	500	20
Prashanth Jain	HDFC	B.Tech./MBA	20	2150	21

[AUM – Asset Under Management]

They are professionally trained and experienced to look at share market through the prism of data, analysis and rationality. When you invest into Mutual Funds, such qualified persons are indirectly employed by you to manage your money.

2] Fund Managers are supported by a team of Analysts

Fund managers are supported by a team of equally qualified analysts. They analyse and prepare reports on various sectors and companies. They visit customers, suppliers and competitors of targeted companies. Very often they meet company CFO or attend their press briefings. They prepare research reports which are based on not only desk-research but also feedback from the field. Such in-depth analysis and research are not possible for individual direct investors. How many hours can you spend every day or every month on analysing Companies or sectors? For you, it is an "extra job" that you do. For these analysts, it is their full-time job.

3] Mutual fund managers have a formal structure of decision making and not based on "whims and fancies".

For each fund, there are well-laid-out strategies and processes set for investment. One cannot make a serious deviation from these processes and systems. For example: If the fund has an upper limit of 5% cap on any company, the fund Manager cannot increase contribution to 10% without a process of analysis and discussion. This reduces risk at sector or company level. Whereas, when it comes to an individual, he can have any % in any sector or company which puts his entire portfolio to serious risk of "over concentration". If something goes wrong, his portfolio could be almost wiped out.

4] Fund managers are far ahead of individual share investors with information

The sources of information to an individual investor are common – Newspapers, TV shows, journals, etc. When the information is known to everyone it is no more a "secret". When it is known to everyone the market price is adjusted along with it, whereas a fund manager can forecast company performance based on such information and take trading calls.

Example: If the Rupee-to-Dollar rate jumps from Rs. 68/- to Rs. 73/- it may have an impact on export-oriented units. The MF Manager is likely to forecast the financial impact or profit jump almost immediately. The individual investor has to wait for days and weeks to know the impact. By that time price of the share would have gone up, or down in other cases.

5] Mutual funds returns are better on long term

Research has shown that the return from MF is far better than individual direct investments into share market on long-term basis.

6] MF Investors get great services at fraction of the cost

As an MF investor you are supported by technology of the fund house and indirectly, high quality talent is working for you. All these are available to you at a fraction of the real cost than any individual trying to deploy such high-quality talent.

7] MF ensures high returns with minimal risk

MFs have clear mandate to give returns better than average returns of the share market, while ensuring low risk for the investors. It is almost impossible to hear stories of any fund going bankrupt. That is because funds are diversified enough to protect the interests of investors.

8] MFs are subjected to regulatory scrutiny

MFs are governed by rules and regulations laid out by SEBI. Further, their actions are subjected to regulatory scrutiny. This ensures safety for investors' funds.

9] With MF one can choose the risk level

There are mutual funds available for various types of investors based on their risk profile, age, short term or long-term goals, etc. If you want stable low-risk return there are debt funds. If you want long-term growth, there are pure equity funds. If you want above-average growth but are willing to take a bit of risk, there are different types of balanced funds. If you want to protect your invested principal even at the cost of low return, there are money-market funds.

10] MFs save you from crooks and frauds

MF investments are transparent with facts. There is limitation on the promised return. They cannot make wild claims like unregulated finance Company sales sharks. Hence MFs save you from crooks and frauds, and offer peace of mind.

11] MFs offer highest liquidity

Other than bank deposits, most investments have low liquidity. With MFs you can invest in a few hours and if you need funds you can send request for redemption and money will get credited in maximum of 3 working days.

12] MFs help you get ownership of best of companies

When you buy MFs you get indirect ownership of best-run private companies. Suppose you wish to invest into banks and NBFCs it would be impossible to understand and invest into one dozen such institutions. If you buy banking and finance funds, you will indirectly own shares of all well-known names like HDFC, ICICI, KOTAK, YES, SBI, BAJAJ and various top Insurance companies.

13] With MFs the fund manager does all shifts on your behalf

If you own shares, you need to take calls on buying or selling of individual shares, based on your forecasted performances. With MFs, the fund manager will increase or decrease stakes in different companies or sectors and will try encashing greatest available opportunity or reduce holding if the manager feels that risk is high.

14] With MFs, you can take a long holiday

If you own shares you need to keep track of events on a frequent basis. You are under perpetual tension of decision-making. However, when it comes to MFs such tensions are handled by the Fund manager and team of experts. You will be saving considerable amount of time and attention.

15] With MFs you can spread your risk and decision-making among different teams

With MFs, you can invest through different fund houses. You can get benefit of "best fund manager" in each category.

If you want to invest into ELSS funds, you can invest through top two names. And, when it comes to another category [Multicap or Banking and Finance fund or any other], you can choose another fund house that you select. With this strategy, you get services of all top names and you spread the risk.

vii) Basics of Mutual Fund Investments

Highly Confusing World of Mutual Funds

Mutual Fund investments are extremely confusing for newcomers. And, debt-fund mutual funds are even more confusing for even veteran investors.

Look at the following statistics when it comes to Mutual Funds in India.

Number of MF houses – 40

Total Mutual funds – 900

Pure Equity Mutual funds – 400

Hybrid Mutual Funds – 168

Debt Mutual funds – 304

Within each category, there are many funds with different flavours.

Example: In equity funds there are Large cap, Midcap and Small cap funds and their combinations.

Then there are 35 ELSS funds and 70 Sector funds for banking, Infrastructure, IT Sector and so on.

Around two years back SEBI tried to bring in control and set its own classifications. That classification brought in greater clarity where Equity-based mutual funds are concerned.

But Debt-funds are still highly confusing even for veterans.

What Is the Impact of These Confusions and Complexities?

An average investor in stock market is exploited by agents and fund houses. His ignorance about such a complex market is frightening him from taking rational decisions. When he takes decisions, it lands him with wrong set of investment instruments which give returns far less than expectations. When returns do not match expectations, he takes irrational decisions like suddenly pulling out of market or going back to investment choices which give hardly 8% returns like Bank FD or gold. This book is an attempt to help him take rational long-lasting decisions which will make him wealthy and he can hope to retire peacefully.

How Do I Propose to Remove Complexity?

I will exclude stuff which may not come to your use in the near future. I will focus on Mutual funds which you can choose to invest within next few days or even months.

viii) Types of Mutual Funds

[1] Difference between Equity and Debt Mutual Funds

DEBT MUTUAL FUNDS

Debt Mutual funds are very similar to bank deposits and are meant for those who want high safety of capital, but are willing to settle for 6–8% p.a. returns.

Debt Mutual funds are not Income Tax friendly. If you hold these for less than three years, the returns that you receive will be treated similar to your other income and taxed accordingly.

Debt Mutual funds cannot give returns much higher than inflation and can never make you rich. Be very clear about this.

For who are Debt Mutual funds meant?

Situation – 1

You want to hold funds with the intention to shift to Equity-based Mutual funds in the 6–18 months period.

Situation – 2

You want to park the sale proceeds that you received from property-sale or Share-sale till you decide to redeploy funds, but, would like to get returns higher than 3.5% that Bank SB offers.

Situation – 3

Holding your emergency fund, mentally prepared to hold for 3 years plus.

Situation – 4

If you wish to get SWP payment as a source of Income, gains from debt funds are useful to those outside I-T bracket.

Which Debt funds to choose?

If you want to hold for period less than 90 days – LIQUID FUNDS

Average return for 3 years – Around 7.3%

Axis liquid – 7.3%

Birla Liquid – 7.3%

If you want to hold for 3 months plus – SHORT TERM/ULTRA SHORT-TERM FUNDS

Average 3 years return: 6.9–7.1%

Franklin India short term: 8.7%

Birla short term: 7.7%

If you want to hold for 3 years plus-BANKING & PSU FUNDS

Average return in 3 years: 7.3%

Birla: 8.1%

Axis: 7.7%

[2] Mutual Funds' Classification Based on Structure

Open-ended:

These are known as "open-ended" because units can be purchased or redeemed almost anytime. This gives complete freedom to the investor.

Close-ended:

These are known as "close-ended" as these can be purchased only during initial offer period or popularly known as NFO [New Fund Offering]. After these, the fund is locked and can be redeemed only on a pre-determined date; it could be 3 years or more. These are often listed in the stock exchange to bring liquidity in the fund.

Recommendation: As closed-ended offer hardly any advantage over open ended, go for latter.

[3] Mutual Funds – Sector Based or Multisector-Based

SECTOR-BASED MUTUAL FUNDS are those which make investments only in one particular sector of the economy. All other Mutual funds are multi-sector mutual funds. An average multi-sector mutual fund may invest in 12–15 different sectors.

Some of the popular sector funds are given below:

- Natural resource – Oil, Metals, etc.
- Power/ utility – Electricity, coal, etc.
- Infrastructure – Construction, Cement, Steel, etc.
- Finance/banking – Banks, NBFCs, Insurance, etc.
- P S U focussed – PSU Companies
- Media/ communication – TV, Newspapers, Radio
- Healthcare/ Pharma – Hospitals, Pharma Companies
- IT – Information Technology, E-commerce
- Precious metals – Gold, silver and their mining
- FMCG – Consumer goods Companies
- Transportation – Vehicles, Tyres, Car batteries, etc.
- Housing – Housing construction Companies

What are the issues with sector funds?

At any given time, a few sectors are booming and other sectors are depressed. This may not be due to poor performance of any individual companies, but general speculative trend in the marketplace.

Examples:

- In 2018-year, Pharma companies' market performance was very poor. This was mainly due to regulatory issues faced in the US.
- In the second part of 2018, all Banking firms were performing poorly due to after effects of ILFS crisis.

- In 2017 most IT Companies faced problems due to US issues and recovered smartly by 2019 beginning.

What happens to market performance of sector funds?

After you have made investments in sector funds, if the particular sector shows huge upswing, you are benefited. This may not have anything to do with your brilliance.

In case you made big investments in one sector when it is at its peak, if it falls, your investments may show huge downfall. The decline can be 30% at times and it may stay for 3–4 years. Imagine a situation where your Rs. 1 million investments have come down to Rs. 700,000/- two years after investment! This can completely unnerve you and most people sell off the sector fund at a loss and get out. After such a bad experience, the investor stays away from mutual funds for a long term as his confidence is completely shaken. He does not realise that he did a serious error of investment by putting a large amount of his hard-earned money into sector funds.

My recommendation:

* Unless you have "in depth" understanding of a particular sector, do not invest in any sector funds.

    Do not get drawn to any advertisements by Mutual funds or fall for sweet talk of any agent.

* In case you happen to have reasonable understanding of the sector, never put more than 10% of your total money into sector funds.

[4] Mutual Fund Classification Based on Market Cap

In the previous part of this chapter we discussed the difference between sector mutual funds and multi-sector mutual funds. If sector differentiated between types of products that such companies operated in, here the differentiation is based on market cap of Companies. Market cap refers to the combined market value of all its shares at marketplace. This may not be a reflection of the turnover of the Company. It reflects the market value perceived by the market. A Company can have high turnover and low market cap. There are a number of Companies where turnover is low but, market cap is high. So long as the market cap is high, it will figure in the list. It has nothing to do with type of sector or product that they deal in.

Large Cap Funds

These mutual funds invest in top 100 stocks according to market capitalization, meaning, these companies are the most valuable in the Indian stock market.

Characteristics of Large cap funds

1] Stability

These Companies have well established market reputation and long duration of experience in running the business. Because trust levels are high amongst customers and investors, these companies offer stability to the Portfolio as their stock prices do not fluctuate violently.

2] Dividends

These companies generally have stable growth in revenue and profits. Such companies have good history of dividend pay-outs.

3] Data for evaluation

Not only data about these companies is available for long period of time, but also there will be a huge quantity of data, which will be available. Since these are prominent companies, detailed company analysis done by analysts, fund houses, Banks and other financial institutions are valuable in the online and offline spaces.

4] Quality of management and Systems

These companies have reputed Directors and senior Management structure. Well established systems and processes give stability and growth focus.

5] In Sync with economic trends

These companies are generally leaders in their sectors and are in tune with economic trends of the times. Most of these companies are aligned with the powerful political system too.

6] Expected Performance

Large cap MFs are likely to perform much lower than overall stock market. However, these will offer stability even during bear phase.

For who are Large cap MFs beneficial?

For all those who are seeking returns better than debt funds and fixed Income investments, but wish to get stability and protection of capital.

Large cap mutual funds can also experience fall during bear phase and do not be surprised if it shows NIL growth or – 5% in worst periods.

Time frame should be 5 years plus and never less than 3 years.

Midcap Mutual Funds

Midcap Mutual Funds invest 65% of their portfolio into companies which figure 101–250 ranks in market capitalization. They are expected to perform with focus into the universe of 150 companies.

Midcap companies are well established with good level of systems and experienced management Structure. However, their price stability would be much lesser than large cap companies. In a bull phase they may rise a notch higher than the market and in bear phase their fall could be slightly greater than the market.

For who are Midcap MFs meant?

For those who are seeking return a little higher than overall market and have the mental stamina to withstand fall in the bear phase, which could be [-]25% at times.

Selection of midcap stock requires far greater understanding of stock market and business than large cap business and we do not recommend anyone to buy these shares.

The time frame of these mutual funds should be close to 7 years, never less than 5 years. Not recommended for those who have crossed 50 years.

Small cap Mutual funds

Small cap Mutual funds invest into the universe of companies which figure in market cap below top 250, and likely to have market cap lower than Rs. 5000 million. Many small cap companies are comparatively new to market and are led by aggressive entrepreneurs based on an idea which could make a mark in the market. It could be technology, cost advantage or creation of a new segment, etc. One can overlook small cap companies which are old or stagnant in their business outlook.

Small cap Mutual funds come with a host of risks which must be clearly understood by all investors.

1] Leadership and management risk

Typically, these companies are driven to success by a charismatic leader or a group of 2–3 people. If there are exits in the senior team, the entire company may get shaken up which will impact the entire fund.

2] Fluctuation in prices

Small cap companies can fluctuate prices at stock exchange wildly – up or down. These will get reflected in the performance of the fund.

Liquidity

Small companies' shares many not be traded frequently which will impact the fund itself.

The plus point is that small cap mutual funds deliver better returns in long term [7–10 years] than Mutual funds which are focused only into Large cap or Midcap.

Small cap mutual fund is for whom?

Small cap mutual funds are meant for younger people who are typically less than 40 years old. However, to get returns better than index, small cap funds shuffle investments frequently which are unavoidable. The price fluctuation could swing wildly. In the worst phase of bear market, the fund may come down by 35% which can break the confidence of investors.

You must hold small cap funds for 7–10 years to get the best returns. If you cannot patiently wait and see its wild swings, do not opt for small cap fund at all.

Multicap Funds

Multicap funds have no restriction on market cap focus. They can shift from large cap to midcap to small cap depending on the opportunity available. They need not restrict themselves within a market cap of large, mid or small. But, their Midcap and small holding may not be abnormally high to reduce risk. Since they need to hold only 65% in equity, they have the option to shift to debt instruments in an overheated market situation.

Price fluctuation

The price fluctuation is likely more than large cap, but lesser than Midcap and much lesser than small cap funds. However, be prepared for swings between – 5 to +25%.

MULTICAP is for whom?

Multicap is a good investment option for first-time investors as well as seasoned investors. The greatest advantage of multicap is that it covers most vibrant sectors and market caps at the right times. The fund manager shifts from one sector to another sector and from one market cap to another to get the best of returns. If he sees too much danger ahead like fall in prices, he may shift to debt instruments.

Performance of Various Market Caps [CUM Dec 2018]

Category	3 years	5 years	10 years
Large Cap	11.2	12.90	14.80
Mid Cap	9.6	19.90	21.30
Smallcap	9.30	21.50	20.10
Multicap	10.30	15.70	17.30

Index funds

These are mutual funds that invest in equities in sync with a specific stock market index so as to capture the overall characteristics or performance of the selected index.

Examples: Nifty 50 Index – Of the top 50 Indian [NSE] market

Sensex 30 index – Of top 30 as per [BSE] market

US S&P 500 Index – Of top 500 as per [USA] market

Investing in Index funds through the SIP route is becoming the most popular way across US and India. *I strongly recommend Index fund investing for all investors.*

[5] Hybrid Mutual Funds

Hybrid funds are a combination of equity and debt components in differing proportions.

We will discuss three major ones and ignore the rest to avoid confusion.

	Equity %	Debt %	TAX-FRIENDLY	RISK IN 3 YEARS
Aggressive Hybrid	65–80	20–35	YES	HIGHER
Balance Hybrid	40–60	40–60	NO	LOWER
Conservative Hybrid	10–25	75–90	NO	LOWEST

Aggressive Hybrid funds

These funds are amalgamation of growth and income funds. This is the most popular balanced fund wherein 65% of the portfolio will be in equity and balance will be mainly in debt investments.

Benefits

- Returns are likely to be far better than income/pure debt funds while some amount of risk is covered with 35% in debt instruments.
- The benefits of long-term capital gains tax can be applied here if held for more than one year as this is treated at par with other equity funds as regards Income Tax, LTCGT are concerned.

Note – Some fund houses increase the equity portion to almost 75% which increases the risk of investments. Hence if you are so much risk-averse you need to go for an equity-oriented balanced fund which restricts equity portion close to 65% of the portfolio. When the time is ripe, such funds increase equity holdings to get the best out of the market. If the fund managers feel that the holding is high % of equity, they shift to debt.

Balanced Advantage Fund

This is a new variant of hybrid funds and is recommended for risk-averse investors and the elderly and is suitable for 3+ years of investment horizon.

Balance Advantage Funds invest in a mix of stocks and FD-like instruments. However, they keep changing this allocation based on the market conditions to provide you with optimal returns with minimal risk. Balance Advantage Funds also known as Dynamic Asset Allocation Funds.

Time duration

It is ideal to hold these funds for around 5 years; however, benefits of long-term capital gains tax will kick in after one year.

For whom is Aggressive Hybrid mutual fund ideal?

* It is ideal MF for plus-50-years individuals and those who wish to reduce exposure to equity world and its resultant risk.
* Not for those who are retired and want to invest their retirement corpus. They can have maximum exposure of 20% if they are well-placed.
* Those with multiple sources of income during post retirement period can expose some % to this fund.
* It is a good fund as a "starter fund" if the investor is new to mutual funds, as this can teach him the basics of stock market and funds without risking too much.

Balanced Hybrid funds

These funds are amalgamation of predominant debt portion and minor equity portion. In most cases equity portion could be 40–60% of the total portfolio.

Benefits

Returns are likely to be better than income funds but less than aggressive balanced funds or growth/ on long term basis equity funds. Risk will be less than aggressive hybrid funds if held for only three years.

Negative

Not eligible for long term capital gains tax benefits as the equity portion is less than 65%. It will be taxed similar to income funds based on I-T bracket of the individual.

Time duration

To get I-T benefits, hold it for 3 years plus.

For whom?

- For those who are in the lower tax bracket.
- For freshly retired individuals, they may take some exposure, not more than 20% to improve income. However, this will depend on the individual's appetite for risk.
- Ideal for parking "emergency" corpus

Top three Balanced Hybrid funds

UTI CCF – Saving Plan

UTI Retirement Benefit Pension Fund.

Franklin India Pension Fund.

Conservative Hybrid Funds

These are conservative funds with combination of high debt component and very low equity portion which could be as little as 10–25%.

Conservative Hybrid funds are for whom?

* It is meant for those who are highly averse to risk and wish to protect their capital.
* Low I-T payees and retired people.

Top three Conservative hybrid funds

HDFC Hybrid debt

Birla SL regular savings

UTI Regular saving

Performance of Hybrid Funds [% return cum Dec 2018]

Hybrid Fund Category	3 Years	5 Years	10 Years
Aggressive Hybrid	9.5	13.70	14.80
Balanced Hybrid	8.10	11.20	11.70
Conservative Hybrid	7.60	9.60	9.50

My Recommendation for Hybrid Funds

- All those who are above 50 years and placed well financially and have a little risk-taking ability can go for Aggressive Hybrid mutual funds, but hold for 5–10 years.
- Those who are conservative, retired and those who have income lesser than I-T limits can go for Balanced Hybrid funds, but, must hold for 5–10 years.
- One can overlook Conservative hybrid altogether.

[6] Growth vs. Dividend Option of Mutual Funds

Mutual funds come in the two options – Growth and Dividend

Which one should you choose?

Let us understand the difference:

Growth option – when you choose growth option the profits that you earned in the MF are invested automatically and NAV per unit goes up automatically.

Example – if you invested Rs. 100,000/- in a mutual fund and assuming that the fund gives you 10% return every year, at the end of 5th year the market value of your assets will be as follows:

1st year – 110,000, 2nd year – 121000, 3rd year – 133100, 4th year-146410, 5th year – 161051

Dividend option – Should you go for it?

In dividend option, the profit that is earned will be paid to you on regular basis (monthly or quarterly). After the last budget, dividends of equity mutual funds are getting taxed at the hands of mutual funds @10%.

Let us take this example of 1st year.

Principal – 100,000

Dividend – 6,000

Taxes at 10% – 600

Balance dividend paid to you – 5400

At the end of 5 years, your principal will remain more or less at the same level of Rs. 100,000/- and you would have lost over Rs. 6000/- as taxes. Hence under dividend option, the possibilities of growth of invested amount are almost NIL. If the fund has grown beyond 10% PA, the tax on dividend also would have gone up proportionately.

Recommendation:

Do not opt for Dividend option to protect your principal.

In case you need regular income from MFs, you can opt for SWP [Systematic Withdrawal Plan]

[7] Index Funds

These types of mutual funds were popularised in the US by the legendary investor John Bogle.

Mutual funds come in two types the way they are managed:

ACTIVE funds – These funds are managed by fund managers to outperform market. But, there is considerable cost to it which could go up to 2.5%.

PASSIVE funds – Also called INDEX funds. These funds are created to mimic the stock market. These go up when the entire market goes up and go down when the market goes down. To get the best returns, one has to wait for bull phase of the market. These have very little operational expense cost. These funds are popular in US where it has been in vogue for decades.

Five principles of Risk vs. Return on equity Mutual funds.

1. *The higher the equity, the greater the possible return, but, the greater the risk.*
2. *The longer you hold the MF [as much as above 5 years], the greater the possibility of return.*
3. *The shorter the period that you hold the equity MF, the greater the risk.*
4. *The higher the diversification, the lower will be the risk.*
5. *Go for SIP to reduce risk and to make it a saving habit.*

ix) Why Do Investors Lose Money with Mutual Funds?

A good % of investors lose money even with mutual funds. Let us look at the basic reasons.

1. Investing lump sum amount when market is at peak.

   [Always invest through SIP or over a period of months or years.]

2. Exiting funds too soon. In a recent study it was found that only 40% stayed with investment after 2 years. Those who stayed on with investment after 5 years would be far less.

   [Stay on for 7 years plus ideally. Certainly not less than 5 years.]

3. Investing into sector funds and small cap/mid cap funds for less than 3 years.

   [You need to stay with 5–10 years with these funds.]

4. Investing into mutual fund after watching 1–2 years performance.

   [Investors must have 5–7 years view – back or front.]

5. Funds chosen without study and thought.

   [Choose funds carefully with life's goals in mind.]

6. Treating mutual funds similar to Bank FD.

   [Go for SWP if you want regular income and choose fund with less equity if you want less risk.]

CHAPTER 8
Major Tax Saving Investments

Under Section 80 C of I-T Act, deduction of Rs. 1,50,000/- can be claimed from your income while working out your I-T. In simple terms you can reduce up to Rs. 1,50,000 from your total taxable income through 80 C by opting for any of the following, alone or together.

[DEDUCTIONS UNDER SECTION 80C]

8.1 PPF (Public Provided Fund)

Small saving rates are linked to the Govt. bond yields in the secondary market. PPF has come down over the last few years. However, compared to inflation which is around 4–5% the returns are close to 8.0%. Those who are senior citizens can get 8.7%, which works out to be attractive. Further, interest earned in PPF is tax free. PPF offers safety and flexibility. One can start PPF account with post office or with most banks. However, there is better alternative available to salaried taxpayers covered by EPF.

Recommendation – Suitable for those who are not covered under EPF and those who are in low tax bracket.

My rating – 4 Star

8.2 Senior Citizens Saving Scheme (P.O./Some Banks)

Investment into Senior Citizen Saving Scheme is eligible for 80C benefit under IT Act. This Scheme is open to investors aged 60 years plus. In VRS cases it may be available from 55 years. It could be ideal for those seeking guaranteed returns. Currently this scheme offers 8.6% interest. There is a cap of Rs. 1.5 million in this scheme and the tenure of the scheme is five years. For premature withdrawal there is penalty 1.5–1.0%.

Interest earned up to Rs. 50,000 is exempt for TDS. However, if total interest earned is above Rs. 50000/-, the rest of the interest above Rs. 50000/- will get added to the slab of IT payee. For those Senior Citizens having taxable income, this investment has to be done after looking at the tax implication.

Recommendation – Suitable for low Tax investors and those who are retired.

My rating – 4 Star

8.3 National Pension Scheme (NPS)

The NPS can help save tax under three different sections. Firstly, contributions upto Rs. 1,50,000/- can be claimed as deduction under overall Sec 80C. Secondly, there is an additional deduction up to Rs. 50,000/- under section 80 CCD (1b). Thirdly, if the employer puts up to 10% of the basic salary of the individual in the NPS, that amount will not be taxable. These three benefits have attracted a lot of investors to the pension scheme.

- The investor is expected to choose any one PFM [Personal Fund Manager], among eight currently available – HDFC, ICICI and SBI are the big three.
- The subscription is allocated in four asset classes:

- EQUITY and related
- Corporate debt and related
- Govt. bonds and related
- Alternate investment funds like REITS.

– The investor is expected to choose among two choices:

AUTO CHOICE – This is ideal for those who have less knowledge to manage NPS funds across asset classes. In auto choice, funds will be deployed depending on the age of the investor. Example: As one gets older, equity content will be reduced.

ACTIVE CHOICE – This is for those who can manage contribution amongst four asset classes.

NPS Returns

Higher returns were accomplished by investors who had higher exposure to equity.

Investor profile	Equity exposure (%)	3yrs. return (%)	5 yrs. Returns (%)
Aggressive	50	9.6	11.8
Balanced	33	9.4	10.9
Conservative	20	9.3	10.3
Ultra-safe	0	9.2	9.4

Our Recommendation for NPS Investments

- If NPS scheme option is available with the organization where you work, it is a good idea to subscribe to it irrespective of the age of the participant.
- If you have only limited knowledge about financial markets, opt for "Auto Choice-Life cycle Fund" which automatically reduces exposure to equity with advancing age.

- To get the best benefits of NPS, you must stay invested for 10 years plus.
- It is useful to those who want to go beyond Rs. 150,000 as it offers additional Rs. 50,000 benefits.
- Those who are not going for ELSS must try to go for NPS if it is available.

My rating – 3 Star

8.4. ULIP (Unit Linked Insurance Plan)

ULIP or Unit Linked Insurance Plan is a mix of insurance along with investment. From a ULIP, the goal is to provide creation of wealth along with life cover where the insurance company puts a portion of your investment towards life insurance and the rest into a fund that is based on equity or debt or both and matches with your long-term goals. These goals could be retirement planning, children's education or another important event you may wish to save for.

When you make an investment in ULIP, the insurance company invests part of the premium in shares/bonds etc., and the balance amount is utilized in providing an insurance cover. There are fund managers in the insurance companies who manage the investments and therefore the investor is spared the hassle of tracking the investments. ULIP allows you to switch your portfolio between debt and equity based on your appetite for risk as well as your knowledge of the market's performance.

Lock-in-period of ULIP

ULIPs have a lock-in period of 5 years.

Things to consider as an investor

Following are some important factors you should weigh in before investing in ULIPs:

- **Personal financial goals:** If your financial goal is about creation of wealth and you want to save money for retirement, ULIP could be one good option available.

- **Compare ULIP offerings:** Look for a comparison in the form of background expenses, premium payments, ULIP performance, etc. Also, investigate the nature of funds that the ULIP invests in to ascertain the returns from investments in the particular ULIP.

- **Risk factor:** Since ULIP investment is not as diversified as compared to ELSS, the risk in ULIP is probably a bit high compared to schemes like ELSS.

- **Investment horizon:** ULIPs have a lock-in period of 5 years. If a ULIP is surrendered in the first three years, the insurance cover would cease immediately. However, the surrender value can be paid only after three years.

Types of ULIPs

ULIPs are categorized based on the following broad parameters:

8.4.a. Funds that ULIPs invest in

8.4.a. i. **Equity Funds:** Where the premium paid is invested in the equity market and thereby is subject to higher risk.

8.4.a.ii. **Balanced funds:** Where the premium paid is balanced between the debt and the equity market to minimise the risk for investors.

8.4.a.iii. **Debt Funds:** Where the premium is invested in debt instruments which carry a lower risk but in turn also offer a lower return.

8.4.b. Death benefit to policyholder.

8.4.b.i. **Type I ULIP:** This pays higher of the assured sum value or the fund value to the nominee in case of death of the policyholder.

8.4.b.ii. **Type II ULIP:** This pays the assured sum value, plus the fund value to the nominee in case of the death of the policyholder.

ULIPs vs. Mutual Funds

Here is a comparison between the two:

Particulars	ULIPs	Mutual Funds
Nature	Investment cum insurance product	Pure Investment product
Withdrawal	Only after lock-in-period of 5 years	Can be withdrawn anytime
Switching	Alternating between funds is permitted and not subject to taxation.	Switching is permitted between schemes of the same fund house. However, it's treated as redemption and the resulting capital gains are taxable.
Charges	Mortality charges, premium allocation charge, fund management charge and administration charges	No entry load, the annual fund management charges apply and an exit load, if applicable.

How does ULIP differ from traditional life insurance policies?

	Traditional plan	ULIPS
Investment	* Tilted towards savings	* Tilted towards investment
Objectives	* Rate of returns may or may not match inflation * Works towards capital protection	* Underlying investment objective is to outpace inflation * Works towards wealth creation
Risk and Return	* Low risk return * Same investment decision is taken by the insured for all policyholder	* Risk and return are linked to the selected fund option * Choice of fund option enables policyholder to select a fund that fits their risk profile

Transparency	Investments are less transparent	Complete transparency with investment and cost
Charges	Inbuilt, not shared	Complete transparency under various heads
Liquidity	Depending on the policy type the only element of liquidity is through loans subject to conditions	Offers financial liquidity against the policy after the lock-in period depending on the market value of the fund
Flexibility	Fixed sum assured and premium	These is scope to enhance cover as additional premium payment
Death benefit	Fixed	Option between higher of fixed Sum assured and fund value or death Benefit along with fund value offered

How ULIPS have fared?

Allocation	3 years returns%	5 years returns%
Aggressive allocation	9	12
Conservative allocation	8	10
Flexible allocation	8	10
Moderate allocation	8	11

My Recommendation for ULIP

1. One should go for aggressive allocation if age is below 35 years and equity content to be reduced as one gets older.
2. If investing in lump sum, opt for liquid or debt fund of the ULIP and gradually shift to equity funds.

3. Stay as far as 10 years – It is a good option of investment for all those who are not knowledgeable about stock market and wish to get a good corpus as one gets older.

4. Given an option, ELSS Funds with SIP will be a better option for Tax purpose. And, a separate Term insurance could be taken for life cover.

My Rating – 3 star

8.5. NSCs (National Saving Certificate)

NSCs are eligible for deduction under 80C of the I-T Act. The interest earned is 8.0% and senior citizens get 8.7% at the end of 2018. Further, interest earned on NSC is also eligible for deduction under 80C in the following years. Suppose investor buys Rs. 50000/- with NSC, he can claim Rs. 4000/- (8%) in the following years as additional deduction. This is especially useful for those also are in low tax bracket as they may be able to not cross Rs. 15000/- deduction limit set.

NSCs are backed by Government of India and are 100% safe.

Our Recommendation

This is ideal for those who are in the low tax bracket and those who are above 50 years. One can create a ladder of NSCs so that after the maturity, it can be reinvested every year.

By this, a good corpus is created as one retires and every year one investment will mature. The matured amount can be shifted to Senior Citizens' Saving Scheme.

The only issue is poor service rendered and bad behaviour by post office staff.

My rating – 3 star

8.6. Tax Saving FD for 80 C

Tax saver FD is a type of fixed deposit, by investing in which you can claim tax deduction under 80C of the IT Act. One can open such an FD with most banks. But you can claim only up to Rs. 1,50,000/- deduction limit fixed.

The "lock-in" period is 5 years, but the interest earned is taxable at the tax bracket of the investor. Tax saver FDs offer almost 8% in a few banks to senior citizens.

Our Recommendation

Compared to other avenues for getting 80C benefit, these FDs are not attractive. It can be a "last minute" attempt to save I.T for a financial year.

My rating – 2 star

8.7. Sukanya Samrudhi Yojana

This is eligible for 80C deduction under IT Act with max limit of Rs. 1,50,000/- for two daughters and meant for taxpayers with a daughter below 10 years. The interest rates are 8.5%, compounded annually, which is higher than PPF. Account can be opened in PO or designated banks.

Our Recommendation

If you are living in a rural area and have no understanding of other avenues to invest for the future of your daughters, it may be a good idea.

My Rating – 4 star

8.8. ELSS (Equity Linked Savings Scheme)

ELSS is one of the best ways to save IT under 80 C up to Rs. 1,50,000/- for all investments put together.

ELSS has short "lock-in" period compared to all other avenues under 80 C.

When you invest in 80C, your money is going to be locked in for a long period; why not get maximum return over long period? In ELSS, your money is invested into equity and your returns are market linked.

From FY 2019, you have to pay 10% tax on long term capital gain Tax (over one year) for equity gains above Rs. 1,00,000/-. Though ELSS funds have lost some of the sheen compared to the past, still it is one of the best investment avenues under 80C.

Let us look at how it compares with ULIP, another equity linked unit linked insurance plan.

	ULIP	ELSS
Combination	Insurance & Equity or debt or balanced	Only Equity
Lock-in period	5 years	3 years
Expected return	Returns can vary because investor can choose any combinations of equity, debt or hybrid schemes for his investments (9.4 – 11.8% in recent 5 years	Market linked returns which has returned 15% plus in Dec 2018 for 5 years
Tax benefits	Eligible under 80C Gains are taxable	Eligible under 80C Gains are taxable under LTCG
Charges	Complex and multiple charges	Exit Load and fund management Charges are clearly communicated
Liquidity	After 5 years	After 3 years
Insurance cover	Yes	No (but that can be taken separately)

Among the various options available to save taxes under 80C of the IT Act, ELSS has not been given adequate attention by many taxpayers. It could be due to the following reasons.

A typical employee depends on EPF (Employees Provident Fund) for taking care of tax savings. And, most self-employed take care of 80C investments at the last moment (typically after 15 March) based on what the Tax consultants suggest.

Most people look at 80C investments as an action taken merely to save on a bit of income tax and not looking at it from the point of view of long-term returns. Traditionally, people have been dependent on Insurance, PPF and NSC to save on taxes.

All these reasons are not going to be helpful. One of the best ways to save tax based on 80C benefit is through ELSS funds.

What are ELSS funds?

ELSS is "Equity linked" because it is an MF which invests in the stock market. Because it invests into stock market, it is affected by day-to-day fluctuation in the prices of equities in the stock market.

Among all the 80 C investments available for investment, ELSS funds have the least "lock-in" period of 3 years. Because it is market-linked, there is strong possibility that the investments will fetch you returns much higher than fixed returns investments into PPF, VPF, NSC or similar Govt. products.

ELSS vs. other debt-oriented 80 C items

While ELSS is equity linked, Employees Provident Fund, Endowment Insurance, National Savings Certificate, Tax free FD, and PPF invest in debt instruments.

No debt instrument can give return higher than 8%

When it comes to saving for the long term, equity investments are better than debt investments as they tend to give returns much higher than inflation.

If your debt investments yield about 7.5% when the rate of inflation is 6% effectively you are earning just 1.5%. On the other hand ELSS returns have been 15.7% at the end of Dec 18 for 5 years' duration. There are many ELSS funds which returned 19–21% for this period because of more aggressive portfolio. Let us look at how ELSS funds returns affect your long-term wealth creation.

How Rs. 50,000/- in 80 C can create wealth in 15 years.

PPF/NSC	8.5%	1,77,000/-
Endowment Insurance	3.5%	84,000/-
ELSS [forecast]	16%	5,26,000/-

If you are investing Rs. 50,000 into 80C investments in each year, the difference will be phenomenal if you invest into ELSS funds instead of PPF/NSC/Insurance.

Another important argument in favour of ELSS is the necessity to lock in investments for long period of time. If your money is locked up for long periods, why not earn much higher returns?

ELSS vs. other Equity-linked 80C investments

In addition to ELSS, ULIPs and NPS also come as equity-linked and can be considered for 80C benefits. ELSS is far more investor-friendly compared to NPS and ULIPs.

ULIPs have high fees and upfront commissions. This brings down the returns considerably. Their investments into equity market lack transparency whereas ELSS funds disclose performance and portfolios regularly. ELSS funds face intense competition with other funds to deliver performance and to cut cost of operation. That is not the case with ULIPs. ULIPs are sold claiming to take care of both insurance and investment needs of the investor. However, when one makes closer scrutiny we can see that ULIPs underperform on both counts. The insurance cover is too insufficient and return on investments (ROI) is much lesser than ELSS.

Types of ELSS funds

A vast majority of investors who choose ELSS funds do not go into the details of ELSS funds. There are close to 40 ELSS to choose from and it could be confusing. These details are:

Who is the fund Manager and what is his track record?

What type of portfolio does it have?

(Large cap oriented, Small and Mid-cap oriented, etc.)

How has it performed? Is it built in bear-phase?

What type of rating has it received from well-known fund analysts?

Broadly, all ELSS schemes are Multicap in nature and all of these invest into equity markets, however these may have an orientation towards a certain category of equity.

This characterization of their orientation is as follows:

- Large cap oriented ELSS funds-(LC-ELSS)

    These funds invest in mostly large cap funds up to 70 – 80%. The investments into small cap could be less than 5%

- Midcap oriented ELSS funds(MID-ELSS)

    Then ELSS funds have high % of investments into Midcaps. This investment into large cap could be equal or less than Midcaps.

- Midcap + Small cap oriented ELSS funds (MID+SC-ELSS)

    These ELSS funds have almost 20% investments in small caps and pretty high (+30%) investments in Midcaps. Together many have above 50% investments into Small cap + these Mid-caps equity.

Now let us look at how these ELSS funds differ in terms of performance/Volatility.

Fund Name	Fund size	Large cap%	Mid cap%	Small cap%	5 yrs. returns
Large cap oriented ELSS funds (LC-ELSS)					
Axis	17000	63	27	1	20
HDFC	6800	84	8	8	15
ICICI	5300	72	22	7	16
DSP	4300	71	22	7	17
Franklin	3600	82	14	4	16
Mid-cap oriented ELSS funds (MID-ELSS)					
Birla	7000	42	47	11	19
L&T	3200	55	35	10	16
Midcap+ Small cap oriented ELSS funds (MID/SC-ELSS)					
Reliance	9600	55	30	15	18

Fund Name	Fund size	Large cap%	Mid cap%	Small cap%	5 yrs. returns
SBI	6200	14	16	37	16
IDFC	1600	50	29	21	17

	LC-ELSS	MID-ELSS	MID/SC-ELSS
Price Volatility Original Capital	Less	High	Very High
Risk in 3 years	Less	Moderately High	High
	Suitable for +50 years (High Risk averse)	40–50 yrs. (Medium risk takers)	< 40 years (aggressive risk takers)

How much to invest in ELSS?

The current limit available for 80C benefit is Rs. 150,000/-. After having invested into EPF and NPS which may be more or less mandatory for employees, all the rest of the limit can be invested into ELSS. Let us say your current investment under 80C is Rs. 90,000/-; the rest Rs. 60,000/- can be invested into ELSS. The amount can be arrived at after talking to your Tax consultant.

How to invest in ELSS? Lump sum or SIP?

A large % of IT payers decide on the 80 C investments only by the end of the year, which is unhealthy for various reasons. Such lump sum investments can hurt your short-term and long-term returns as the stock market may be at the peak during this period.

In the beginning of the financial year (April) itself, you are aware of the likely amount to be invested in the ELSS fund. If it is Rs. 60,000/- start SIP (Systematic Investment Plan) for Rs. 5000/-. at the beginning of the year itself. This has the following advantages.

- This brings in "Saving discipline" which is very important for long term wealth creation.

- Over a long period of time, with SIP you will be able to average the prices and get the best deal of equity.

- You will not forget investments so that you do not miss out deadlines.

ELSS – How many funds to be chosen?

Depending on your age and your appetite for risk, you may choose maximum two ELSS funds. If you are plus 50 years or highly risk averse, choose one fund from large cap-oriented category and one from Mid cap.

Category: If you go for ELSS from the same category, you may end up with two identical portfolios. The very purpose of choosing two fund houses is defeated. If the amount to be invested is low, there is no point in going in for more than one ELSS fund and it would be a waste of time.

Should you exit after 3 years?

ELSS funds are generally Multi cap funds and they give the best returns on long term basis. Long term means 5–10 years. Unless you have a well-researched and better option, you need not exit from a performing ELSS fund even after the lock-in period of 3 years. If the ELSS fund is giving you returns equal or better than the average of ELSS funds, there is no case for exiting such investments.

Recommendation

- Always look at minimum 5 years-plus cumulative return while evaluating any ELSS fund.

- While selecting an ELSS fund, try going in for funds which have 4/5 star rating in www.valueresearchonline.com or silver/ gold in www.morningstar.in.

- Do not invest into ELSS funds beyond Rs. 1,50,000/- as the invested amount will be restricted with 3 years' lock-in period. If amount is available for investment, one can consider other Multi-cap funds.

Top four ELSS Funds – Star rating

These are the Star ratings given by two leading investment online portals – Morning Star and Value Research Online.

ELSS fund	Morning Star	Value Research Online
Axis	5	4
DSP	4	4
Birla	5	4
L&T	4	4

8.9 Top Four - 80 C Tax-Saving Options

	ULIP	NPS	ELSS	PPF
Minimum Investment	Rs. 24000 p.a. + (Depending on insurer)	1000	1000	500
Maximum Investment	Rs. 1,50,000 for 80C	No Limit (Rs. 1,50,000 for 80C)	No Limit (Rs. 1,50,000 for 80C)	1,50,000
Lock-in Period(yRs.)	5	until 60 years of age	3	15
Extension after lock-in period	-	Till 70 years	No	+5 YEARS
Tax on Maturity	Not Taxable. Pension is taxable	Pension taxable	Taxable under LTCG	Free
Amount on Maturity	Yes	Yes	Yes	Yes

	ULIP	NPS	ELSS	PPF
Average returns	11% – 12%	9.5% – 11.8%	16%+	8–8.7%
Our Rating (Stars)	3 ★	3 ★	5 ★	4 ★
Comments	Suitable for Medium bracket I-T payees and low understanding of stock market	Suitable for Medium bracket I-T payees and low understanding of stock market	Suitable for Medium-to-top tax bracket, people with 10 years-plus views	More suitable for those who are not covered in EPF and have low tax bracket

IMPORTANT NOTE

The income tax and capital gains tax structure and rules may undergo changes from time to time.

Investors must check the latest position before taking investment decisions in any asset class including debt funds.

CHAPTER 9
Great Investing Strategies

Traditionally, most Indians hold higher percentage or share of assets in real estate, Gold and Bank FDs, compared to stock market. In earlier chapters we discussed about various asset classes. Here, we will discuss the need and strategy to shift from one asset class into another.

9.1 Why Diversify?

Traditional wisdom says "Don't put all your eggs in one basket". It affects and restricts your financial wellbeing, if one asset class or an instrument within an asset class goes for a spin.

For example, equity crashed by 39% during 2008–09. If you were planning a major event like retirement, daughter's marriage or children's admission to a professional course that year it would have been a disaster. Similarly, in Nov. – Dec. 2018 many small cap shares were down by 40 – 50% and the small cap MFs were down by 15% on year-to-year basis while large cap showed growth of (-) 1%. If you had invested all your savings in small cap MF in 2017 with the hope of retiring in 2018 Dec., things would have been very unpleasant.

However in 2008 – 2009 if your investments were spread across Equity, Debt, Cash and Gold, the average return would have been 0.70% (see chart given below). That is because gold returned close to 24% and debt returned closed to 10% when equity returned (-) 40%

A few lucky investors got positive returns in 2008 – 2009 as well as 2018 Dec. while buying in one asset class or one instrument within an asset class. Vast majority got negatively affected. To be safe, one must diversify between asset classes and even within an asset class, among various instruments.

9.2 Shifting from One Asset Class to Another

The following are the popular shifting of asset classes as part of reorganizing one's risk and asset concentration:

- Real Estate to Stock Market

- Bank FDs to Stock Market
- Bank FDs to Real Estate
- Lump sum cash to Stock market/Real estate/Gold

9.3 Strategies for Shifting from One Asset Class to Another

The following are some of the broad strategies/tips that could be kept in mind while shifting from one asset to another.

1. The asset-class-shifting must be taken based on long-term interest and stability. One must not change from one asset class to another as "flavour of the season". Some these asset-class-shifting may take a decade or so to be implemented.
2. Asset-class-shifting must not be done frequently without a clear strategy.
3. Tax-implications must be studied before shifting class of assets.
4. No one knows what is going to happen in the market in another 30 days or 6 months. At best one could give intelligent estimates.
5. Soon after you shift the asset-class the market could go up or down; either way, do not get excited or depressed. Stay cool and stay focused on long-term basis.
6. All of us know that an asset has to be sold at its peak price and another asset has to be purchased when it is available at the bottom. But when is the peak and when is the bottom? This is a calculated risk.
7. The acquisition of new assets like stocks must be done slowly as much as possible. Such slow decision-making is not possible when you buy any real estate. Unless you pay full amount, the seller will not transfer the property into your name.

9.4 Real Estate to Stock Market

After one sells a real estate asset, suddenly the bank account has significant amount of cash. It could be few hundreds of thousands to millions.

Stage 1

Settle matters relating to capital gains tax. It may require you to invest in capital gains bonds upto Rs. 5 million and pay advance I-T as capital gains tax. Your investment and plans for building assets can start only after meeting your obligations of tax.

Stage 2

Shift balance amount into 2–3 parts and invest into liquid funds/ultra-short-term funds/low duration funds. One could be for retaining as a debt fund with target maturity of 3 years to get long term capital gains benefits. Others which you hold for returns will be added to your income tax bracket and taxed accordingly.

Stage 3

Opt for STP to move from debt fund to equity-based fund for higher return.

I will give three examples as follows:

Ashok's strategy – CONSERVATIVE APPROACH

Ashok sold property worth Rs. 20 million and he gets Rs. 19.80 million into his bank account after compulsory TDS of I-T.

- He invests Rs. 5 million into capital gains bonds which has maturity of 5 years
- He keeps aside Rs. 1.80 million to pay I-T
- He splits Rs. 1.80 million into 3 bank FDs with differing dates to match the tax payment deadlines. While choosing FDs he goes for Banks which offer highest interest rates.
- He has Rs. 13.00 million in his bank which he splits as follows:
  - Rs. 5.80 million in short duration fund with targeted maturity of 3 years
  - Rs. 7.20 million in ultra-short term fund with STP of Rs. 2,00,000/- into two aggressive hybrid funds
- After 3 years Rs. 5.80 million in the short duration fund is shifted to two aggressive hybrid funds for a period of 24 months @ Rs. 2,40,000/- per month

- After 5 years the capital gains tax bonds that Ashok invested in has matured. He shifts the amount to ultra-short term fund and shifts Rs. 2,50,000/- per month as STP into aggressive hybrid fund in a bond for 20 months.

Ashok shifted his asset in real estate to stock market linked investments in a period of 7 years.

Mohan's strategy – AGGRESSIVE APPROACH

Mohan sells property and gets Rs. 9.90 million after TDS. He invests 2.0 million into Capital Gains Bonds and keeps Rs. 4,00,000 for paying I-T. He decides to invest Rs. 7.50 million into stock market as follows after keeping entire amount in ultra-short term fund.

He transfers by STP as follows:

To Large cap fund = Rs. 5,00,000/- per month * 12 months = 60,00,000/-

To Midcap fund = Rs. 1,00000/- per month * 15 months = 15,00,000/-

Pradeep's strategy – LUMPSUM APPROACH

Pradeep sells property and gets Rs. 14.80 million after TDS. He invests 50% into shares of 10 Companies (Rs. 7.40 million total) and other 50% into two funds, Rs. 3.70 million into a small cap fund and Rs. 3.70 million into a Midcap fund.

Our Assessment of Three Approaches

Protecting your capital is as important as getting returns higher than 8% from the investments that you make in the above three examples. The return if forecast in 4 – 5 years may be as follows.

Ashok may get return of 12 to 14% return.

Mohan may get return of 6 to 15% return.

Pradeep's returns could be [–] 10% to 10%.

Our Recommendation

Never try making lump sum investment into shares or equity-linked investments like MF. You may end up with a negative return like Pradeep.

- Opt for STP from an ultra-short term or similar fund to equity-related investments on a long duration
- Unless you are an expert and have considerable understanding, do not invest into individual shares directly. Always route equity investments through mutual fund.

If you are too confused about most of these stuffs, try to follow the pattern below:

- First preference   –   Large cap funds
- Second preference   –   Large + Mid-cap fund
- Third preference   –   Multicap fund
- Fourth preference   –   Midcap fund
- Fifth preference   –   Small cap fund or sector fund

9.5 Bank FD to Stock Market

Bank FD interest may look more attractive than liquid/ultra-short term debt funds, but with debt funds if you hold for 3 years + you can apply long capital gains tax rules. Hence, your post-tax returns could be higher than bank FDs.

Hence if you are shifting from bank FDs to stock market you can consider two options:

- If you are shifting the investment in less than 3 years you could shift in every alternate month or once a quarter to space out and reduce risk.
- You can park funds in Ultra-short term funds and opt for STP.
- You can have a mix of above two options too.

9.6 Bank FD to Real Estate

Considering the benefit available under long term given for the debt funds if you have more than 3 years it is better to hold in debt fund and shift after that.

If it is less than that, the only option for you is to hold in highest-interest-short-duration FDs, and then shift when the property is ready for registration.

9.7 Lump Sum Cash to Stock Market/Gold

All markets undergo price fluctuations within a year and over the years. In both stock market and gold one can make staggered investments. In stock market one can opt for mutual fund route and in gold you can opt for E – Gold – both staggered manners. Such a strategy will help you get the average price rather than probable highest purchase price.

The years of 2017 over 2016 saw drop in real estate prices in various metros.

City	2017/2016[All Negative]
Delhi/NCR	2%
Mumbai	5%
Bangalore	5%
Hyderabad	3%
Chennai	3%
Kolkata	5%

In this period equity investments were showing rapid growth and growth of gold was muted.

Purpose of diversification

To reduce risk it is important to diversify with asset class. If someone does not want any risk at all, go for ultra-safe investments like PPF, POMIP or NSC and debt funds, but the average return will be less than 8%, post-tax.

One has to have a balance between Risk and Return. Also it will depend on the risk-taking ability of an individual.

Please read chapter on Risk capacity vs. Risk; age determines type of investments.

Everyone would love to earn higher returns without taking any risk, but in real life one has to take reasonable risk for getting a reasonable return.

The following factors can influence asset-allocation changes.

- Current allocation in relation to age and life goals.
- "Willingness" to take risk.
- "Ability" to take risk.
- Time period available to achieve the life goal.
- Market and regulatory situation.
- Income tax and capital gains tax considerations.
- Balance between over-diversification vs. under-diversification.
- Need to have liquidity.
- Influence of family, division of assets among family members, pending will for implementation and other compulsions like business, partition, etc.

9.8 Dealing with Bull and Bear Market

Let us understand the difference between two scenarios – Bull Market vs. Bear Market

1. The market is mentioned as 'bullish' when the overall market scenario is positive and the market performance is on the rise. A 'bearish' market is when the performance of the market is on the decline.

2. In the bullish market the outlook of the investor is very optimistic and this is visible from the fact that investors take a long position in the market. This way the anticipation is stock prices will rise further and investors have opportunity to maximize profit opportunities. In a bearish market, the market sentiment is quite pessimistic and is reflected by investors taking a short position, i.e. selling securities in anticipation of falling market.

Great Investing Strategies

3. Economy will grow in a bull market and in a bear market the economy will slow down.
4. In a bull market, market indications are strong whereas in a bear market indicators are weak.
5. The job market is strong in a bullish market whereas job market is sluggish in a bearish market.
6. Liquidity flow is good in a bull market whereas in bear market it is slow and investors go to comfort zone of gold, real estate, etc.
7. IPO activities are encouraged in a bull market.
8. International investments increase in a bull market.
9. In a bull market, banking sector reduces interest rates on loans encouraging growth of business.
10. In a bull market, dividends will be low, whereas in a bear market yield will be better to attract investments.

BULL VS BEAR MARKET	BULL	BEAR
Attitude	Optimistic	Pessimistic
Economic Movement	Growth	Recession/Decline
Price Movement	Rising	Falling
Stock Price/Trading	Increasing	Decreasing
Stock Position	Long Position	Short position/ Short Selling
International Investment	Faster Pace	Stable or Receding
News Reports	Positive Stories	Less Stories
MF Investments	Rising	Falling Withdrawals
IPO	More	No
Rise in Salaries	Increase	Decline/Stable
Risk Taking	High	Low

Typical behaviour patterns in Bull and Bear markets

		Bull	**Bear**
1	MF Investment	Rising	Falling/Very hesitant
2	SIP	Rising	Stopping
3	Allocation to equities	High %	Low %
4	Allocation to Sector funds	High %	Low %
5	Profit Booking/Loss Booking	Very low profit booking/Waiting for further rise in price	Sell at a loss/Try getting out
6	Feel Smart	Feels smart and boasts about it	Depressed and keeps quiet
7	Conversation	High in parties and social occasions	Low at all places; avoids discussion, to reduce internal pain
8	Spending attitude	Feels like buying more goodies	Afraid of spending
9	Looks at future	Very optimistically with dreams	Pessimistic, worried
10	Risk taking altitude	Feels strong and brave	Feels weak and vulnerable
11	Cash in hand	Deploys maximum cash in equity	Least cash in hand

Recommended behaviour/Actions in a bull market

1. Do not get excited and invest disproportionate % of investments into equity. Keep your asset allocation more or less under control.

2. Do not look at 3/6 months' or 1 year's return and take your decisions; look at 5 – 10 years' horizon to target returns.
3. Look at extraordinary rise in stock prices and extraordinary success stories with healthy scepticism.
4. Try replacing "super growth" stocks and equity MF with more stable/healthy ones.
5. Try keeping reasonable % in short-term funds or debt funds in keeping with your asset allocation.
6. Avoid IPOs and "tips" from experts and TV discussions.

Recommended behaviour/actions in the bear market

1. Do not get depressed and worried and start selling your equities or Mutual funds. If you have invested with rational thinking, hold on. Remember this bad phase will get over soon and the problem may not be your selection, but the market cycle.
2. Do not stop SIP.
3. Do not switch shares and MF based on 3/6 months' or 1 year's performance. You are here for 5 years-plus, remember that.
4. Do not check portfolio every day. Think of your portfolio as jewellery lying in bank locker or a plot that you have been owning for a couple of years.
5. Do not keep getting reminded about the peak value of shares or MF. It can only make you sad.
6. Do not try shifting share or MF abruptly. Remember, no fund manager in the world has been right 100% of the time. The best of stock market investors in India had bad periods and bad decisions in their life. You are not an exception.
7. Do not compare with other returns. Remember people brag about their success stories and exploits in parties and social occasions. Almost no one will talk about their setbacks and wrong decisions in their life.

8. If 6 months or 1 year return of MF is much lower than 5 years' return, you can look at it positively and consider investments, preferably in a staggered manner.

9.9 Age and Choice of Investments

AGE AND CHOICE OF FOOD

Doctors recommend different choices of food depending on your age.

For a young and active person – High-carbohydrate food to give fuel to body to meet high physical activity.

For a young sportsperson – High-protein food to build muscles.

For a middle-aged person with BP/Diabetes – Low carb or sugar food, low oily food.

For older person – Easy to digest, high leafy food, less oils and carbs.

Age, physical activity, health and status are key determinants while deciding on food.

Similarly, age, risk-attitude and risk-capacity are key determinants while deciding on investments.

AGE AND INVESTMENTS

The strategy for investment when you are young, middle aged or when you are nearing retirement should be different. Investing for retirement is important at any age, but the same strategy cannot be applied across all age profiles.

Investment planning in age 20's:

You must have recently graduated and taken up your first job. You may still be paying student loans. Unless you are in a high-paying job, you may not be able to save more than 10–15%.

Suggested income allocation is given below.

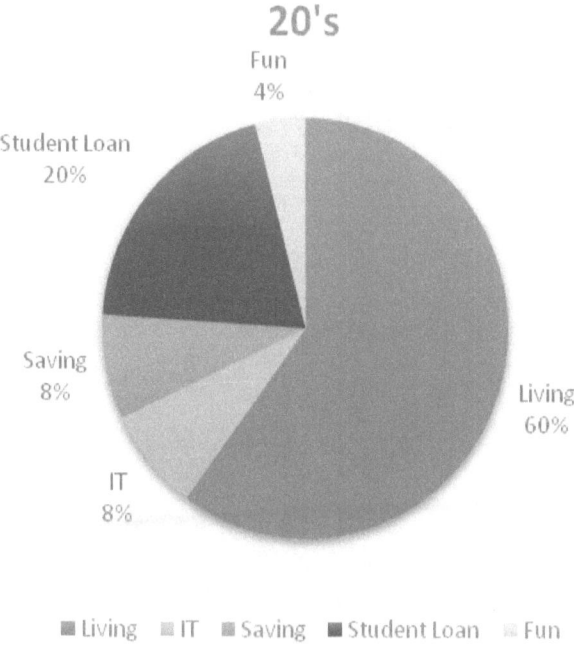

[Suggested income allocation in 20's]

Focus: Start keeping track of income/expenditures

- Start filing Income Tax returns
- Save mandatory 8–10% through PF or ELSS scheme

Investment planning in age 30's

You have come out of paying student loans, recently been married and are career-focussed. Typically, you would have almost doubled your income compared to the previous decade.

You will have multiple responsibilities.

- Newly married with kids
- Need to start paying for children's education
- Need to start long plan for retirement
- Buy/plan to build your house by taking housing loans

- Family outings, short holidaying, picnics, etc. to build up family togetherness

Each of these responsibilities must reflect in your plans. Suggested distribution of income is given below.

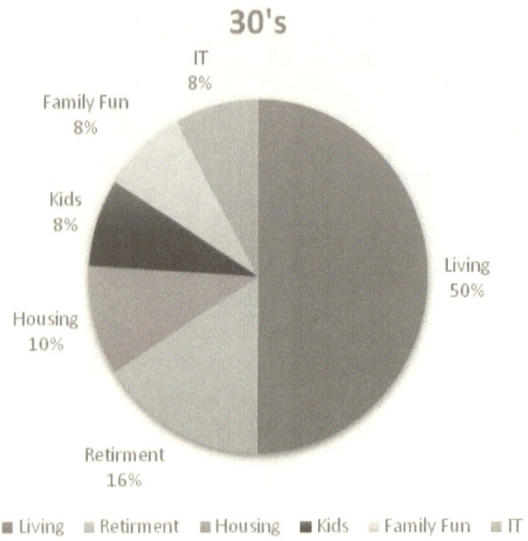

[Suggested income allocation in 30's]

Investment planning in your 40's:

You started owning a house with long term housing loan contribution. Your kids are moving into high school or college and which have to be funded. Probably, your career and earning-potential are at peak. Have you procrastinated saving decisions for retirement? You need to seriously plan for retirement. You probably started getting grey hairs and a bit of health issues like Diabetes or Hypertension or a little overweight. Your savings and investments must be well thought-out. You may need to visit a personal financial planner and it is a must that you start reading this kind of book or journals. Start taking serious decisions on financial goals. The suggested income allocation could be as follows.

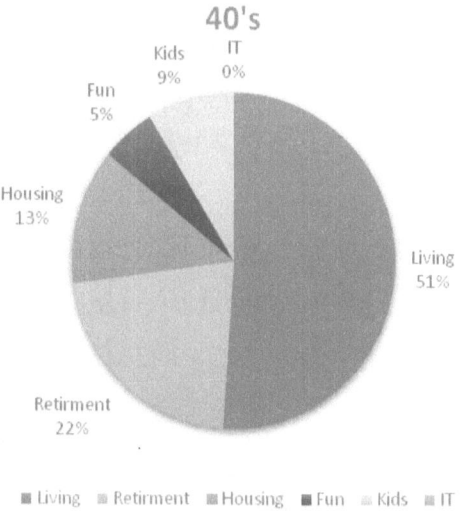

[Suggested income allocation in 40's]

Danger ahead! Pre-retirement decade of 50's:

Let us face facts. You can see your retirement date. It could be 60 years or in some cases, 58 years. Thing may not go as per your plan. Your company may suddenly declare VRS and you may be persuaded to accept VRS. If that happens, you may not get another job with similar salary package.

There are many unethical Companies who may wish to get rid of you, because you are no longer sexy like the 30-year-old guy who is able to make a better impression than you. If there are mergers or acquisitions, you may end up with tragic consequences. They may post you some 1000 Kms away, or they may ask you to report to a guy who was your junior a few years back. Or ask you to do some work which you did two decades back. Whichever way they will justify it and you have very little options. That is as good as being sacked at the age of 55 years!

However good you are, in many companies HR people are so conservative that they may not call you for an interview. Or somebody may offer you a job out of pity but with 40% cut in salary!

This is a dangerous period of life and must be planned carefully and shocks at career-front must be handled with emotional balance. The key concerns are:

- Ensuring a kitty for retirement.
- Clear housing loans and do not invite further debts.
- Ensure proper Mediclaim policy for family and parents.
- Learn an alternative career either with the help of books or attending some training.
- Do not undertake risky financial ventures or investment decisions.
- Consider second home if you can leverage housing loan and existing loans are cleared.

CHAPTER 10
Insurance – Protect Life and Assets

10.1 Annuities

Annuity is an insurance product that pays out regular income, often used as part of retirement portfolio. The most common type of Annuity plan works like the reverse of a typical term-life Insurance policy.

In the term-insurance policy, a person pays premiums during the policy period and the nominee (family) gets sum assured in the policy in case the policyholder dies during the policy period. In the Annuity plans, a person pays lump sum or regular instalment in the accumulation period and gets regular payment as long as he/she lives or for a prefixed period.

Life Insurance covers the financial risk of "dying too young", leaving family destitute, while an Annuity Plan covers financial risk of "living too long" without adequate money for a comfortable living.

Types of Annuity Plans

There are broadly four types of annuity plans based on Timing, Benefits, Variability of Benefits and Coverage of Benefits.

10.1.a) Annuity plans which are based on timing

10.1.a.i) Immediate annuity plan

In this case, annuity payments can start almost immediately. This is ideal for those who are likely to retire soon and wish to have a periodic income after retirement.

10.1.a.ii) Deferred annuity plans

This is an annuity plan which can start payment of annuity at a future date on which the contributor plans to retire. During his work-life, he contributes towards the annuity and gets the periodical (monthly or quarterly) pay-out after retirement.

10.1.b) Variability of performance

If the planned annuity amount is fixed it is called 'Fixed annuity' and if it varies based on performance, it is called 'Variable annuity'.

'Fixed annuity' is for those who have low risk appetite and 'variable annuity' is for those having high risk appetite. The higher the risk, higher the possible return.

10.1.c) Coverage of lives

An annuity plan can cover one life (say husband) or two lives (husband and wife) wherein after the death of one person, the other person continues to get annuity payment in his/her lifetime. Single life payment is better if you have no dependants. At the same time, Single Life Annuity payments are higher than Joint Life Annuity.

10.1.d) Benefits

There are optional features like partial withdrawal facility, Indexation benefits, etc.

10.1.e) Criteria for choosing an Annuity Plan

We feel that one should look at five criteria before selecting an annuity plan:

- ✓ Safety
- ✓ Returns
- ✓ Liquidity
- ✓ Service
- ✓ Retirement Kitty mix

10.1.f) Safety of annuity payments

One tends to make Annuity contributions for 20–30 years, followed by another 20 – 30 years of annuity pay-outs. The financial firm that you have chosen must not only survive for 60–70 years, but also service the annuity efficiently in spite of having various challenges like inflation, interest-rate-fluctuation, competition, etc.

It is ideal to go for a well-established financial institution with great management and history of performance.

10.1.g) Returns

As annuity products are very long-term, most companies are conservative in terms of returns. These Companies do not pass on returns earned to the customers, but retain a substantial portion of earnings as reserves to meet contingencies. This could be detrimental to the interests of older people who depend solely on annuity pay-outs for day-to-day living expenses. And, inflation adds further to the misery of older people. One must look at the history of its returns while choosing the annuity offered by a company.

10.1.h) Liquidity

Annuity products are not structured to be highly liquid. However, reasonable liquidity should be there in times of extreme emergencies or a financial contingency.

10.1.i) Service by annuity companies

The Financial Institution must have good customer service system and prompt response mechanism.

10.1.j) Retirement Kitty mix

Annuity Products must form one of the elements of retirement-kitty mix planning. Like any other financial planning, never put all the eggs into one basket. One needs to have an ideal mix of SCSS deposits, PO MIP, bank deposits and if need be, SWP of mutual funds.

10.1.k) Top Annuity Plans available in the market

10.1.k.i) LIFE INSURANCE CORPORATION

- **Jeevan Akshay VI Plan**

This is an immediate-annuity pension plan, based on lump-sum payments. It offers six annuity options and one can receive pension monthly, quarterly, half yearly or annually.

- **Jeevan Nidhi Plan**

This is for those who want to accumulate annuity amount over a period of time. It also offers insurance cover on the accumulation phase. If the pension seeker dies in this accumulation phase the nominee will get Sum Assured and bonus.

10.1.k.ii) HDFC LIFE

- **Click to retire plan**

This is an online unit linked plan (ULIP) that offers the individual a return that is linked to market performance. Premium can be given as single payment or 8, 10 or 15 years and benefit period can be 10–35 years. In case of death, the nominee will get higher fund value of the policy or 105% of the premium amount paid till the death of the policyholder.

- **Assured pension plan**

It is a unit linked plan that offers market linked returns with loyalty additions to the policyholder that can meet the retirement goals of the individual. Along with applicable tax benefit, this plan offers single and limited payment option to the policyholder.

10.1.k.iii) ICICI PRUDENTIAL

- **ICICI Pru Immediate Annuity plan**

This plan offers pension for the policyholder as well his/her spouse for life. It has different payment options: has single premium paid as lump sum or in instalments.

- **ICICI Pru Easy Retirement Plan**

It is a unit linked insurance plan, designed to take care of post-retirement income. The policy helps to build up the corpus as per policyholder's risk appetite. The participant pays premium for maximum 10 years and gets the benefits during income phase through any of the vesting age options. It also takes care of market volatility through an assured benefit.

10.1.k.iv) SBI LIFE

- **SBI Life Annuity Plus**

This is a pension plan where the premium amounts have to be paid in one lump-sum. And pay-outs start almost immediately on monthly or quarterly basis. There are many annuity options and annuities can be advanced under certain conditions.

- **SBI Life Retirement**

This is a unit linked pension plan with limited or regular payment options.

There are three funds available for investments.

Equity/Bank/Money market. On vesting, the benefits can be used to purchase immediate annuity plan or deferred annuity plan.

10.1.k.v) BAJAJ LIFE

- **Retire rich pension plan**

It is a unit linked pension plan and the retirement corpus grows as per market performance. It also provides insurance coverage during plan tenure. Premium amount and tenure can be changed during tenure. On "vesting" [starting of pension] one can choose immediate annuity or deferred annuity plan.

10.1.k.vi) BIRLA SUNLIFE

- **Empower Pension**

It is a unit linked pension plan. The company invests premiums in a pre-determined ratio between two available funds with different risk profiles. As the vesting date approaches the units are automatically transferred from high-risk to low-risk funds.

10.1.l) Return on Annuities

The average annual returns on an annuity have been 6.4–7.5%. This has been lower than other investment avenues available for retirement. Example: SCSS and PO MIS. As with all investments one must not put all the eggs into one basket.

10.1.m) Advantages of Annuities

1. Sense of security.

An annuity gives a sense of security. You will keep getting your monthly income for the rest of the life on a pre-determined day. You do not have to worry about what is happening at the marketplace. Also, you will get the guaranteed income irrespective of your financial literacy.

2. Remove reinvestment risk

For a matured amount in most fixed income securities when you try reinvesting, the interest rates may have fallen. This could happen even in PO MIS. However, with annuity, the pay-out is fixed.

3. No limit on investments

For fixed income investments like SCSS and PO MIS there are limits fixed, Rs. 15,00,000/- and Rs. 4,50,000/- respectively. But, for annuity, there are no limits. However, the pay-out is subject to IT slabs applicable.

10.1.n) Disadvantages of Annuities

1. No access to capital

After taking up Annuities most investors lose access to capital. The principal amount is more or less locked up for a long time which makes investors uncomfortable.

2. Lower rates of return

The annuities' return is far less than other options like SCSS and POMIP; works out to be lesser than 7%.

3. Annuities do not fight inflation

Annuities do not fight inflation which goes up by 6–7% every year. In 20–30 years, the returns received from annuities will be grossly insufficient to meet the rising costs.

4. Premature withdrawals not allowed

Annuities do not allow premature withdrawals in the event of emergencies of the investors. This makes investors helpless in spite of having made investments.

5. Simple interest

Annuities work on simple interest whereas SCSS [Senior Citizens Saving Scheme] compounds interest on quarterly basis.

10.1.0) Tips for investing into Annuities

1. Do not keep all the eggs in one basket; you need to diversify to reduce risk in the retirement age.
2. Go for a strong, big insurer who is offering Annuity.
3. Irrespective of what, you need to have an emergency fund.
4. Plan your investments to beat inflation.
5. Compare among different Annuity offerings before taking your pick.
6. Read all clauses and conditions and their implications.
7. Exhaust SCSS and POMIP limits before opting for single payment, immediate annuity plans, as they are likely to give better returns.
8. To get maximum. post-tax benefit, go for a Bank FD which gives returns higher than SCSS.
9. Income from dividend of company shares is tax-free. (Try owning shares of Large cap and avoid others.]

10.2 Term Insurance

FAMILY MUST BE PROTECTED WITH TERM INSURANCE

Term insurance is a type of insurance product that provides a large sum assured to the policy-buyer at a relatively affordable premium. It can be purchased for period 5 – 40 years. Such policies do not carry any survival benefit unlike money-back or endowment policies.

Q: Do you need a term insurance?

A: That depends on whether other people are dependent on you or not.

Q: What about single person with no dependents including parents?

A: No need to buy term insurance as no one is dependent on you.

Double income couples with no kids – Term Insurance

The need to buy term insurance is very low as the other partner can carry on with his/her income levels, unless you have made a joint financial commitment which cannot be handled with one's income.

Recently married with dependents Spouse and parents

You need term insurance urgently as a lot of people are dependent on your income and life.

Couples with children and dependents parents

You need to buy term insurance urgently as a number of adults and children's futures are dependent on you.

Term Insurance for retired people

If you have no people dependent on your income, you may not need term insurance.

How much term insurance do you need?

You need to look at life as "What if" Scenario: If you unfortunately fade away what financial impact will you leave behind to your dependents?

Loans:

Housing loans, vehicle/white goods loans.

And, other personal debts/loans.

Future expenses

You need to account for future expenses of the loved ones. This includes children's education and normal living expenses, keeping in mind, the inflation.

We will explain as below through a hypothetical case.

Housing and other loans – 5.0 million

Current household expenses-50,000 × 12 = 6,00,000 p.a.

Expected financial requirement for the next 20 years – 12.0 million

Minimum Term insurance required-17.0 million [Including to cover inflation]

TERM INSURANCE Thumb Rule

Minimum 20 times of your Annual Income

Different types of pay-outs in term insurance

While buying the term insurance, you need to select the right pay-out option.

Lump sum

The entire death benefit is paid to the nominee at one go. This is OK if the nominee is financially literate. If wrong decisions are made, most of the benefits received would be lost through wrong choices made regarding investment. There is also a possibility of other members of the family blackmailing to get part of the benefits received.

Monthly Income option

In this option, the death benefit is paid in equal monthly instalments over a period of 10–15 years. This can help the dependants (nominee) to meet living expenses for the premium chosen. With this option, the premium would be lower.

Increasing monthly income option

This is similar to monthly income option, but amount would get increased every year. You can choose to increase amount of 7% or more every year.

Lump sum + Monthly Income options

This is a combination of lump sum and monthly income option. Here the nominee would receive a specified portion as lump sum soon after the demise to take care of immediate financial needs, followed by monthly income over a period of time: 10–15 years.

My Recommendation

1. Go for lump sum pay-out if the nominee is well-educated and has good financial literacy.
2. Monthly Income will suit if the nominee is not good at managing money.
3. Choose lump sum +monthly Income plan if you have various financial commitments to take home and at the same time you want to ensure long-term safety.

Tips for taking Term Insurance

1. Ensure that you give correct disclosures to Insurance Company so that the nominee does not face problems if it ends up with claims.
2. Buy policy under MWP Act so that no one other the nominee can stake a claim on the pay-out in case of your death.
3. Choose pay-out option after a lot of thought. Do not go for lump-sum if the nominee is not having good financial literacy.

4. You can choose to have two term insurances: one for your housing loans and another for family's long-term living insurance coverage.
5. Choose the years and policy amount very carefully.
6. If there is any change in nominee and contact details it must be communicated immediately. Or it will end up in various problems at the time of claim.

You may not require term policy beyond 60 years. You may end up paying premiums even when your nominee may not require your coverage anymore.

Where to buy term insurance

The cheapest way to buy term insurance is online. You will get it directly from insurance company without any commissions, either short-term or long term.

Not only look for premium, but also look at the following factors:

- Reputation and longevity of the Insurance Co.
- Claim settlement ratio.
- Pay-out options – (Do not go for cheapest option).
- Number of years and Amount covered. If your life's value is Rs. 50 million, go for Rs. 50 million whether you get benefit under 80C or not.

Tax benefits

Term insurance premium paid is eligible under Income tax benefit under 80C limits of IT Act.

10.3 Endowment Policy

It is essentially a life insurance policy; however, apart from covering life, these help the policyholder to save regularly. There are broadly two types of endowment policies: with profit and without profit. Within these classes there are many variations structured to meet child education, whole life protection and pension, among others. However, all these policies have three broad benefits:

- Goal-based savings
- Financial protection of loved ones
- Income tax benefits

Who could consider endowment policies?

Endowment policies are meant for any average common man with regular income and wish to meet three important goals – Savings, financial protection and tax benefits. It can be considered by all small-salaried small-business people and Small-time Self-employed professionals.

Enrolling and taking benefits under such policies are least complicated, trustworthy and very safe. One must look at the following:

- Premium vs. life cover/benefits.
- Past performance of the policy including bonuses.
- Claim rate of such policies with the Insurance Co.
- Where and how it will get serviced.
- Payment options which are friendly.
- Surrender value and terms.

It may be ideal to go for simple uncomplicated endowment plans if your income levels are limited and you wish to be simple or uncomplicated in life.

10.4 Money-Back Policy

It is a type of Life Insurance policy wherein some money is returned at regular intervals. It could be every five years.

- The insured gets life covered for the policy value
- Certain % of the accumulated premium with profits and bonuses are returned to the insurer
- When the plan matures, the remaining portion of the premiums and bonuses are given back.

Money-back policies meet goals of the policy-taking: Savings at regular intervals, life cover and tax benefits. Added benefit would be return of some amount at regular intervals; it adds to the liquidity to the insurer. However, if the returned amount is not properly utilized or invested, his returns will be even worse.

Returns from endowment and money-back policies

As returns are poor on long-term basis [hardly around 3%], not recommended. One can go for Term Insurance for protection and go for any other saving schemes. For conservative investors, it is ideal to go for a Hybrid Mutual fund as funds will be locked up for very long periods like 15–25 years.

10.5 Home Insurance

A home insurance offers a sense of security for all members of the family. Comprehensive policy has more covers. It covers the building and contents therein. Building means the current building cost.

Tips

1. Read the "fine print" of the insurance policy.
2. If your house is located in a place where earthquake or floods are possible, make sure that these are included.
3. Review house cost (excluding land) and contents list/cost every year.
4. Keep as many receipts or bills as possible to avoid dispute with insurance agency.
5. if it is an Apartment, the building needs to be covered by Co-op Society of building owners.
6. Insuring jewellery is expensive and it has to be done only if it is kept at home.
7. Avoid small items for insurance as the admin. cost and time required for settlement of claim may outweigh the benefit of insuring these.
8. If your family members are frequent travellers, ensure that baggage is added to the policy.
9. It is better to avoid personal accident in this policy as it is better to take term insurance separately.

10. If the building is unauthorized, the claims can get rejected even if you paid for the policy.

11. While making insurance claim, the insurer may ask for police report/FIR or inspection report. Be prepared.

12. All general Insurance Cos offer house insurance policies and it is recommended that you make comparisons before buying any policy.

10.6 Vehicle Insurance

For private vehicles there are two types of vehicle insurance:

1. Liability-only policy: covers third party liability or bodily injury and or death and property damage. It also covers personal accident cover for the owner/ driver. It is mandatory for vehicle-owners to take this policy.

2. Private car Package Policy – This covers loss/damage of the vehicle along with third party liability cover.

Private car Package policy is broadly divided into 3 categories:

Section 1 – Loss or damage to the vehicle due to accident, fire, natural calamities like flood, landslide and cyclone, riots, terrorism, etc.

Section 2 – It covers loss or damage caused to third parties on account of your vehicle. It also covers death or injury caused to pedestrians, passengers, employees, etc.

Section 3 – Personal accident cover to the driver or owner and occupants of the vehicle.

Add-on coverage

There are many 'add-on' covers to the vehicles:

- Zero depreciation.
- Engine protection.
- Roadside assistance.
- Loss of key.
- Free pick-up, etc.

Some of these may be available 'FREE' at the time of renewal. All vehicle insurance companies offer 'ZERO-claim' bonus too.

Where to buy vehicle insurance?

These days it is ideal to buy vehicle insurance 'online' which works to be cheapest. Also, you need to compare the rates, benefits and service and before deciding on the insurer, you will be able to negotiate rates with the insurance firm.

10.7 Family Healthcare Policy

(PROTECT ENTIRE FAMILY WITH A FLOATER HEALTHCARE POLICY)

A healthcare policy is a must-have even before starting to invest for any financial goals in life. You need to cover your entire family which consists of spouse, children and parents, if they are not covered. There are companies which offer healthcare policy as part of the salary package. You need to confirm whether your dependent parents are covered in the Company's healthcare policy or not. If they are not covered, you need to cover them through a separate policy. Also you need to ensure that your family keeps getting coverage of healthcare policy if you move from one company to another – either company-sponsored or self-financed.

We strongly recommend that you go for "Family Floater Policy" which has many advantages.

1. Family Floater Policy works out to be cheaper.

2. It is ideal to cover all members under one single policy. Most of the family floater policies are designed in such a way that premiums are fixed on the basis of the eldest member of the policy. Hence, you need to work out the advantage of splitting the policy.

3. Family floater policy helps to get higher coverage and it is unlikely that all members will fall sick at the same.

4. Additional healthcare policy cover can be taken by different members of the family, each for a lower amount and get benefits under I-T exemptions. By this the entire family can stretch the coverage amount. Example: If there are two sons in the family, father could be covered along with one son and mother with another son.

5. Usually, persons above 45 are required to go for medical examination to get health policy. It is ideal to take a healthcare policy before reaching 50 years and then continue with it the whole life. If this is not done, you may be denied a normal healthcare policy or they may offer a healthcare policy with stiff premium.

6. Pre-existing diseases may not be covered for 4 years. If you have BP, Diabetes, Asthma etc., declare it in advance or you may face problems while making claims. It does not matter whether said that you are a diabetic or blood pressure patient, the fact that you were put on anti-diabetic or anti-hypertensive at some point of time will be taken as "Pre Existing Disease". On this basis, your claims may get rejected. Be careful while filling up forms. Do not blindly sign enrolment form.

7. Look for cashless facility, so that you do not have to spend money upfront when confronted with hospitalization.

8. Your insurer is likely to offer 'no claim bonus' year after year. Check for this. No-claim bonus can make a major difference for a senior citizen.

9. Read 'exclusion clause' carefully before deciding on the insurer.

10. Critical illness riders are available for illnesses like cancer, Kidney failure, stroke, etc. Before taking such a rider, it is better to check out the illness. If this is not attractive it is better to go for a maximum coverage for the entire family

11. Look for the limits mentioned for Hospital room rent. Compare this with other plans.

12. Senior citizen coverage may be required in some cases either as an 'add-on' or first policy. There are insurers offering special senior citizen policy for 60-years-plus people with higher premium. It is important that senior citizens are adequately covered with healthcare policy whether they have earning children or not.

13. Though healthcare policy portability is possible it is better to stick to same insurer after 50 years.

14. Those who are in employment and their families are covered under group insurance of company, must ensure separate policy before they retire or they will find it tough to get healthcare policy with reasonable premium. Always compare the coverage terms and premium among 3–4 major insurers before choosing one.

15. "Co-pay clause" – Co-payment means the policyholder will bear a specified percentage of the claim amount. Example 80:20 clause: 20% of the treatment cost to borne by the policyholder.

16. Sub-limits – Health Insurance Company may specify limits for certain illness or treatments. For example, the policyholder can claim money only up to Rs. 20,000 for a cataract operation whereas the policy's sum assured may be Rs. 3,00,000.00. The policies without sub-limits are better, but may charge higher premium.

17. Alternate treatments – some policies also cover non-allopathic or alternate treatments like Ayurveda or homeopathy.

18. One needs to check up two important aspects:
    a. Claim settlement history.
    b. Whether the insurer is having well-established, long history of operation or not.

Healthcare Policies

A few selected healthcare policies are given below.

Company name	Plan name	Premium	key features/benefits	Negatives
ICICI Lombard	health complete	Rs. 14668	Lifelong renewal No Sub-limits (optional) No claim bonus Pre-existing diseases covered after 4 years	non-allopathic not covered
Max Bupa	health companion Silver	Rs. 13,718	all-day-care procedures covered Lifelong renewal Free Health check up No claim bonus Pre-existing diseases after 4 years	NA
Oriental Insurance	happy Family Floater silver	Rs. 9297	Non-allopathic covered Home hospitalization covered Existing diseases covered after 4 years lifetime renewal	Room rent limit Rs 5000 Co. pays 10%

Company name	Plan name	Premium	key features/ benefits	Negatives
Star Health	Family optima	Rs. 11055	no co-pay lifetime renewal 100% restore benefit Health check-up No claim bonus	Room rent limit – Yes Non-allopathic not covered

(Above example is for family of four: two adults 28 and 30 years and two children 5 and 3 years, Sum Assured Rs. 5,00,000/- and no pre-existing diseases.)

How much Healthcare Insurance, do you need?

- If you are young, single or it is just a couple, you need to have not less than Rs. 0.5 million.
- If you are a family, older and live in Metro city, the minimum amount must be Rs. 1.00 million plus.

IF YOUR FAMILY IS NOT COVERED UNDER HEALTHCARE POLICY, TAKE A POLICY TODAY ITSELF

CHAPTER 11
Dealing with Banks & Loans

11.1 Savings Bank Accounts

Every person must have an SB account in his or her name either as "single" or "Either or Survivor" with spouse. It is not a good idea to open more than two SB accounts as there are hidden charges and minimum balance requirements.

SB Interest Charges

There are private Banks which offer 6% on SB Accounts compared to 3.5% offered by SBI and many other PSU Banks. This must be an important consideration while opening SB account. You need to be aware of many hidden charges that banks charge.

Hidden charges on SB Accounts

1. Non-maintenance of monthly/quarterly balance
2. Cash transaction charges – Number of times and amount
3. Money transfer charges
4. Debit card annual fees
5. ATM usage charges beyond fixed number
6. Charges for SMS alerts
7. Charges for Bank statements
8. Cheque bounce charges
9. Stop payment charges
10. Additional cheque book charges
11. Debit card replacement fees
12. Charges for resetting ATM pin
13. Charges for redeeming reward points

14. Attestation charges
15. Balance Certificate charges
16. Interior certificate charges for additional copies
17. Account closure charges
18. Account transfer charges (from one branch to another)
19. International debit card charges
20. Charges for returned couriers
21. Debit card decline due to insufficient funds
22. Known charges – D/D, RTGS/NEFT charges

My Recommendation:

* Do not have more than 2–3 SB accounts as you need to maintain minimum balance in each account.
* Go for a Bank close to your house and which has fewer crowds.
* Maintain max two debit cards, as these have annual charges and it is difficult to remember so many PIN nos.
* Please ensure that nominee name is properly entered into Bank records.

11.2 Bank Fixed Deposits

FD rates undergo frequent changes as given below:

45 days	91 days	6 months	1 year
4.00 – 6.25%	4.00 – 6.75%	4.00 – 7.50%	5.25 – 8.00%

Senior Citizen may get 0.30–0.50% extra.

There are Banks giving higher rate for 46–90 days and lower interest for 6 months.

There are Banks giving 0.50% extra for Senior citizens. Example: Yes Bank gives 7.00% for 46 days for general public and 7.50% for Senior citizens. There are others who give only 0.25% extra.

Bank deposits Tips

1. Always compare interest rates before booking. Many private banks offer bank FD rates much higher than PSU banks. The differences of 2–3% p.a. can make huge differences on long term basis.

   Recently in a public park an elderly man showed me his SB passbook to check the balance. He had Rs. 18,00,000/- which he received as PF settlement in the SB account. This account was giving him hardly 3.5% p.a. If he had made FD in the same bank, he would have received an additional interest of 2.5% and if he had opted for a well-known private bank, he would have got an additional 3.5%. This may appear small, but such amounts it works out to be Rs. 40,000–65,000/- on such huge amounts.

2. Spread deposits under different durations 46 days/ 6 months/ 1 year to get maximum spread and to ensure liquidity. This could be done with different banks too. It may not be a good idea to commit FD beyond 1–2 years, unless the rates look very attractive.

Your ignorance and laziness may cost you heavily. Please check out your SB accounts and take corrective action today itself. You need not be a financial wizard to take such baby-steps to protect your wealth.

11.3 Managing Loans

11.3.1 Understanding Loans

Almost no one can live without taking some kind of a loan. What one needs to be conscious of are the following.

- Can you repay this loan without compromising on your essentials of life?
- How long will this loan tie you down – months or years? Are you prepared?

- Are you taking this loan for an appreciating asset or depreciating asset or is it for fun?
  - Appreciating assets – Plot, Apartment or Houses [Appreciation may take over 5 years plus]
  - Education loan can be considered an appreciating investment.
  - Non-Appreciating Asset – Cars, white goods
  - Fun/Pleasure – Holidays and clothing

If it is a big loan, you may be tying up your near ones with an albatross around their neck. Be careful.

You need to seriously evaluate your desire to take loans before getting carried away by "attractive EMI offers".

11.3.2 Loans and Credit Scores

Whatever the loan that you wish to take, your credit score will have major influence in sanctioning of the loan as well as interest rates –high or low.

If you have high credit score, almost everyone wants to offer you a loan. Your mailbox will be flooded with EMI and other offers. If your credit score is low, you will be shunned by these firms as if you suffer from a contagious disease.

Most important principle of loan is – You will be offered money if you do not need it and they will run after you. If you badly need money, you need to run after them!

11.3.3 Credit Information Companies

Credit information companies are the specialized financial institutions that collect and maintain information related to credit and loans of commercial institutions and individuals. On the basis of financial records, they prepare a credit report and score, on the basis of which the financial institution decides to give loan or a credit card. The report gives the credit history of the applicant, based on which loans or credit cards can be quickly processed. The credit score is the basis on which the application is initially processed.

11.3.4 Understanding Personal Credit Score

1. **Four top credit information companies and their credit scores**

[CREDIT SCORE]

	Equifax	Trans Union CIBIL	Experian	High Mark
Credit Score range	300–900	300–900	330–830	300–900
Cost	Free once a year	Free once a year	Free once a year	Free once a year

Credit Score is arrived at using credit information of the individual as 250–300 different variables each with different weightage.

- Track record of past payments
- Previous settlements, defaults and write-offs
- Loans as proportion of income
- Secured loans vs. unsecured loans and credit cards
- Loan enquiries' frequency

2. **Score range and what it means**

0 or 1 – It means you have no credit history

350–550 – This is a bad score and your chances of getting loan are minimal

550–650 – This is an acceptable region; however, the loan-giver may charge you higher interest

650–750 – This is considered to be a good score; however, the loan giver may charge higher interest

750–900 – This is an excellent range and you will be provided with loan offers, though you may not ask for it

3. Essential tips to have great score

A score of 750 and above is considered ideal; keep the following tips in mind

Be disciplined – Credit card and loan repayment have the strongest impact on your score. Hence timely payment of this should be your priority.

Low credit utilization ratio – For a credit card, get maximum limit, but after having got such a limit, stay below 35% of the limit to get a good credit score.

Seek variety – You need to have a mix of secured and unsecured debt to get a high score. Credit card is an unsecured debt whereas car loan is a secured debt.

4. Things that affect your credit score negatively

1. Too many credit report enquiries by Banks and other institutions
2. Cheque bounces and dishonours
3. Defaulting or late payment of credit card payments
4. Multiple unsecured loans
5. Frequent rejections of unsecured loans
6. Defaulting as a guarantor
7. High % utilization of credit limit
8. Errors in the records of Banks and other financial institutions

5. Important Note:

Banks are under no compulsion to correct records in time. Hence very often low credit score is due to incorrect or incomplete entries in the records of credit information companies.

6. Tips to improve credit score

1. Check and monitor your credit score for its errors and incorrect entries which you need to "dispute" officially. If things do not change you can file complaint with 'Banking Ombudsman' in a metro city close to you. Very often, Banking ombudsmen are slow or their orders may not get enforced. In such a situation, the only option for you is to go to consumer court. That is like going from frying pan to fire. Even if you are right, you may not get a positive verdict for a decade!
2. Limit your credit usage to bare minimum
3. You can increase your credit limit, without increasing usage
4. Make all payments on time
5. Even if you dispute often, it may be better to negotiate and settle rather than carrying on with poor score. This is true particularly when the amount involved is far less compared to the financial loss due to high interest that you may pay or the mental tensions that you may undergo. Your valuable time can be utilized for more productive goals in life
6. Under the current scenario, you can systematically build up credit score by the following actions:

- Have 2 free credit cards with maximum limits, but limit usage to bare minimum, i.e.: less than 20% but pay in time (Get credit cards even if you do not require!)
- Have 1–2 secured loans, pay in time
- Correct the records for incorrect entries
- Check your credit score once a year and systematically build up your credit score

11.4 Credit Cards

Credit cards are the most pushed and sold product after insurance. You will be persuaded by banks and credit card companies to take their credit cards. Your mailbox will be flooded with credit card offers from various Companies.

How do Credit Cards work?

These represent a type of financial account and nothing but a loan. Banks are persuading to take their loans so that they will earn interest on these loans. They are neither loving you nor offering charity!

By using credit cards, customers can offer bank's money instead of their own to pay for products or services today and over time they repay the bank. For the benefit of using bank's money, you need to pay interest after specified period which is the free period.

You need to pay back within 21 – 25 days from your own incomes. If you are not able to pay, the bank will keep collecting interest. Over time, the amount payable may become far more than your immediate income. To keep you from this perpetual debt trap, Banks will offer facilities like EMI.

If you are a well-behaved timely-paying credit card customer, bankers make less profit from your interests. With credit cards, bankers make far more money than other loans and they wish to see you continuing in this debt trap. Why kill a hen which lays golden egg?

Let us look at hidden and "not so hidden" credit card charges.

a. **Interest** – Bankers charge 2–3% interest per month on the delayed payment. This is an all-out robbery considering the fact that almost no bank gives monthly interest on deposit higher than 0.75%.

The delay in payment can happen for a variety of reasons:-

- Not having enough time to look at bills and clear the dues
- Laziness/forgetfulness
- Sickness
- Payment cheques not reaching or getting misplaced
- Indiscipline in personal life, etc.

b. **Finance Charges** – A lump sum amount is added to the bill if payments are not made in time

c. **Cheque** Bouncing **Charges**

d. **Annual Charges** – Many credit cards offer zero joining fees as a bait, but from the second year onwards there is an annual fee charged

e. **Overseas transaction cost** – This is charged if you have credit cards abroad and it could be 3.5% to 4% per month

f. **Late payment fees** – Typically these are slab-wise, forcing to pay higher fees for higher delayed payment

g. **Duplicate statement fees** – This is charged if you ask for a duplicate statement of accounts

h. **Surcharge** – If you buy petrol using credit card, a surcharge of 2.5% or a flat fees of Rs. 10 – 25/- may be charged

i. **Service Tax** – This is charged on the entire fees that you pay and could be 12.5% +

Complaints – If you complain to the credit card customer service, they will drive you nuts. These are driven by robot-like girls who have standard set of answers for everything. If they resolve your complaint, they will stop earning interest; hence, mostly they do not resolve complaints. If you write to Head office [which will be a Post box!], it will make you still madder. At the end of it they will ask you to contact on phone again.

Personal Experience of Nightmare Called Credit Card

I have personally experienced a case where for a false entry and associated minor wrong claim, I made over 50 written communications including a few to the MD of the Bank. Since the matter was not resolved even by the MD of the Bank, I approached Banking Ombudsman and got two judicial orders favouring me. Still the matter is not resolved even after 10 years! Then, there were over a hundred irritating or threatening calls at odd times of the day to me. I complained to RBI which resulted in zero action. I had even gone to the Police for such blackmail tactics. As a matter of principle, I did not pay this small false claim made on me: an amount of Rs. 12,000/.

If you do not have tenacity like me, my advice – DO NOT OWN ANY CREDIT CARD. If you own one, it may haunt you for decades.

Baits used by banks to trap you with credit cards:

1. No joining fees
2. Reward system and prizes
3. Credit transfer
4. Joining gift
5. Free credit card for spouse
6. Credit card usage linked to restaurants, shops and airlines, forcing you to spend money, using Bankers money as credit
7. salespeople sitting at banks persuade you to join
8. Cash backs at select outlets
9. Annual movie or drama tickets

My Recommendation

- If you want to be wealthy and lead a peaceful life, DO NOT OWN A SINGLE CREDIT CARD
- If at all you have a credit card, put a limit on spending at 20% of monthly income
- Unless used for business trips, avoid using credit cards altogether
- Teach your kids and family members about the danger of credit card. They must know the difference between credit card and debit card

Live Within Means

11.5 Housing Loan

The first step before taking a decision to buy/build a home is to check your eligibility for a home loan.

The housing finance companies take a decision on your loan based on the following

Functions:

- Your monthly income net of standard deduction like PF, insurance, etc.
- Your income history of the three years (if salaried, Form 16 and if self-employed, P/L settlement of your firm's history of three years. They will certainly ask for I-T returns acknowledgement for 3 years
- Your credit score as per CIBIL or similar rating agencies

   (If you're taking a joint loan, the above details of spouse also to be added)

   They may ask for the following documents as proof

- Address/age proof
- Pan/Aadhaar
- Appointment letter/salary certification
- Bank statements for six months
- Proof of other source of income, if any

Broadly HFCs decide the loan amount based on numbers of years and maximum EMI that you can afford to give based on your current monthly income.

A broad indication of monthly income, loan amount and EMI are given below.

If rate of interest is 8.7% the table will look like this

Monthly income	No. of years	Loans Amount (Rs. lakhs)	EMI
50,000	10	17.99	22500
50,000	15	22.57	22500
50,000	20	25.55	22500
75,000	10	30.00	37500

Monthly income	No. of years	Loans Amount (Rs. lakhs)	EMI
75,000	15	37.63	37500
75,000	20	42.57	37500
100,000	10	36.00	44000
100,000	15	45.15	44000
100,000	20	50.00	44000

Three smart actions get maximum loan amount

    a. **Increase number of years to maximum level, all reaching retirement age**

    b. **Add spouse's income**

    c. **Find an HFC who can give loan with lower interest rate**

11.6 Personal Loans

Personal Loans help an individual to meet financial emergencies. These emergencies are hospitalization, college admission, marriage, etc. Such loans are used for renovation and furnishing of house, family holidays, buying white goods, etc. Usually no guarantor or security is offered for such loans. The preferred class to which loans are given are salaried people.

Comparison of personal loans

Bank/NBFC	Range	Min tenure – Max tenure	Interest %	Fees and Charges
Axis	50,000 – 15,00,000	12 M to 60 M	15.5 – 24.0%	Process fees 1.5% – 2% Tax
Bajaj Finance	100,000 – 2500,000	12 M to 60M	12.00 – 15.5%	Process fees 2.25% – 3%
HDFC	100,000 – 2500,000	12 M to 60 M	15.15 – 20.00%	Process fees 0.25% – 1.50%

ICICI	100,000 – 2500,000	12 M to 60 M	11 – 22%	Process fees 0.25% – 1.50%
Kotak	50,000 – 2000,000	12M to 60 M	11 – 24%	Process fees 1.00 – 2.00%

Eligibility for personal loan

- Annual or monthly income
- CIBIL score of 750 + is ideal
- Stable employment, preferably salaried
- Age 21 – 60 years
- Good repayment history

Points to consider before applying for loan

1. Make doubly sure that you need a loan. In business, sudden shortage of working capital can affect your business. In other cases, the loan can wait unless urgent.
2. Compare the best offer in terms of interest and processing fees.
3. Check eligibility in advance with CIBIL Score.
4. Look at EMI and other repayment options.
5. Look at possibility of repayment before time and penalty if any.
6. Generally, interest rates are very stiff; hence proper thought to be given before applying for loans.
7. Keep all documents ready before applying for loan.
8. You may cover the loan amount with a term insurance with a different firm if rates are more attractive.

11.7 Car Loans

The few reasons why people take car loans are as follows:-

- You can own a car almost immediately by paying only 10%, rest through loans.

- You can avoid upfront payment in cash or other means which can get scrutinized by I-T department.
- You can show the interest as business expense if you are owning a business.
- You can go for an expensive model of car which under normal conditions you cannot afford.

Car Loan Rates Comparison

Bank	Interests %
Axis bank	8.50–11.25%
HDFC Bank	8.50–11.25%
ICICI Bank	8.50–12.75%
SBI	8.90–9.25%

Banks charges for the Car loan

- Processing fees – Upto 2% of the loan amount or fixed amount of Rs. 3000/- to Rs. 9000/-
- Documentation Charges
- CIBIL report charges
- Registration & stamp duty related charges
- Pre-payment charges – it could be 5% of outstanding amount
- Late payment charges
- Cheque bounce charges
- Swap charges – Rs. 500 – Rs. 700/- per transaction
- Amortization schedule charges
- Amortization statement charges
- Statement of accounts charges
- NOC/NDC (No due certificate) charges

- Charges for converting from private to commercial vehicle
- Loan cancellation charges
- Legal fees
- On most charges there will be service tax extra
- Some banks forcibly tie up an Accident insurance, premium for which will have to be paid along with monthly interest or EMI.

On a strictly personal finance point of view, taking a loan for buying a vehicle or owning a vehicle are not attractive propositions.

Please read chapter on personal investment Goal No 9 – Buying a car.

CHAPTER 12

Planning and Achieving Financial Life Goals

[SET FINANCIAL LIFE-GOALS]

Almost everyone must have a financial goal: a goal which can be achieved only by having sufficient money. The goals of a young teenager will be greatly different from those of a married 35-year-old with two kids. It will be different for a person aged 52 years staring at retirement. If you have two daughters, your goals will be different from your brother who has two sons.

The biggest problem is that most people do not have a clearly defined goal. A goal based on realities of today – current income and current expenses. And probable income of tomorrow.

If you have set a realistic goal there is a way of reaching that goal.

12.1 Setting Financial Goals

- Please give a deep thought and write down your financial goals on a paper.
- Discuss with spouse or others in family, and rewrite all of those goals after discussion.
- Look at your current income and forecast your income in the next 5/10/20 years taking into consideration probable inflation (for the purpose of forecast, you may take inflation at 6%).
- ESSENTIAL GOALS – FIVE most essential goals must be planned first –
    o Life cover for the earning member,
    o Healthcare coverage for family,
    o Emergency fund,
    o IT investment planning and
    o Investments on books and self-education.

    Then come all other goals.
- Since resources are limited, ensure that you allocate your income in different silos – Retirement, Children's education, Marriage and so on. Do not put all the eggs in one basket of investments. Each must be labelled separately too.
- Write down your action plan [income and saving] to accomplish those goals based on realistic thinking. It must not be day-dreaming!
- Discuss with your spouse about the financial life goals or yours will be a lonely journey.
- Execute the Action Plan in terms of savings and investment plans.
- Monitor the progress of the plan at least once a month.

12.2 SIP in Mutual Fund and Long-Term Financial Goals

If you are a salaried person or owner of small business, investing through SIP investments in Mutual funds is the best way to accomplish your financial goals. That is because equities offer the highest return on investments on long-term basis.

If inflation continues at 5–6%, the fixed income returns may continue to give returns at 7–8% plus or minus 0.5–1% on an annual basis.

How to calculate SIP or investment & Returns

If you are not strong with Maths, do not worry. There are many Apps and Websites which offer help in calculating returns at different levels of annual return/interest and number of years.

Calculating return at different funds of annual return/interest and number of years.

www.sipcalculator.in

There are many Financial Calculator Apps available on net. Two of these are as follows:

www.fncalculator.com

www.rkapps.co

Or you may choose any other which you are comfortable with.

These are interactive websites or Apps through which you can work out SIP requirement for achieving a particular goal in terms of monthly investments.

If anyone promises fixed income return above 8.5%, look at it through a microscope. Check it out with a few experts. Think of all pros and cons. Be open to negative feedback and "warnings" from well-wishers. Well, it is your money, and, it is your call!

Planning SIP for Two People [Example]

Let us say, there are two people planning to buy Apartment worth Rs. 6.0 million and 10 million.. The SIP working could be as follows for these two people:

[Millions]	Person-1	Person-2
Flat cost (including Registration)	6.00	10
Self contribution	1.50	2.5
Housing loan planned	4.50	7.5

Let us make the assumption that SIP will give around 12% return per annum if held for 6–7 years. The working is without taking into consideration the inflation.

Person – 1

He needs to have monthly SIP of Rs. 15,000/- for six years to buy a flat worth Rs. 6.0 million with housing loan of Rs. 4.5 million.

Person – 2

He needs to have monthly SIP of Rs. 19,000/- for seven years to buy flat worth Rs. 10.00 million with housing loan of Rs. 7.5 million.

Ideally the targeted amount should be including inflation. You could assume this at 6%.

> It is better to be a little conservative while forecasting SIP return, hence taken only 12%. If returns are higher than that, your personal financial goal of buying an Apartment could be accomplished one year earlier.

You can modify these by increasing SIP amount for each year. Example: If your salary is going up by 6% every year, you can increase SIP amount by at least 6% every year. With this, you can reduce the number of years required to reach your goal of buying a home.

Now, let us look at a few popular middle class financial goals and how to accomplish them.

12.3 Plan for Each Financial Goal in Your Life and Achieve It!

12.3.1 Financial Goal No. 1 - LEAD A FEARLESS LIFE

Become Debt-Free

Becoming debt-free is a major precondition before planning your other personal financial goals.

- You need to clear all or most of your personal loans from relatives and friends.
- You need to clear "overdue" credit card bills. These may be carrying penalty and interest charges which could be a major drain for you as well as threatening your credit rating score.
- You need to 'factor in' loans and EMI on other loans before setting your financial goals. If your income levels are not able to support the EMI commitments that you have, there is no scope for starting investments with a financial goal.

Remember!

> Credit cards charge 24–36% p.a. for overdue bills in addition to other penalties. There is no "fixed income variety" investment option which can give return of Rs. 15–18% in 5 year Plus period. This interest is a serious drain.

Hence, your monthly saving must go in for clearing all "bad debts". 'Bad debts' are those which push you to pay more than the rate of return that you may get on your investments.

12.3.2 Financial Goal No. 2

Save Taxes and Maximize Savings

The Government wants your income tax irrespective of your financial or personal situation. Govt. will want you to pay Income Tax even if you are in deep debt or are in hospital bed. Hence, planning income tax is a topmost priority. Strictly in legal terms, I-T could figure as your personal goal No.1.

Your income tax liabilities have strict deadlines and predetermined penalties. Further you can do almost nothing after those deadlines. Under these compelling conditions, I strongly recommend that your plan to save income tax must be priority No.1 at the beginning of the year itself. You must PLAN INCOME TAX and related TAX-SAVING INVESTMENTS in the first month – April itself.

Planning Income Tax and Saving Tax

You can have a simple worksheet as follows:

Expected Annual Income _____

Likely Income Tax for the year _____

Running Investments for the Tax saving limits _____

Balance to be invested for Tax Saving for the financial year _____

Net post tax income _____

Forecasted monthly/yearly I-T payable _____

Let us look at three different people who deal with the limit of Rs. 1,50,000/- per annum set for tax saving.

Ram – Invests Rs. 1,50,000 into ELSS to save taxes.

Shyam – Invests Rs. 100,000/- into ELSS to save taxes and subjects rest of the income to taxes.

Ashish – Invests only Rs. 30000/- into ELSS to save taxes; rest is subjected pay I-T.

Let us look at the amount saved in ELSS at the end of 35 years of service.

	Monthly SIP	Return %	Wealth after 35 years
Ram	12500	18%	439.0 mln.
Shyam	8333	18%	292.0 mln.
Ashish	2500	18%	88.0 mln.

We have assumed 18% return for 35 year period. As on April 2019, ELSS funds have returned 18.5% for a ten years period, hence 18% assumption is not outlandish.

Even if you have no other saving other than tax saving investments like ELSS, you will end up with a phenomenal kitty when you retire after 35 years of service by merely taking a wise decision today.

Lump sum vs. SIP investments into ELSS

To save Income tax and plan investments, you have two options for ELSS.

Option 1 – You can do lump sum investments to ELSS at the end of the year, in March.

Option 2 – Start monthly SIP with ELSS from the 1st month – April.

It is far more preferable to go for SIP at the beginning of the year itself as the SIP will catch the market at different levels of ups/downs and deliver you "average cost". It also brings in financial discipline to your life.

Lump sum investments into ELSS are typically done by people under pressure from outsiders. It could be your Accounts officer calling you up for providing "Proof of Investment" by Feb/Mar every year if you are salaried, or it could be your CA calling you up by March 2nd half for making investments. Either way it would be a bad decision to invest into ELSS funds as "lump sum". In the month of March if the stock market is at peak, your ELSS investments may show negative return for the next 2–3 years which will break your confidence itself. The loss of confidence means you will end up taking more foolish decisions.

Invest in to one or two or three ELSS funds?

Choose maximum of two ELSS funds from two different fund houses. Take into account your profile while selecting these ELSS funds.

Please see chapter under TAX SAVING INVESTMENTS-ELSS funds.

12.3.3 Financial Goal No. 3

DEAL WITH ANY EMERGENCY WITH AN EMERGENCY-FUND

Life is uncertain. Things could go wrong when least expected:

- You or a family member could fall sick and may need urgent hospitalization.
- You or your close family member could meet with an accident and may need immediate surgery.
- Your vehicle could break down in the middle of the road.
- Your home appliance like Fridge or TV or Electrical appliance could break down.
- You may have an unexpected tragedy (death/ accident) with your parents or close family members.
- You may lose your job and you get the news only at 5 pm on the last working day!

Any of those unforeseen events will necessitate you to meet urgent financial need. All such events may not happen at the same time. However, if you are unlucky you could have 2–3 adverse events at the same period – Week or Month.

Every person must have an Emergency Fund which you can reach quickly and meet the financial requirement.

    a. Medical emergencies

It is important that you cover yourself and your family with a health care insurance. Please see chapter under INSURANCE

However, for many illnesses and accidents, these policies may not work either because it is OPD level or not covered under certain sections. If your mother is ill and if she is not covered under healthcare insurance it is almost amounting to "personal medical emergency" for you.

    b.   Vehicle and Appliance breakdown

Your vehicle could break down or meet with a minor accident. For minor accidents, it may not be prudent to go for vehicle insurance claims as it involves time and non-availability of vehicle for a few days which you cannot afford.

The electric and electronic appliances at home could break down – your TV, fridge, AC etc. All these require you to repair them within a few hours or days.

    c.   Urgent personal or social expenses

Your close relative or friend may face hospitalization or even death. You may need to visit them and if it takes overnight travel, you need to take care of train or flight tickets or taxi bills. At times you need to extend short term emergency loan to them. All these require funding from emergency funds.

    d.   Loss of Job

This is the single biggest emergency situation that you are likely to face. Almost suddenly your incomes come to an end. For millions of salaried employees such situation comes suddenly one evening. The boss or HR Manager calls you to the cabin and says "You need not come from tomorrow. Here is your dues' cheque!"

Anger, frustration or even depression, nothing is going to help. Next day morning, you will realize the impact of losing your job.

You need to pay monthly rent, pay utility bills (Gas, electricity, phone, Newspapers, milk, etc.) and school fees and school van bill for your children.

How will you manage the next few months?

It may take 3–6 months to get another job. If you are in an Executive or senior position, it may take even longer period to get a break. Maybe 6–9 months.

If it takes 6 months to get a job, the situation would have been less painful if you had at least 3 months expenses as emergency fund.

If you fall back on credit cards to sustain for a few months, the situation could go from bad to worse. Almost everyone who had financial relationship with you will be after you. The Bankers, credit card companies, the provision-store fellow, milkman and so on.

Every salaried person must have an emergency fund to meet probable loss of job. Not less than 3 months' salary in any case.

How Much Should Be Your Emergency Fund?

If your monthly salary is Rs. 25,000/- your emergency fund could be as follows

	Minimum	Ideal
For home and utilities – For medical emergency/Appliance breakdown/	75000 (3 months)	1,50,000 [6 months]
Social emergency	75,000 (3 months)	75,000 [3 months]
Total	150,000	2,25,000

Important Note:

If you have a family with school-going kids, the ideal emergency fund must be not less than 12 months' normal expenses.

Some tips for accumulating emergency fund:

1. Operate emergency fund through a bank different from the one where your salary gets credited. Choose the Bank carefully, as it must have high SB interest on its day-to-day balance. There are a few private sector Banks which offer 6.5%-plus interest in SB Account. If you have any fear, split it into two different Banks, each with high SB interest.

2. Maintain not more than 30 days' average expense in the SB Accounts and the rest must be in short term deposit of 45–90 days. There are banks which offer 7.5% for 45–90 days term

deposit. You can also explore ultra-short term or liquid funds which may offer around 6–7% return in 1–3 years. One can try to keep around 35% in debt-oriented hybrid funds too.

3. All unexpected income that you get could be shifted to emergency fund. It could be bonus, sales incentives, tax refunds, gifts from relatives, etc. till emergency fund targets are met.

4. You need to have a debit card for the SB account with PIN number known to your spouse too. **BUT NEVER WRITE DOWN YOUR PIN NUMBER ANYWHERE!**

> Treat "emergency fund" as emergency fund and do not use it for anything else.

12.3.4 Financial Goal No. 4

Plan Daughter's Marriage in Style!

For any Indian parent, daughter's marriage will be one of the greatest events of life. Most likely your daughter will move out of your home into the boy's house. In traditional Indian families, major part of assets is to be transferred to her keeping the marriage in mind. Even assuming that ancestral assets, if any, will be transferred to daughter only after your lifetime, you need to plan her wedding as per Indian customs. The least one must do is to plan expenses for her wedding well in advance. It may involve two types of expenses:

- Gold ornaments
- Cash expenses

How to plan marriage expenses?

Gold – If you keep buying gold ornaments 15–20 years before time, you will be spending large amount of your income on "making charges" which could be as high as 5–15% of the total cost of gold. To save your money you can opt for E-Gold. To buy E-Gold you need to have a Demat account with a depository participant (DP) of NSEL in India. It will be different from equity Demat account. As and when you wish to get physical gold at a future date, it can be achieved with quantity accumulated over time.

E-Gold is gold held in electronic form. This is purchased at today's prices without any making charges. It has all the advantages of gold, except that you cannot physically see it.

You can buy 1–2 gm at a time at the prevailing prices. There is no holding cost; however, you need to pay 0.4% as service charges. There is a nominal custody charge too.

You can choose to buy the gold once a year when you read in newspapers that prices have fallen or you can choose to buy on monthly/bimonthly/quarterly basis.

Remember! If you spread out the purchases to a number of times in a year, you will be benefited with cost price averaging.

Planning marriage expenses

Depending on your family and community tradition, please evaluate the current marriage expenses. An example is given below.

Marriage dresses for bride and family	100,000
Transportation cost	25,000
Marriage hall charges	50,000
Buffet for 500 people (@ Rs. 700/ head)	3,50,000
Video/ photo charges	50,000
Hall decoration	30,000
Religious function cost	45,000
Stay for guests	25,000
Event management cost	50,000
Miscellaneous	25,000
Gold/jewellery	25,00,000
Cash Deposits	17,50,000
TOTAL	50,00,000

If your daughter is 6 years old and you plan to arrange her marriage when she attains 21 years of age, what would be the probable expenses after 21 years @ 6% inflation every year?

50,00,000 × 6% inflation every year × 15 years = 1,20,00,000 (Approx.)

There are many online (Free) tools which can be used for working out cumulative inflation cost. (One could use www.smartasset.com) or similar or www.vertex4z.com

Options for Investing for Your Daughter's Marriage

Option-1 Sukanya Samrudhi [with 80 C benefits]

Max. allowable limit for investment under this scheme is Rs. 1,50,000/- per year for two daughters. Rs. 75000/- per daughter is allowable. You can invest approx. Rs. 6000/- p.m. for 15 years, if your daughter is currently 6 years old. This can give maximum Rs. 34,70,000/ @ 8.5% interest PA. [15 years' average return could be less than 8.5%]. There will be a huge gap against your financial goal of Rs. 120,00,000 when your daughter attains 21 years of age if you go with Sukanya Samrudhi.

Option-2 Recurring deposits

Your post-tax return after investing into RDs for 15 years would be similar to option 1 only i.e. you may get 8.0–8.5%. But, RDs are taxable under IT Act at your I-T slab, which will result in returns much lower than Sukanya Samrudhi.

Option-3 Buying Gold jewellery every month or 2–3 times a year

We have explained as to how you will lose 5–15% in terms of making charges every time you buy Gold jewellery. If you opt for gold or gold coins, you will have to bear additional cost in terms of Bank locker charges. For Bank locker, banks charge annual fees of Rs. 2000/-, plus compulsory FD of Rs. 20,000/ on which you may get only 7.5 – 8% interest p.a. That will be double the loss for you.

Option-4 SIP in Mutual funds

Recommended categories if you have 15 years

34% in Multicap fund of one fund house.

33% in Multicap fund of another fund house.

Or 100% in Nifty 50 index fund.

On 15-years scale, the likely return could be 17–18% for Multicap fund; 20% could be expected for Midcap funds: an average of around 18%.

Rs. 12000/- p.m. SIP (Rs. 4000/- × 3 mutual funds).

Increase SIP amount by 6% every year.

Total period – 15 years.

= Maturity amount forecast Rs. 12.6 million.

Mutual Fund monthly SIP for 15 – 20 years will be the best option to choose for your daughter's marriage.

Opening Mutual Fund Account for your daughter

The first step towards opening a mutual fund portfolio under your daughter's name is to have an SB account in her name, though mutual funds under minor's name can have payments from parent's SB A/C.

- Most Banks have child bank account facility with Parents being signatories to the account till child attains 18 years.
- One can start MF SIP portfolio under your daughter's name.
- Parents can be signatories till your daughter attains adulthood of 18 years.
- Generally, the minor has to be first and sole holder of the portfolio.
- MF house will require birth certificate copy, and KYC details of the parent.

If grandparents want to contribute towards SIP, it would be preferable if they make a standing instruction to transfer amount every month to the child's Bank account. Similarly, a standing instruction can be created for "Automatic electronic payment of SIP" on specified dates.

Tips for SIP in MF for daughter's marriage

Start SIP with an amount which you can sustain for long period of time. It could go on for 15–20 years.

- Never withdraw the accumulated amount till the desired date or marriage as you wish.
- Once in 3 years, evaluate the performance of SIPs and shift (if necessary) to another fund house. Remember, this requires performance analysis of the MF vs. the rest of the funds (Example: Multicap vs. Multicap Universe)
- As the stock market is likely to have major fluctuations, do not get worried and stop SIPs.
- Come what may, the accumulated amount must not be withdrawn and invested in low-yielding assets like Gold, Bank FD, Debt funds, Endowment insurance and NSC.

Start early planning for your daughter

2–3 years delay can significantly impact return on 15–20 years period; hence it is strongly advised to start very early.

> **First Birthday gift to your daughter must be MF SIP!**

The earning parents must adequately insure themselves against unforeseen events in life. If your daughter's education or marriage require Rs. 70,00,000/- in another 20 years, it is advisable to cover yourself for at least Rs. 100,00,000/- through Term insurance. Do not take endowment or similar insurance as it may not be prudent financially. (See section under Insurance). Also ensure that your family is covered with a healthcare policy.

Late planning for daughter's marriage

If you failed to plan for your daughter's marriage well in advance, you need to allocate assets based on the time available for the marriage date.

If the number of years available to you is less than 7 years, you need to have a high % allocated to balanced funds, particularly Balanced Hybrid funds which have 40–60% as debt and conservative Hybrid funds which have around 75% in debt.

One can look at allocation of assets as follows based on number of years available for your daughter's marriage and each asset class in % of the total investments.

No of years	Gold	Equity	Aggressive Hybrid	Balanced Hybrid	Conservative Hybrid
15+	Nil	100	—	—	—
10–15	5	40	55	—	—
7–10	10	20	50	20	—
5–7	10	10	40	40	—
4–5	10	NIL	20	50	20
< 4 years	10	NIL	10	30	50

Tip:

Since your daughter is not working and she may not fall in tax bracket, with hybrid Balances funds, the tax implication is likely to be low. Please consult your CA before each major switch.

Option 3 – ULIP policies

There are many child-centric ULIP plans in the market. All of these come with fancy names. ULIPs are nothing but equity or debt linked insurance plans. They mix insurance (which is for protection) with investments in Debt or Equity

We do not recommend these for the following reasons:

1. They divert part of your investments towards term insurance cover which can be bought at much lower cost separately. The money saved over 15–20 years is very significant which could have created significant wealth for you or your children.

2. The labelling is very opaque and it is difficult to compare cost and performance across ULIP funds to make the best-informed decisions.

3. There are high exit costs and charges under varied heads all resulting in ULIP giving returns far less than normal equity Mutual funds.

Compared to Bank RDs and Sukanya Samrudhi or fixed income options, ULIPS – Equity linked may be a better option. However, we recommend a combo of Equity-linked Mutual fund and Term insurance for planning your daughter's marriage.

12.3.5 Personal goal No. 5

Plan for the Best Education for Children

A lot of personal finance advisors mix up daughter's marriage and children's education. We beg to differ for the following reasons.

A. Your daughter needs education as much as your son and requires both – education and marriage.

B. If you are able to put both in different silos your thinking and planning will be more appropriate.

C. In the worst-case scenario, you can shift savings from one Silo to another for your daughter.

The process of planning for children's education will be similar to daughter's marriage planning, with some differences.

Planning education expenses for University

These days, school education has become almost as expensive as college education. However, if your children opt for professional degrees or foreign education, the costs are far higher than normal University degrees. Let us look at approx. cost of education for your children.

These costs could vary based on Institution, UG/PG or country.

The following chart to be taken more as directional rather than exact calculation.

	Coaching	Degree	PG	Hostel/ living	Total
Pvt. MBBS	1	40	—	4	45
Pvt. Engg.	1	10	—	4	15
MBA(Premier)	2	3	20	3	28
MBA(Normal)	2	3	10	2	17
US (3 yrs.)	1	40	—	12	53
Other foreign (3 yrs.)	1	20	—	8	29

[Figures in Rs. hundred thousand]

For a variety of reasons, higher education costs are rising at a pace much higher than other inflation. It may be 10% plus per annum in the next 20 years.

A private Engineering degree of today (Rs. 1.50 million) will cost Rs. 10.00 million and private MBBS' cost of education could be Rs. 30.00 million (at the end of 20 years)

With the rising population, the competition to get seat on merit will rise rapidly. For an Arts or Science degree at Delhi University, the current admission cut-off is at 99% marks. What any political party or Govt. will do in future is wishful thinking. As a parent, you need to take care of the interests of your child, irrespective of what Govt. may or may not do.

DO NOT BLAME GOVT. OR SOCIETY; PLAN YOUR CHILD'S EDUCATION

Except investment in gold, rest of the planning required for children's education will be similar to planning for daughter's marriage, given in earlier pages.

for Children's education:

Ideal funds for children's education is as follows.

- If the period is 10+ years – the Nifty Index fund
- 7-10 years – Balanced advantage fund/Hybrid fund

A few tips

- Start SIPs very early when child is less than 5 years old.
- Have a term insurance for the parent and health insurance for the family.
- Split SIPs among three fund-houses.
- Do not withdraw or transfer to a fixed income instrument till a few years before targeted year.

Start a Bank A/c in your child's name and make him/her aware of the financial implications.

(Teach him/her to save from pocket money or gifts.)

If your child gets admission on merit or scholarship treat the MF investments as a gift for future.

12.3.6 Personal Goal No. 6 – Plan to Retire in Peace

[Retirement Planning]

When one takes up employment on the first day you are handed over a set of forms. These include Biodata details, Forms for Employees' Provident Fund and Health/ Personal Accident Insurance and so on. In the excitement to start your new job, you will fill up all these forms, put your signatures and then forget it for months or even years together.

Let us look at the list of wrong decisions made by an employee on the first day of employment.

- Fills up form for an additional EPF deduction without looking at other options of tax savings/ investments.

- Fills up health Insurance without considering parents or spouse though as per company policy of group Health insurance, they may be covered.
- Fills up nominee as mother even though he is married. (I knew a case where, a young wife lost her husband after 3 years of marriage, and all her legal claims went to husband's mother. And she was kicked out by the mother-in-law. Sad, but true story.)

> **Your Planning for Retirement must start on your First Day of Employment**

Three essential things to do before the start of retirement planning.

1] Term Insurance

Every person [who is the breadwinner of the family] must have a life cover equal to 10–15 times the current annual income. Please see chapter under Insurance.

2] Health Insurance

Either from the company that you work for directly or supplementing with your company, you must have reasonable healthcare policy for the entire family. "Reasonable" means not less than Rs. 4–5 hundred thousand for the family. Of course, the more, the better!

Family means including dependant parents; please see chapter under Insurance.

3] Planning for children's education and daughter's marriage

This must start soon after they are born. You may start planning for retirement on the first day of employment and it must get modified soon after your kids come into scene.

Please see chapter under children's education planning and daughter's marriage planning.

Retirement planning within 80 C limit

Our Income tax structure is created in such a way that you are under indirect compulsion to save maximum Rs. 1,50,000/- through 80 C benefit.

As an employee, you must exhaust this limit before looking at other avenues for retirement planning.

Workout the EPF contribution, Term insurance policy premium amount and any other 80 C investments; the balance amount can be considered for ELSS investments within Rs. 1,50,000/- limit. Let us say, you have made the following investments and it goes up by 8% every year.

Investment	Amount	Monthly	Return%	30 years[Rs. hundred thousand]
[1]EPF	50,000	4166	8%	145
[2] Term Insurance	15000	—	NIL	NIL
[3] Other investments				
NPS	12000	1000	10%	46
PPF	6000	500	8%	17
NSC	2000	166	8%	6
TOTAL[3]	20,000	1666		214
ELSS	65,000	5416	16%	669
	1,50,000			883

Assumptions

* Section-3 of the above investments has been done on fixed income securities. Instead, if the investor makes investments through higher ELSS, the likely return will be even higher.

* If taxable limit goes up every year and investments also go up correspondingly, the likely returns will be even higher.

Key Lesson

After covering for EPF and term insurance, invest maximum under ELSS instead of fixed income tax saving instruments like PPF and NSC. Further, ELSS will give greater return than NPS.

> **IF YOU MAKE WISE INVESTMENTS WITHIN 80C LIMIT ITSELF, YOU CAN BE WEALTHY WHEN YOU RETIRE IF YOU OPT FOR ELSS**

Retirement planning beyond 80 C limits with MF

At the early part of one's working life the equity based investments must be high. As you go up by age, the debt content of Mutual funds must go up. While doing so, the following factors must be kept in mind.

1. 5–10% of the total wealth could be in Gold [E Gold is better] as one gets older.
2. One must have one self-occupied house and other investments could be in mutual fund/related investments.
3. As one gets older, ideally you need to have multiple sources of income.
   - Income from 2nd profession/income from part-time job.
   - Income from Rentals.
   - Some amount of Pensions.
4. You need to cover the entire family with healthcare policy.
5. You need to take care of all essential investments like children's education/ marriage and investments to save on Income Tax.
6. At latter part of one's life, housing loan and other commitments must be reduced to bare minimum.

For the entire basket of mutual funds, the following allocation could be used as a directional guide. This is based on age versus type of mutual fund allocation.

Age-Wise Investments through Mutual Funds

	Pure Equity funds			Hybrid funds	High debt fund	Total %
Age	Small cap	Mid cap	Multi cap	—	—	100
<35	30	35	35	—	—	100
36–45	30	30	40	—	—	100
46–55	NIL	20	60	20	—	100
50–60	NIL	NIL	NIL	70	30	100
60+	NIL	NIL	NIL	20	80	100

It could be 'balanced Hybrid' for 56–60 years and 'conservative hybrid' for the 60+ years-old.

For 60+ years-old, high SCSS could be maintained upto the limit of Rs. 30,00,000 subject to I-T limit considerations.

Allocation depends on the total kitty that you have and the amount that you require to run your life. I will explain this through the following example.

Let us say, there are three people Mr. A, Mr. B and Mr. C and they are having total investments Rs. 30,00,000/-, Rs. 60,00,000/- and Rs. 100,00,000/-. If they have identical expenses, their spread in investment may be as follows.

Rs. hundred thousand	Total investments	SCSS	Bank FD	Equity linked Debt funds
Mr. A	30	15	15	NIL
Mr B	60	15	15	30

Mr C	100	15	15	60
Monthly income	Rs. 21,250/- @ 8.5% return p.a.			

If Mr. A wants higher monthly income than Rs. 21,250/- it is not possible.

However, Mr. B and Mr. C can opt for higher monthly income by opting for a concept called SWP (Systematic Withdrawal Plan) from equity-linked debt funds. (Please see chapter SWP)

Key Lesson

As one gets older, maintain fewer investments in equity-based investments and have high content of debt mutual funds of fixed income products.

12.3.7 Personal Goal No. 7 - Plan to Buy a Home

Buying a home for self is the single biggest dream for an Indian. This requires considerable planning.

1. While buying a ready-to-move-in house you need to pay 25% of the cost towards the following:

   - Your share of the home before taking home loans.
   - Registration, Stamp duty and related charges.
   - Basic furnishing charges.
   - Maintenance amount for a few months till housing society is formed.
   - Electrical and other fittings.

These have to be funded from your own savings.

2. Typically, EMI outflow has to be maximum 30% of the current income. Approx. 70% of the rest has to be allocated to household expenses, children's education, savings for health policy and so on.

   [Unless you are in high income/low outflow bracket]

3. You need to cover yourself with a term insurance at least equal to the loan that you wish to take from the Bank/ Finance Institution.

4. The home must be for self-occupation; then only it may be viable or attractive. If it is for rental, it has to be looked at differently in terms of investment vs. return.

5. Period available to you for accumulating enough funds to meet 25% must be carefully weighed. Also you need to take into account the possible inflation in the property prices in the intervening period. If the current property price is approx. Rs. 50,00,000/- in the area or size chosen, in another 7 years, it may be costing around Rs. 76,00,000/- if 6% inflation is taken into account. If that is so, you need to plan for an upfront amount close to Rs. 20,00,000/-.

You need to plan your investments which are likely to deliver returns above 7% p.a. [post tax] to be way ahead of property inflation forecast of 6%. Such returns are possible only if you rely heavily on equity-based investments.

	1–3 years	4–5 years	6–7 years	SIP
Multicap MF	—	—	Yes	Yes
Aggressive Hybrid MF	—	Max 30%	Yes	Yes
Conservative Hybrid	+75%	Yes	—	Mix of lump sum + SIP
Bank FDs	May be 25% — —			

As with most investments, it is advisable to spread the investments in more than one instrument.

12.3.8 Personal Finance Goal No. 8

Enjoy Life – Holiday Planning

Life is not about working, working and working. One needs to have a good mix of fun and work. Also one needs to take care of children's education, children's marriage, investing for retirement and buying a home. Also provide sense of security with term insurance and healthcare policy.

Assuming that you have created silos for each of these, you need to have fun in terms of picnics and holidays.

One-day picnics

These could be "low cost" outings to picnic spots or national parks. These could be organized with minimal cost. At best, you need to hire a Taxi for a day. This does not require serious planning, but needs money.

Holidays within India

These may cost Rs. 30,000/- to Rs. 60,000/- for the entire family. It could be a trip to a hill station, beach resort or religious destination. For most middle class and lower middle class families, these may happen once in 2–3 years and will require planning on investment.

Holidays outside the country

These are expensive and may happen once in a decade or once in a lifetime for most middle class or lower middle-class families. It may cost Rs. 1,50,000/- for a couple if the destination is nearby and may cost Rs. 6,00,000/- – 10,00,000/- if it is Europe, US or Canada. Such international holidays require long-term planning.

There are two ways to fund your holiday.

- Through a holiday loan extended by Banks or other financial Institutions.
- Through accumulated investments.

Holidays through loans

Let us discuss the financial implications of having a holiday funded through loans with an example.

Loan amount	Tenure of loan(yrs.)	EMI	Principal repayment	Interest payment
600000	5	14,274	600,000	2,56,000

If you have taken Rs. 6,00,000/- loan for a foreign holiday, for 5 years' period, you end up paying back Rs. 8,56,000 including interest. Most Banks charge 14–15% interest on such personal loans against normal FD rates of 8%.

For a pleasure of 10–15 days, you will be debtor for 5 years. Once you have taken such a loan, you may not be able to take any loan for appreciating assets like homes or make investments which could give you 12–18% return per annum.

It would be far wiser to go for long term investments to fund your dream foreign holiday.

Investments strategy to fund foreign holidays

	1–3 years	4–5 yrs.	6–7 yrs.	SIP
Multicap MF	—	—	Yes	Yes
Aggressive Hybrid MF	—		Yes	Yes
Conservative Hybrid	+75%	Yes	—	Mix of lump sum + SIP
Bank FDs	Max 50%	—	—	lump sum

Timeshare holidays – Is it wise to invest?

The purchase of "timeshare" – a way to own a vacation property that you can use, generally once a year – is often an emotional and impulsive decision.

Types of timeshare

A. Fixed week – The buyer usually owns the rights of a specific unit in the same time of the year for as long as the contract stipulates.

   (Example – June 1–10 every year)

B. Floating – The buyer can reserve his own time during a given period of the year.

   (Example – August every year)

C. Points club – This is similar to floating timeshare, but buyers can stay at various locations based on points accumulated.

D. Right to use – In this arrangement, the buyer leases the property for a given amount of time for a set amount of years.

Advantages

- Low rental rooms available at holiday destinations for a few decades.
- Often you can gift it to friends or relatives.

Disadvantages

- You may not be able to go on holidays on the fixed week and end up paying extra for peak season. Very often, room is available only during off-season.
- Getting right for 50–100 years has no meaning, as you may not live that long!
- The tariff of the rooms/accommodation may be immune to inflation, but other major costs go up significantly. In any case, major costs of holidays are travel, food and local transportation which may be 70% of the total cost.
- It is boring to go to similar/same locations year after year.
- You may not be able to use timeshare for years together due to various reasons – illness, marriage within family, official commitments, natural calamities, etc.

Is Timeshare Holidays a good investment?

Not at all! If you manage to sell your timeshare, you may get far less than your investment.

If you take into consideration the initial investments that you made, it would be huge in a 25-year period.

For some of the known time holiday companies you need to invest Rs. 2,00,000/- – 4,00,000/- within 2–3 years. In a period of 25 years Rs. 2,00,000/- would have multiplied to Rs. 163,00,000/-!

My Recommendation

Invest your money into a Multicap MF through SIP route and keep it separately for the next 25 years for all your holiday dreams.

12.3.9 Personal Investment Goal No. 9

Buy a Car and Drive with Family

The primary need to have a car is for transportation. Either to go to work or use by family. But, most often the reason for a buying a particular model or brand of a car is for reasons beyond transportation. It could be to satisfy your ego by impressing others.

Car is a "depreciating asset" unlike properties, Mutual fund, Gold or any other investments. On each passing day, the market value of your car drops. If you bought a car in January for Rs. 10,00,000/- and if you try selling it by February you are unlikely to get quotes beyond Rs. 800,000/-. Within 12 months, it may drop to Rs. 750,000/-.

Should you buy a new car or an old car?

The financial advantage of a new car is that it will have least repairs compared to an old car.

In the initial 2–3 years the depreciated market value of the car drops rapidly.

After 3 years, the car may be available at 40–50% lesser than the buying price, whereas the repair cost may have gone up by 20%. It makes financial sense to buy a 2-year-old car than buying a brand-new car.

Should you buy a car at all?

These days there are options like online taxies and rickshaws which are wide-spread. If you calculate the vehicle loan's interest cost, running cost, maintenance cost and parking cost, the proposition of owning a vehicle may not be attractive. If you live in a city which has good transport facilities including online vehicles, you need to evaluate the benefits of owning a vehicle vs. costs and complications of owning such a vehicle.

Let us look at the costs involved. If you are planning to buy a Rs. 10,00,000/- worth car, the Bank may give Rs. 800,000/- loan @ 15% interest p.a. [All in Rs.]

EMI – 15889/-

Duration – 7 years, Interest-16%

Capital repaid – 800,000

Total interest paid – 5,33,000

Total paid 13,33,000

Value of car after 7 years – 200,000

Total money spent 11,33,000

Approx. KM travelled in 7 years = 80,000

Per km cost – 14.00

Other expenses

Insurance – Rs. 30000 per year 1st year × Approx. 15% less each year

Total insurance paid in 7 years – 133,000

Per Km insurance cost – 1.70

Petrol cost

Rs. 80/- per litre of petrol × 80000 km = Rs. 80,000/-

(Assuming that there is no increase in price of petrol) per km cost = Re. 1/-

Maintenance cost

Assuming that it is around Rs. 100,000/- in 7 years per km cost – Rs. 1.25/km

Total cost – 14,46,000

Per km cost – Rs. 18.00

We have not taken into account other costs like Parking, servicing and cleaning.

[Hey! We have not added Traffic fines and small thefts like mirror!]

On a strictly financial assessment, buying a car is not an attractive decision in a big city.

Investment planning for buying a Car

Most of the car-buying decisions are taken with 1–3 years period advanced planning. Your investment planning has to be done using high Debt content funds. If you have to buy a car of Rs. 10,00,000/- and you wish to contribute

Rs. 300,000/- into it, and balance through vehicle loan, you can consider the following.

- Conservative hybrid funds.
- Corporate bond funds.
- Bank FDs with 1 year plus period (which has high interest).

12.3.10 Goal No.10 - Financial Planning for the Already Retired

With the rise in life expectancy in India, post-retirement life span is now much longer than it was earlier. According to a World Bank report, life expectancy in India has risen from 54 years in 1980 to 70 years in 2015. In states like Kerala, the life expectancy is 75 years. Looking at our parents and grandparents, we assumed that we may last only till 60–65 years. Now, we are looking at the possibility of living up to 75–80 years and beyond 90 years, if very lucky!

This puts serious challenges on the financial situation of the post-retirement period.

At one end, we have to deal with day-to-day expenses of food, clothing and medicines for an "additional" 15–25 years.

At the other end, since we have so much of free time, we have to plan to spend it enjoyably.

This means a huge increase in "non-essential" expenses. These could be mobile bills, internet bills, books or periodicals, Vitamin or liquor bills. More entertainment expenses, holidays in India and abroad, more movies, eating out, more social visits and so on. Since you have responsibility for your spouse, the financial challenge is double!

What we thought of Rs. 20,000/- per month possible expense is becoming Rs. 50,000/- per month and it is only rising!

This great financial challenge has to be kept in mind.

1. Henceforth, you may not be having any income coming into your Bank account on account of salary. And, you need to manage life with current resources only. Most likely, you may have only outflow from Bank.

2. If you do not choose your investment options wisely, you could be badly off or if you make serious errors, you could become a pauper. You will end up at the mercy of your children or other family members.

3. If you are badly off financially, you will be depressed and will lead a miserable quality of life.

With so much of free time and active mind, you may feel like doing something.

Be Careful!

Do not do the following:

1. Do not start some business as "time pass" (Small business requires serious investments, business plan, time, great ideas and long hours of working). Running a small store requires far more skills – Financial and people than being a junior Manager in an MNC. This will require much higher levels of negotiation skills, maturity and persistence. In short, starting a new business is not a joke!

2. Do not invest your retirement Kitty into some 'funny' investment idea like "orchard scheme", "chit fund", "agricultural land", "sheep farming", "unregistered benefit fund", high-interest private deposits, partnership in business, etc. If any friend, colleague or relative promises you interest or return higher than SCSS or Bank FD, do not believe it. You will lose money, for sure.

3. Do not start a private loan business. You will not get back money and Police and court will do nothing in your lifetime!

4. Do not join a firm with fancy titles like "Manager", "Partner", wherein you have to bring in customers who are expected to invest money in this firm. This is all the truer if you worked as Executive with Bank or Officer in Govt. or been a Teacher. They may offer you 10–20% commission on the deposits collected, but you may land up in police stations and courts sooner than later!

5. Do not join a firm which is trying to sell developed plots. They may offer fancy salary plus commission for selling these wonderful plots

to your relatives and friends. These plots may never get delivered and you will be a crook in the eyes of your relatives.

6. Do not become trader of shares and commodities. Trading in shares and commodities are for the finest brains in the world of finance: people who understand economy trends, RBI policies, currency fluctuations and so on. You may be very intelligent and experienced in some other area. It is too late in life to become a trader of shares and commodities. In case you wish to get benefits of equity market, talk to a CFP [Chartered Financial Planner] and stick to low-risk mutual funds in the area of hybrid funds only.

While investing, keep the following in mind:

1. Stick to products that you understand.

    Since you have ready money, a lot of people will land up with advice and suggestions, even at your home. It could be Managers from chit funds, insurance agents, bank Managers, real estate dealers, sophisticated wealth managers and so on. Unless you have done sufficient studies and made enquires do not go into products that you do not understand.

2. Think of ways to beat inflation.

    If the inflation is 5 – 6% if you get return anything above 8%, you should be happy. If anyone promises you returns higher than 9% through any fixed income security, you need to be careful.

12.4 High-Safety Instruments

List of investments which are likely to give return higher than inflation%:

	Returns	Taxable	Safety
Bank Deposits	8% plus	yes	High
Company A Grade Deposits	9% plus	yes	High
B Grade company Deposits	10% plus	yes	Medium

SCSS (upto Rs. 30,00,000/-)	8.6%	yes (on tax slab)	High
Post office monthly Income scheme (Max Rs. 4,500,000/-)	7.8%	yes	High
Debt MF	7%	yes	High
Tax free bonds	6.5%	yes	High
Insurance Immediate annuity	5–6%	yes	high
MF Debt	7–8%	yes	Medium
MF Balanced Funds	Market Linked	yes	Medium

(Note – These returns change frequently. Please recheck current returns before taking decision on investment)

3. Think of liquidity

   You need to invest into anything which has high liquidity. You should be able to convert into "cash" at short notice of 2–3 days

4. Need to look at post tax returns

   For every investment that you make, you need to make due consideration of your tax bracket and post-tax returns, particularly if you are in tax bracket.

12.5 Where to Invest Your Retirement Kitty?

You would have noticed that I had given high levels of caution and warning while planning finances in the post-retirement period. This has come after I have seen a number of cases where retired people have been reduced to penury within a few years of retirement. Some of them lost their entire life's savings and even pensions while taking very foolish financial decisions. I have personally witnessed a well-educated gazetted officer landing in a destitute home after losing everything. Post-retirement period is not the period that you can experiment with your finances and income, unless you have considerable spare wealth.

My advice for the post-retirement period will be as follows:

1. Exhaust Rs. 30,00,000/- limit of SCSS by investing into this account. You can open such an account with Post office and most PSU Banks.
2. Exhaust PO monthly income scheme of Rs. 4,50,000/-.
3. Bank Deposits which give maximum plus returns above inflation. (There are a few big Banks offering 9% against inflation of 6%)
4. Balance can be held in Ultra-short term or liquid funds of MF. Then, do a Systematic Transfer Plan (STP) into Hybrid Debt fund over 12–18 months period.
5. Simultaneously workout Mutual fund SWP if the amount is not sufficient.

What if a retired person has only low pensions and low retirement Kitty?

There are many retired people facing hardship in the post-retirement period. They have very low monthly pension and have low investments which are yielding only little monthly returns. They may have a home in which they live with their spouse. For such people, there is an excellent idea called "Reverse Mortgage" of house.

12.6 What Is Reverse Mortgage?

The reverse mortgage is the opposite of a conventional home loan. A reverse mortgage enables a senior citizen to receive a regular monthly stream of income from a Bank against mortgage of his home.

The borrower (owner) continues to reside in the property till the end of his life and receives a periodic payment on it. Some of the basic highlights are as follows.

– Reverse mortgage is only for those who are above 60 years of age.

- Maximum loan amount is 60% of the current value, which is reworked every 5 years.
- Reverse mortgage loan period could be 10–20 years
- Over time, the loan amount and monthly payment can be increased, all within the 60% of asset value
- Rate of interest is fixed on either "fixed" or floating" terms.
- No Income taxes to be paid on the amount of loan taken or monthly payment received.
- The loan-taker or co-owner/spouse can stay in the house till the end of his/her lifetime.
- After the lifetime of both the owner and spouse, the remaining amount can be settled with nominees. They have the option to pay up the loan amount or take part in its sale and get balance amount after deducting loan amount and expenses related to it.

Example:

For a Rs. 20,00,000/- loan @ 12%

	10	12	15	18	20
Monthly (Rs.)	8640	6220	3960	2600	2000

If the rate of interest is reduced to 11% the monthly flow would be Rs. 2289/- for 20 years and Rs. 9133/- for 10 years for Rs. 2000,000/- loan.

Two factors which will influence the monthly flow of income – Duration and rate of interest.

My Recommendation

"Reverse mortgage" is an ideal way to lead a quality-life for those who are retired and have less of other sources of income.

Though it is impossible to forecast as to how long one will live, it is ideal to start it when both spouses are close to 70 years.

Tips for the retired couple

- Do not transfer property till the end of lifetime of the person, especially the house that you live in.

- Please ensure that you keep a "will" ready as you move into retirement. This 'will' can be modified later as many times as you want.

- Keep Xerox of all documents with spouse and children or close relatives as the case may be.

- Operate with maximum two bank SBs close to your residence.

Annuities

Please read Section on Annuities as part of Retirement planning.

12.7 Systematic Withdrawal Plan (SWP)

Systematic withdrawal plan (SWP) is the MF scheme in a prefixed date or frequency; with the SWP one can customize the cash flow as per your requirement. You can decide the frequency monthly, quarterly or annually. That way, you can withdraw to meet your financial needs without totally withdrawing or closing the investment. As for the amount which stays back with MF, it continues to grow as before.

How to plan the SWP?

Let us say you have Rs. 50,00,000/- invested into aggressive balanced fund. Looking at the performance history you know that it has performed @12% in the past 5–10 years and you estimate that it will continue to grow @ 10% minimum in the future.

If you withdraw up Rs. 5,00,000/- p.a., then you withdraw only the amount which has grown.

If you withdraw above Rs. 5,00,000/- p.a., you not only withdraw the grown amount, you also withdraw a little of the invested capital.

You can have any of the following strategies:

Option 1 – Approx. withdraw the grown amount on monthly basis

Rs. 5,00,000/- /12 months – Rs. 41,600 per month on equal instalment for the duration that you decide.

Option 2 – Withdraw only 50% of the amount on monthly basis

Rs. 5,00,000/-, /12 months × 50% – Rs. 20,800/-

In this situation, part of the grown amount is added back and your invested amount keeps growing.

Option 3 – Withdraw lesser than the grown amount every year

[But step up the amount every year in keeping with inflation.]

Example:

You decide to withdraw Rs. 30,000/- p.m. (Rs. 3,60,000 p.a.) in the 1st year and 6% increase in each subsequent year. (2nd year Rs. 31,800/-, Rs. 33780 in 3rd year and Rs. 35730/- in the 4th year. If you can afford it, option 3 is the best option considering all aspects.)

You can continue SWP for your entire lifetime and the balance amount can be transferred to your nominee.

Tax implications of SWP

Mutual fund withdrawals are subject to tax depending on the category of funds you own. Debt funds and equity funds are taxed differently. SWP redemption is as per "First In First Out" (FIFO) method, wherein units first bought are assumed to be redeemed first. Hence your cost for the purpose of taxation will be considered as per FIFO method.

If you redeem your investments in equity funds after 12 months, your investments would qualify for long term capital gains tax (LTCGT). Long term capital gains in excess of Rs. 100,000/- are taxed at 10% currently. If you sell your equity MF before 12 months, you will have to pay short terms capital gain tax at the rate of 15%.

Debt Mutual funds qualify for long term capital gains tax only if investments are held for 3 years or more. The long term capital gains tax on debt fund is 20% with indexation benefit done on your original investments. However if debt MFs are sold before 3 years, the short term gains are taxed as per your applicable income tax slab; your SWPs are taxed as above. Hence SWPs have to be planned accordingly.

Tips for SWP

1. After your retirement, if your net income is more than taxable limit, you have to shell out Income Tax. Except a little concession in slab, you will have no sympathy from Govt.; hence, plan it in consultation with your CA.

2. If you do not require funds, let your investments in MFs stay as such for long term till you decide to bequeath it.

3. If you are financially better placed, retain higher amount in aggressive Hybrid funds as you will get the best of everything: the equity growth benefit as well as stability offered by debts as these have 65% in equity and 35% in debts.

4. As much as possible, do not withdraw more than 50% of the "grown" amount, which will help you to maintain your invested capital.

CHAPTER 13
Money, Friends, Relatives and Family

13.1 Teaching Your Kids about Money

If kids develop good financial skills from an early age, they will be ready for financial challenge of adulthood. Giving kids a good fundamental teaching about money matters is critical for personal development. Look at the range of actions that an adult is expected to do.

Earning	Investing/funding	Taking loan	Banking
Budgeting	Choosing asset class	Lending	Debit Cards Cheques
Saving	Wealth creation	Credit card EMI	Planning to buy a Home
Resisting impulse buying	Dealing with sickness	Protecting with insurance	Planning retirement tax saving
Saying no to scamsters	Funding education		

Each of the money-related planning or action requires a range of knowledge and skills.

Let us look at a range of techniques and strokes used in swimming.

freestyle	breaststroke	sidestroke
Butterfly	backstroke	combat sidestroke
Water Yoga	Synchronized Swimming	Water Gymnastics

Each of these techniques and strokes has to be learnt and practiced. For many of these, you require to learn under experts and learning may last months or even years. Managing money and learning techniques and skills associated with money is no different.

> **START EARLY,**
>
> **GET EARLY-MOVER ADVANTAGE**

Visible vs. Invisible Money

Traditionally, all people used to use currency and coins for financial transactions. This is visible money; over time the usage of currencies and coins has come down. Now, money is invisible. It could be credit cards, debit cards, internet banking and online shopping. It has become harder to explain to kids. They get an impression that unlimited money is available and it is very easy to get and easy to spend. Also, they get an impression that it is unlimited!

Whenever money is discussed, it is ideal to involve kids also. They get used to the idea of money – earning, budgeting, saving, spending, etc.

Budget Planning

Every household can have a small meeting on household budget once a month. Ideally, kids must participate and observe. They will get an early impression on money. Most importantly, they will get an idea on budgeting and expenses.

At ATM

The ATM is a great place to start teaching kids about money. You could explain to the kids that ATM holds some of your money with the banks. ATM will give more money only if you work hard, earn more and save more.

At the Supermarket

At the supermarket you can explain to the kids about product prices vs. quantity (weight or volume). How you can get things cheaper to save money.

Why you need to always look around to make maximum savings. Ask your kid to suggest ways to get cheaper products at supermarket.

Paying utility bills

You can ask kids to keep track of electricity and mobile bills. Ask them to suggest ways to cut down utility bills.

Monthly Pocket Money

Every kid above 5 years can be given a fixed monthly pocket money on a fixed date. You may start with Rs. 10/- They can be given an option to earn more by sharing the household work.

Examples are as follows:

- Making up all beds — Rs. 1/-
- Cleaning all furniture — Rs. 1/-
- Cleaning bathroom — Rs. 2/-

The value of working and earning money gets embedded into the mind at an early age. The collected money can be stored in a "piggy box". As they grow older, an SB A/C can be opened in their names.

Maintaining Expenses Diary

Kids can be encouraged to maintain a notebook on revenue vs. expenses. They may make mathematical errors initially, but, at a later stage they will pick up the right values.

Teaching difference between Credit and Debit card

From middle school, kids must know the difference between credit and debit card. They must know it is very injurious to use credit cards.

Key concepts Kids must learn

At preschool age

- You need money to buy things
- Money includes notes and coins with different values
- You can earn money only by going to work
- There are things that you need (water, food, clothes)

- Things that you want (Ice cream, fancy shoes, balcony tickets)

At primary school

- Comparing prices and weight of things that you buy
- Do not tell your personal details on online and to strangers ("Secret" talk)

At Middle School

- Saving Money into piggy bank
- Difference in fare between Bus, rickshaw and taxi
- Difference in Price between branded and non-branded products
- Visit to poor home or destitute home

At High School

- It is always better to use cash, than credit of any kind
- Credit is money that you borrow and pay back with interest
- Encourage children to take up some part-time job
- Keep track of revenue and expenses in a book
- Start using bank account and debit card. Check balance after each transaction.
- Discuss ways to increase "income"
- Ask grown-up children to work in some store for 2–3 days
- Take part in sale of things at temple or church
- Ask children to make critical comments of advertisements seen on TV or newspapers (let them learn to look at advertisement sceptically)
- Ask them to make a list of NEW OR OLD products in terms of prices

13.2 Teaching Your Spouse about Money

Often only one person in the household is responsible for maintaining the family budget and managing household expenses. But, what if you died or become incapacitated and could no longer manage the budget? Or you wish to involve your partner in some or major part of managing household expense? Your partner can manage household expenses only if you train her/him in the management of household finance. Let us see how this can be managed well.

1. **Make a list of everything and where it is located**

    a. FILES

Go ahead and buy couple of files with labels as follows:

- Utility Bills:- gas, electricity, phone, water, internet
- Insurance:- Household, healthcare, life, term insurance, etc
- Pensions:- Private pension, Govt pension, ULIP Pay-outs, LIC, Superannuation, etc.
- Property Documents:- Xerox of all property documents
- Deposits:- SCSS, company deposits, bank deposits, PO-MIP
- Mutual Funds:- ELSS, MF of all houses
- IT File:- Copies of all I-T Returns
- Demats or Share:- Demat A/C details, list of shares

At the beginning of the file, give a brief explanation as to what the file contains.

Before filing, recheck the "nominee" column properly

   b. SMALL BAG WITH BANK BOOKS

Buy a small nylon bag with zip to keep your SB A/C passbook and cheque books.

You may visit bank branches and give an updated "Nominee" list. Copy can be maintained in the folder

   c. BANK LOCKERS

Make a list of things in Bank locker and maintain list in the bank book bag. Check whether Bank locker has "Nominee" name as per your wish.

The Bank locker could contain the following materials:-

- Property Documents – Original

- Gold and Jewellery
- Certified copy of your will
- Your master list of all assets

2. Make sure that your partner has legal and physical access to everything

You need to make sure that your partner has legal access to all your assets. You can have bank A/C with 'either-or-survivor' status. If that is not possible, your partner must be made the official nominee No 1. It could be bank A/C or Bank lockers or Mutual funds or pensions or whatever.

3. Explain the details of each asset or document

Unless you explain in detail, your partner may not be able to understand the implication of each one. Example – Our health care policy covers us for Rs. _____ million and premium must be paid one month before expiry on (Date) _____.

Remember! If premium is not paid in time the family will not get covered for health insurance.

4. Prepare a monthly household budget and let your partner monitor it

You can prepare a monthly household budget and let your partner prepare a short and sweet monthly expense list. Let him/her assess the position of your finances at the end of the month.

5. Maintain a separate SB A/C for household expenses

This is the best way to keep track of your budget vs. expenses. Have only one ATM card for which PIN numbers is known to both.

6. Prepare a contingency plan

Life is full of surprises. Smart people are better prepared than others in dealing with emergencies.

You need to discuss this as follows:

"If I fall unconscious, do as follows _____"

7. Train your Spouse

In all metro cities there are workshops on investments. It could be 4–6 hours' sessions. Or, it could be an online course. Or it could be a personal book like this one you are holding in your hand. Educating and training your spouse will go a long way to strengthen the entire family.

13.3 Lending Money to Relatives and Friends

All of us have had experience of dealing with the issue of lending money to relatives and friends at some point of time.

> "Neither a borrower nor a lender be, For loan oft loses both itself and friend"
> — **Shakespeare (Polonius, in Hamlet Act 1, scene 3, 75–77)**

Wisdom from ancient days shows that lending money to friends and relatives will result in serious problems like

- Loss of Complete Capital
- Loss of relationship, almost permanently
- Enmity and violence (Even murder in some cases)

1. Open ended loans

Loans to relatives and friends tend to be "open-ended". It does not have a timeline for return. It does not have any interest clause that leaves both parties in limbo. This leaves stress in the minds of the lender as he may require the money to meet some other important commitment like buying a house.

TIP: If you must lend money, make sure that you have a clear understanding on schedule for repayment as well as interest. You can consider asking for at least simple SB interest.

2. Loans are not a priority for the borrower

If you borrow from a financial institution there are consequences for not paying back in time, like

- Penalty

- Punitive Interest
- Higher Interest rates
- Negative impact on credit score, etc.

Since there are no such compulsions, borrowers do not treat loans from relatives and friends as priority.

3. It is difficult to ask for return of money

Even if the lender is desperate, he finds it difficult to ask for return of money. Since the borrower is emotionally connected to the lender, he avoids bringing up this topic to avoid "eye-to-eye" contact with the lender. The whole atmosphere is stressful for both.

4. The family gatherings can be awkward

Family gatherings become stressful and awkward if the lender raises the topic of loan. He will be branded as cruel and unloving. To avoid conflict, people resort to silence and withdrawal.

5. The borrower becomes a servant to the lender

The borrower loses the psychological advantage or sense of equality. And he ends up almost like a servant to the lender.

> "Borrower becomes a servant to the lender"
>
> **– Bible Proverbs 22–7**

6. The borrower may ask for more

Once you lend money to a relative or a friend this may happen:-

- He may come back for more borrowing
- Your name gets around as a potential lender

7. Teach people to manage money better

If you help a person in financial difficulty you are giving an easy way out for the borrower by lending money. He does not learn the importance of earning well, budgeting properly or curtailing expenses. Instead, you can offer to help in the learning process.

8. Loans and interests

It is a good idea to charge some level of interest for the money loaned even if it is awkward.

For Business purpose:- Charge market rates of 12–15% interest.

For personal purpose:- Minimum 5% interest which is equal to SB interest of bank.

9. Never lend money from your emergency fund

You may face emergency situation like losing job, falling sick, meeting an accident and so on. Hence, it is not a good idea to lend money out of your emergency fund.

10. Remember! You may lose a friend or money or both

Lend only what you can afford to lose and lend only if you can afford to lose that friend. Prepare yourself mentally before you decide to lend money.

11. Frank discussion

Before you lend, you need to have a frank discussion on the pros and cons of loans with your borrower friend or relative. You need to say upfront – how, not paying in back in time can seriously impact your life. And, if you choose to loan, give by an A/C payee cheque. Never cash.

12. Draw up an agreement

If the amount is significant for you, you need to enter into a written agreement which is enforceable under law. Remember! You have responsibility to take care of your money, your family and your kids.

13. Be careful before you become a guarantor

It is common for relatives and friends to approach you, requesting for your confirmation to be a guarantor to a financial institution. Unless you are sure about the person do not stand as a guarantor. You need to check the creditworthiness of the borrower before standing as a guarantor. Remember, you as a guarantor have legal liability to pay as much as the borrower, and if the borrower fails to repay in time, your credit score also will be impacted.

13.4 Write a Will and Keep Records

A will is a legal declaration a person makes about the way he/she wants his/her property managed or distributed after his/her death.

- There is no prescribed form
- No need for stamp paper
- It can be handwritten or typed
- Any adult with sound mind can write the will

Basics of a will

Declaration – You need to declare that you are of sound mind and if it is not the first will, you should make a statement revoking all previous wills.

List of your Assets – You must list out all your assets

- All properties that you own
- Money in savings accounts
- All fixed deposits & company deposits
- All Mutual funds
- Bank Locker
- Gold assets
- Company Shares
- Insurance policies
- Demat accounts, etc.

The process of making the list can be tedious and please go over it again to ensure that nothing is missed out.

Divide your Assets – You need to divide your assets item-wise. If the beneficiary is a minor, please make sure that a custodian is appointed.

Sign the Will – You need to sign the will, witnessed by two witnesses; make sure that you countersign all pages.

Storing the will – Your will must be stored in a safe place. The copy of the will must be kept elsewhere.

Common mistakes while writing the will or related to will

1. Avoid technical jargons. Use simple and direct language.

2. You need not mention anything about tenants, if property is rented out.

3. Not having will – It is ideal to have a will once you hit 50 years. In the absence of a will, legal heirs are forced to spend large sum to acquire mandatory documents like succession certificate/court order to transfer titles and high legal fees.

    Succession certificate – Required for movable property

    Letter of Administration – Required for immovable property

    Nomination – This is for transfer of cash and movable assets. Nominee is only a caretaker of other assets and has to pass on the assets to legal heir.

4. Undesirable distribution of assets – Only a will can clearly state which asset will go to whom. In its absence the asset may go to people whom you may not wish to give.

5. Incorrect drafting of will – It is preferable to draft the will with the help of a lawyer or it may land with various drafting errors.

6. Not being Specific – Very often the instructions are not given with specific details which can lead to contest or misunderstanding.

7. Not updating will – If assets have undergone any change like sale or offered as security to bank, updating needs to be done.

8. Wrong Executor – The Executor appointed is preferred with following characteristics:-

    - Younger person than you
    - Trustworthy person
    - Not a good idea to appoint a close relative or friend who may take sides

9. Gifting assets while being alive – This is not a good idea as after getting assets, children or relatives could maltreat you. There are lots of stories going around of parents being kicked out from home after the son/daughter acquires assets.
10. Neglecting illness – It is important to make provision in the will in case you suffer from terminal illness. It can also mention as to how the executor can take health-related decisions on your behalf.

Intestate Succession [death without a will] – In case someone dies without a will there are laws relating to succession based on the religion of the person:

- Male Hindu
- Female Hindu
- Christians
- Parsis
- Muslims
- HUF (Hindu Undivided family)

Who can write the will?

- A will can be written by an individual on a plain paper (Not recommended)
- A lawyer can draft the will
- There are online firms offering writing of will

www.ingramcontent.com/pod-product-compliance
Lightning Source LLC
Chambersburg PA
CBHW020856180526
45163CB00007B/2523